Eleventh Edition

Handbook for Georgia Legislators

Georgia State Government Complex: (1) Georgia Plaza Park, (2) Garden Room, (3) Depot Plaza Parking, (4) Agriculture Building, (5) No.7 Martin Luther King Building, (6) No.1 Martin Luther King Building, (7) Floyd Building (Twin Towers), (8) State Capitol, (9) Butler Street Parking Deck, (10) Parking Lot No.1, (11) State Archives Parking Lot, (12) State Archives Building, (13) Transportation Building, (14) Legislative Office Building, (15) Judicial Building, (16) Labor Building, (17) Health Building, and (18) Trinity-Washington Building. Also shown are (19) Atlanta City Hall Annex and (20) Atlanta City Hall.

Eleventh Edition

Handbook for Georgia Legislators

by Edwin L. Jackson and Mary E. Stakes

**Carl Vinson Institute of Government
The University of Georgia**

HANDBOOK FOR GEORGIA LEGISLATORS, Eleventh Edition

Editing: Inge Whittle
Design and production: Reid McCallister
Typesetting: Lisa Carson, Brenda Keen
Proofreading: Charlotte Eberhard
Publications editor: Emily Honigberg

First Edition published 1958. Eleventh Edition 1994.

ISBN 0-89854-176-X

Library of Congress Cataloging-in-Publication Data Pending

Photo credits: Georgia Department of Archives and History, xiv; Phyllis B. Kandul, 138; Edwin L. Jackson, frontispiece and all others.

Foreword

Thirty-six years ago, the Carl Vinson Institute of Government published the first *Handbook for Georgia Legislators* as a service to members and staff of the Georgia General Assembly, particularly those new to that body. Intended to bring together in one volume the fundamental laws, procedures, and practices that govern the legislative process in Georgia, the handbook has proven useful to a wide audience, including state and local government officials, attorneys, teachers, students, and other citizens interested in the legislative process in Georgia. While experience is still the best teacher, this handbook seeks to augment the educational process for state lawmakers.

Edwin L. Jackson is senior author and Mary E. Stakes is associate author of this eleventh edition of the *Handbook*. Both are public service faculty in the Citizen Education Division of the Carl Vinson Institute of Government at the University of Georgia.

The first edition of the handbook was prepared in 1958 by R. Perry Sentell, Jr., now Carter Professor of Law at the University of Georgia. Mr. Jackson has been responsible for the *Handbook for Georgia Legislators* since 1973, including a comprehensive revision in 1976. Ms. Stakes became coauthor for the ninth and tenth editions.

Over the years, numerous legislative officials and staff members have answered questions, supplied information, and otherwise provided assistance useful in the preparation of the publication. Particular thanks for this edition are due Robbie Rivers, Clerk of the Georgia House of Representatives, and Frank Eldridge, Secretary of the Georgia Senate, for reviewing this edition of the handbook. Special appreciation also goes to the staff of the clerk and secretary's offices; Paul Lynch, Legislative Fiscal Officer; and Shawn Davis of the State Ethics Commission for their invaluable assistance with this edition.

At the Institute, third-year law student Jeanna Marie Mastrodicasa ably assisted with the revision by identifying relevant holdings of Georgia appellate courts over the last six years that required discussion and/or citation. Laura Haase, graduate research assistant in the MPA program, spent long hours compiling the committee assignments for over 10,000 bills and resolutions in the House and Senate during the last six sessions.

November 1994   Melvin B. Hill, Jr.
                                                 Director

Contents

Chapter 3—Standards of Legislative Conduct...29

Chapter 4—Convening and Organizing...53

Chapter 5—Powers and Limitations...73

Chapter 6—Bills and Resolutions...89

Chapter 7—The Lawmaking Process...139

Appendixes...225

Index...205

Tables

Figures

Eleventh Edition

Handbook for Georgia Legislators

STATE OF GEORGIA
SENATE

 **Georgia's General Assembly**

Georgia's constitution establishes three separate branches of government—the legislative, judicial, and executive—and declares that they are to remain forever separate and distinct.[1] Each, however, is given a number of checks over the other branches, so that "The separation is not, and, from the nature of things, can not be total."[2] Nevertheless, in a republican form of government, the courts have said, the legislative authority necessarily predominates among the three coordinate branches of government.[3]

In Georgia, as in 18 other states, the official name of the legislative body is "General Assembly."[4] In common usage, however, it is frequently referred to as the "Georgia legislature," and the two names are used interchangeably in this handbook.

Like all states except Nebraska, Georgia has a bicameral, or two-house, legislative body, consisting of a Senate and a House of Representatives. However, this has not always been the case, since Georgia is one of four states to have experimented with a unicameral legislature.[5]

ORIGINS OF THE GENERAL ASSEMBLY

This history of legislative assemblies in Georgia began in 1750, two years before Georgia became a royal colony.[6] Prior to that time, Georgia's trustees, by virtue of their 1732 charter, exercised legislative, executive, and judicial powers to the extent that their actions conformed to English laws and met the approval of the King in Council.

There was no representative assembly in the colony until a trustees' resolution in March 1750 authorized Georgia's colonists to hold an assembly of elected deputies in Savannah, with representation to be based roughly on population. Although little is known about how they were elected to the assembly, 16 representatives met in Savannah for the first time on January 15, 1751. They had no legislative powers, however, since the assembly had been created to advise the trustees on conditions in the colony and to report on various census data from each district. During the 24-day session, a variety of measures for improvement of the colony were debated, with grievances submitted to both local authorities and the trustees. Many grievances were favorably acted upon by local authorities, and while the trustees did not accept all of the assembly's recommendations, several were adopted. This assembly never met again, however, since the trustees surrendered their charter to the Crown the following year.

Under royal government, provision was made for a General Assembly, consisting of an elected lower house, called the Commons House of Assembly, and the Governor's Council (whose 12 members were appointed by the Crown), known as the Upper House of Assembly. The Commons House first met in January 1755, with 19 representatives elected by landowners of 50 or more acres within the colony.

Meetings of the General Assembly were called by the royal governor, with members' terms lasting until he dissolved the assembly. Laws passed by the body could be vetoed by the governor (with no legislative override) or by the British Privy Council. Despite its restrictions and the frequent dissolutions in later years, this assembly met at various intervals during the next 20 years, enacting important laws for the colony which included the levying of taxes, appropriation of money, limitation of interest on loans, and regulation of the Indian trade.

Incidentally, many of the legislative offices and procedures used by today's General Assembly can be traced back to the 1755 body. These include the practice of three readings of a bill, the requirement that money bills originate in the lower house, use of "the previous question," use of "Committee of the Whole," and such officers as the speaker and clerk of the House.[7]

As discontent with British rule grew in Georgia, a call was issued in January 1775 for convening a Provincial Congress in Savannah on the same date that the royal Commons House of Assembly was to open. However, since only five parishes sent delegates, it was ineffective as an alternate representative body.

The outbreak of hostilities against British forces in May 1775 again stirred sentiment for an end to royal government in Georgia, and a Council of Safety was established in June, followed by a call for election of members to a Second Provincial Congress. More than 100 delegates, representing every parish, met on July 4. In the months that followed, this one-house Congress assumed executive, legislative, and judicial functions, with the Council of Safety exercising governmental authority when the Congress was not in session. A Third Provincial Congress met in January 1776, and though forced to flee Savannah in the face of British attack, reassembled in Augusta, where it adopted Georgia's first temporary constitution in April 1776.

The Constitution of 1777 provided for a legislature composed of representatives elected annually from each of the counties and from two cities. Seventy-two representatives were elected according to the apportionment plan. They then met to select a governor, and they elected from their own number 12 representatives to serve as an Executive Council. The remaining 60 members served as the House of Assembly.

Full legislative authority rested with the House of Assembly. The Executive Council could only recommend changes in proposed laws and had no formal legislative authority. Thus, Georgia joined two other states of the revolutionary period—Pennsylvania and Vermont—in providing for a unicameral legislative body.[8]

Following independence, Georgia continued its one-house legislative body until the Constitution of 1789 provided for a "General Assembly" composed of two separate houses—an arrangement continued through all succeeding constitutions. Under this constitution, the legislature elected the governor, who did, however, now have veto authority over its acts, subject to override by two-thirds of both houses. In 1824, provision was made for popular election of the state's chief executive.

CHANGES IN MEMBERSHIP AND SESSIONS

Since 1789, Georgia's legislative body has undergone a number of changes affecting its size, basis for apportionment, frequency of meetings, length of sessions, and terms of office for members.

Changes in Terms of Office

Except for the periods 1789-95 and 1868-77, senators and representatives have been elected for identical terms. This has meant that the entire General Assembly has usually been before the voters for reelection at one time, resulting in the reorganization of the legislature following every election.

Initially, representatives served one-year terms, with three-year terms for senators. In requiring more extensive qualifications for the Senate than the House, Georgia is reputed to be the first state to so discriminate between the two houses.[9] In 1795, however, senatorial terms were reduced to one year, and the entire General Assembly was elected annually, a practice continued until an 1841 constitutional amendment extended terms to two years for both houses, beginning in 1843.

During Reconstruction, terms for senators were increased to four years, but they were returned to two years in 1877 and have remained at this length to the present.

One interesting practice adopted by the state Democratic party earlier in this century and formalized by the General Assembly in 1939 was that of rotating senators at each biennium among the different counties comprising a district.[10] All but two senatorial districts were made up of three counties each, and a procedure was instituted whereby each county within a district took a turn at electing the senator for that district. The senator had to reside in the county whose turn it was under the rotation, and in the Democratic primary only voters of that county could vote on the office. Occasionally, a county would defer and allow an incumbent to stay in office, but usually there was a wholesale turnover in the Senate every two years. Georgia's rotating senatorial scheme was declared unconstitutional, however, by a federal district court in 1962,[11] and the General Assembly subsequently abolished the practice at a special session that year.

Changes in Frequency and Length of Sessions

Sessions of the General Assembly have been held on an annual basis since 1777, except for the periods of 1843-57 and 1925-43, when biennial sessions were held. (See Table 1.)

The current session length—40 days—was first set by a 1955 constitutional amendment, later amended in 1962 to authorize 45 days in odd-numbered years. The 1962 change also instituted a split session in odd

Table 1: *Legislative Sessions since 1777*

Year Instituted	Session Held	Length of Session
1777	Annually	No limit
1843	Biennially	No limit
1857	Annually	40 days[a]
1880	Biennially[b]	40 days[a]
1893	Annually	50 days
1925	Biennially	60 days
1933	Biennially	70 days[c]
1944	Biennially[d]	70 days
1955	Annually	40 days
1963	Annually	45/40 days[e]
1977	Annually	40 days

[a] This limit could be extended (and often was) by two-thirds vote of both houses. In the 1869-70 biennium, for example, the General Assembly was in session for a total of 328 days, and in 1889, for 140 days. (McElreath, *A Treatise on the Constitution of Georgia*, pp. 169-74.)

[b] Although biennial sessions were formally dictated, in practice the legislature was in session at some time during every year between 1880 and 1893.

[c] Based on a split session of 10 days for organizing in January and 60 days for a regular session later in the same year.

[d] Though biennial sessions were formally dictated, the legislature could adjourn during the first year and reconvene the following year, as long as the total 70-day limit was not exceeded. From 1944 to 1955, the legislature met in regular sessions every year except 1944, 1948, and 1954.

[e] See *Handbook*, pp. 4, 6.

years whereby the legislature convened in January for no more than 12 days to organize and receive a general appropriations bill from the governor. Afterwards, the legislature adjourned for a budget recess of several weeks, reconvening in February for no more than 33 additional days. Even though a 1972 constitutional change provided for annual appropriations acts, the 45/40-day limit associated with the former biennial appropriations process remained in effect through 1976. The Constitution of 1976 reinstituted the 40-day session limit for both odd and even years, effective with the 1977 General Assembly, and abolished the formal split session in odd years.

Changes in the Size of the General Assembly

Historically, apportionment of House and Senate membership has been based on counties, population (sometimes roughly apportioned), or a combination of both. The size of these bodies—especially the House of Representatives—usually has been free to fluctuate (invariably upward) as new counties were created and populations increased, although there have not always been direct correlations between population and representation in the legislature. During some periods, precise sizes have been constitutionally set; this has necessitated redrawing apportionment districts or further amending these constitutional limits as counties were added or as populations shifted.

House Size

Until House elections in 1965, every apportionment plan for the House in the state's history has given each county then in existence at least one representative, with some formula for giving additional representation based on population. Table 2 illustrates the changes in House size, the number of counties in existence with each change, and the representation possible to each county.

The Georgia Constitution of 1945 incorporated a formula for apportioning members of the House, whereby the 8 largest counties received three representatives each; the next 30 largest counties, two representatives each; and the remaining counties, one each. In June 1964, however, a federal district court declared this provision void and inoperative on the grounds that the system violated the voters' equal protection under the Fourteenth Amendment to the U.S. Constitution.[12] Under court directive to reapportion on the basis of population alone, the General Assembly adopted a new plan for the House in 1965. While the court rejected this method of apportionment because of population variances among districts, it allowed the plan to operate until further redistricting could be accomplished.

At the 1967 session, both houses adopted new apportionment plans, with the House reducing its membership from 205 to 195. Court objec-

Table 2: *Changes in the Size of the Georgia House of Representatives since 1789 (Year size became effective)*

Year	Size	Counties	Representatives Allowed per County
1789	34	11	2-5
1795	41	16	2-4
1798	58	23	1-4
1838	208	92	1-4
1844	130	93	1-2
1851	135	95	1-2
1860	169	132	1-2
1868	175	132	1-3
1904	183	137	1-3
1908	184	146	1-3
1914	189	148	1-3
1918	193	156	1-3
1920	206	160	1-3
1924	207	160	1-3
1932	205	159	1-3
1969	195	159	*
1972	180	159	*

*Representation not based on counties.

tions to some districts led to further reapportionment at the 1968 session, but the new 195-member size was allowed to go into effect in 1969.

The 1970 census necessitated further reapportionment, resulting in a 1971 reduction of House size to 180 members, effective with the 1972 session. No changes were made in the number of representatives in the 1981 and 1982 reapportionment acts.

The Constitution of 1983 added a constitutional mandate that the House of Representatives consist of *not fewer than* 180 members. However, since 1972, the size has remained set at 180—the minimum now allowed by the state constitution. Reapportionment acts could increase the size in the future should legislators so choose.[13]

Senate Size

Creation of the Senate in 1789 included provision for equal representation of counties within that body, a plan similar to the equal representation of states in the U.S. Senate adopted the same year. Each county—regardless of population—was to be entitled to one senator.

As the number of counties increased, so did the size of the Senate, and by 1838 it had 93 members. (See Table 3.) An 1844 constitutional amendment instituted a plan of 47 single-member districts, but in 1852

Table 3: *Changes in the Size of the Georgia Senate since 1789 (Year size became effective)*

Year	Size	Year	Size
1789	11	1859	132
1800	24	1861	44
1829	76	1919	51
1838	93	1939	52
1845	47	1947	54
1855	98	1969	56

the former basis of representation—one senator from each county—was restored. By 1859, the Senate totaled 132 members, leading to a return to single-member districts and a reduction to 44 members in 1861.

Since 1861, the Georgia Senate has been apportioned on the basis of single-member districts, though federal courts in the 1960s ruled that these districts must be based solely on population, and not on counties.

From time to time, constitutional amendments have not only reduced but enlarged the Senate's size. A 1968 amendment provided that the body consist of not less than 54 or more than 56 members, the precise number to be set by the General Assembly. The Constitution of 1983 dropped the minimum size requirement, stating that the Senate shall consist of *not more than* 56 members elected from single-member districts.[14]

ENDNOTES

1. GA. CONST. art. 1, §2, ¶3.

2. Beall v. Beall, 8 Ga. 210 (1850). See discussion of separation of powers in Chapter 5.

3. Walker v. Whitehead, 43 Ga. 538 (1871); Myers v. U.S., 272 U.S. 52 (1926). See Chapter 5 of this handbook.

4. Two states use the term "Legislative Assembly"; two states use the name "General Court"; and the remainder use the term "Legislature" as the official designation of their legislative bodies. See *The Book of the States, 1994-95* (Lexington, Ky.: Council of State Governments, 1994), p. 108.

5. In addition to Georgia, Pennsylvania and Vermont used a unicameral legislature during the revolutionary period. Georgia abandoned a one-house legislature in 1789, followed the next year by Pennsylvania. However, Vermont continued its unicameral legislature until 1836. In 1934, Nebraska voters approved a constitutional amendment to replace their bicameral legislature with a unicameral body, and its first session was held in 1937.

6. For a discussion of the historical background of legislative bodies in Georgia, see Albert B. Saye, *A Constitutional History of Georgia, 1732-1968* (Athens: University of Georgia Press, 1970); Walter McElreath, *A Treatise on the Constitution of Georgia* (Atlanta: The Harrison Co., 1912); and Robert Gerwig, "Colonial Georgia: Path to Self-Government," 12 *Georgia State Bar Journal* 130 (February 1976).

7. Saye, *A Constitutional History of Georgia*, p. 61. Many of the practices adopted by this early body, of course, were adapted from British parliamentary rules and tradition.

8. It has been argued that Georgia did not have a true unicameral legislative body, because even though the Executive Council could not veto actions of the other house, it did play an important role in the lawmaking process. See Henry Luce, *Legislative Assemblies* (New York: Houghton Mifflin Co., 1924), p. 24.

9. McElreath, *A Treatise on the Constitution of Georgia*, p. 88.

10. Ga. Laws 1939, p. 311; Ga. Laws 1946, p. 44; Ga. Laws 1950, p. 165. For a discussion of this system, see William G. Cornelius, *Southeastern State Legislatures* (Atlanta: Emory University School of Law, 1967), p. 58; and Doyle Mathis, "Georgia's Reapportionment History and Process," in Brett W. Hawkins (ed.), *Reapportionment in Georgia* (Athens: Institute of Government, 1970), pp. 6-7.

11. Toombs v. Fortson, 205 F. Supp. 248 (1962).

12. Toombs v. Fortson, (N.D. Ga., June 30, 1964).

13. GA. CONST. art. 3, §2, ¶1(b).

14. GA. CONST. art. 3, §2, ¶1(a).

 *Membership*

COMPOSITION OF THE GENERAL ASSEMBLY

Georgia's legislature is composed of a 56-member Senate and a 180-member House. The General Assembly is free to enlarge (but not reduce) the size of the House by general statute.[1] The Senate consists of not more than 56 members, with the exact number to be set by the General Assembly.[2]

With a total membership of 236, Georgia's General Assembly is the third largest state legislature in the United States. The Georgia House ranks third in size among lower houses of state legislatures, and the Georgia Senate fourth among state senates.[3]

QUALIFICATIONS FOR MEMBERSHIP

Formal Qualifications

The constitution of Georgia requires members of both houses of the General Assembly to be United States citizens, Georgia citizens for at least two years, and legal residents of their district for at least one year.[4] Should a senator or representative move from the district from which elected, that seat is automatically declared vacant.[5]

The only difference in qualifications between the two houses is that a senator must be at least 25 years of age, while a representative need only be 21.[6]

Other Provisions Relative to Membership

In addition to the specific qualifications for office, a number of constitutional and statutory provisions bear on eligibility to seek and/or hold office in the General Assembly.

Registered voter. Georgia's constitution contains a general mandate that only registered voters may hold public office or be appointed to any position of honor or trust in the state.[7]

Criminal record. Any person who has been convicted and sentenced for any felony involving moral turpitude is prohibited from holding any public office in the state, unless the State Board of Pardons and Paroles has restored that person's civil rights and at least 10 years have elapsed from the completion of the sentence without a subsequent conviction of another felony involving moral turpitude.[8] In a 1983 opinion to the board, Georgia's attorney general interpreted this constitutional provision to mean that, with respect to holding public office, (1) a person is not disqualified by virtue of a nolo contendere plea; (2) all felonies should be considered as involving moral turpitude; and (3) even if the sentence has been served, the board must specifically restore a convicted felon's civil rights before he or she can hold office in Georgia.[9]

Holder of public monies. By both constitution and statute, public office is denied any person illegally holding public funds.[10]

Incapacity. Although there is no mandatory retirement age for members of the General Assembly, Georgia law provides that persons of unsound mind or those who, from advanced age or bodily infirmity, are unfit to discharge the duties of public office are ineligible to hold it.[11] According to the constitution, any person who has been judicially determined to be mentally incompetent is disqualified from being a registered voter, and hence from holding public office.[12]

Should a court determine that any state officeholder has abandoned that office, has ceased performing his or her duties, or has become incapacitated or ineligible to continue (whether by voluntary act or misfortune of the incumbent), that office shall be declared vacant.[13] Failure of an elected member of the General Assembly to obtain the proper commission for that office is also sufficient grounds for vacating the office.[14]

Qualifying for election. All candidates for the General Assembly seeking their party's nomination in a primary must qualify with their state political party in accordance with the procedural rules of their party.[15] Also, all candidates—whether seeking office through party primary, as members of a political organization, or as independents—must qualify within time periods and according to procedural requirements of the state election code.[16]

A candidate for the General Assembly may not seek nomination in the primary of one political party while seeking that or any other office in the primary of another party.[17]

Special rules apply to any person seeking election to the legislature as a write-in candidate.[18] A write-in candidacy is only allowed in a general or special election. No person can seek a write-in candidacy if that person sought the same office in the immediately preceding primary. Also, at least 20 or more days before such election, the candidate (or one or more qualified voters acting in his or her behalf) must notify the secretary of state of the write-in candidacy and supply an affidavit stating that notice of the candidacy has been published in a newspaper of general circulation in Georgia.

Restrictions on holding other offices. No person on active duty with any branch of the United States armed forces may hold a seat in the General Assembly, unless otherwise provided by statute.[19] Also prohibited from holding a seat in the General Assembly is any person holding any other compensated appointive or elective public office in the government of Georgia, any other state, or the United States.[20] According to a 1908 Georgia Supreme Court decision, this provision would invalidate the election to the General Assembly of one already holding state office, but it would not prohibit the person continuing in the prior-held position.[21]

In addition, no one seeking membership in the General Assembly may also run in the same primary or election for constitutional officer in the executive branch (e.g., commissioner of labor, secretary of state, etc.) or for any of the following offices: U.S. senator or representative, public service commissioner, justice of the supreme court, judge of the court of appeals, judge of the probate court, clerk of superior court, tax commissioner, tax collector, sheriff, judge of superior court, county treasurer, county school superintendent, or tax receiver.[22] Further, no elected county or municipal official is eligible to serve as a member of the General Assembly.[23] There are no specific exclusions, however, applying to local government appointed officials or employees (such as those of public schools).[24]

The Georgia Constitution declares that the legislative, judicial, and executive branches shall remain separate and distinct, and no one discharging the duties of one may, at the same time, exercise the functions of either of the others, except as the constitution specifically allows.[25] For example, no judge of a court of record or a judge's clerks or assistants may hold office in the legislature, nor may officers or employees of the executive branch.[26]

This prohibition has been construed by the Georgia Supreme Court to preclude a member of the General Assembly from holding any office or employment in the executive or judicial branches, including membership on boards and commissions (including authorities) involved in executive functions.[27] (However, this preclusion apparently does not apply to legislative memberships on various *advisory* boards and councils in the executive branch.) Georgia's high court also has refused to allow an employee of the executive branch—in this case a state college faculty member—to take an unpaid leave of absence while serving as a member of the General Assembly.[28] While a public school teacher can hold both jobs, a college teacher—if employed by the State Board of Regents—cannot.

A senator or representative cannot be elected by the General Assembly, or appointed by the governor, to any office which has an emolument during the period for which he or she has been elected unless first resigning from the legislature.[29] This provision, however, does not prevent a senator or representative from being elected by the General Assembly or appointed by the governor, with additional compensation, to certain legislative offices—such as the speaker of the House, the House and Senate majority leaders, and the administration floor leaders. Further, no legislator, during the term for which elected, can be appointed to any civil office which has been created during that term.[30]

REQUIRED OATH OF OFFICE AND COMMISSION

Required Oath

The Georgia Constitution requires that each member of the General Assembly, before taking his or her seat, take an oath of office as prescribed by law. Until adoption of the Constitution of 1983, the oath was specifically detailed in the constitution. Now a part of Georgia statutes, the oath reads:

> I do hereby solemnly swear or affirm that I will support the Constitution of this State and of the United States and, on all questions and measures which may come before me, I will so conduct myself, as will, in my judgment, be most conducive to the interests and prosperity of this State.[31]

Georgia statutes also require an oath that the new officeholder does not hold any public money due the state which has not been accounted for; is not a holder of any office of trust under the United States government or under any other state or foreign government; is qualified to hold the office; and has been a resident for the time required by the Georgia Constitution and laws.[32] Finally, the legislator must take a loyalty oath stating that he or she is not a member of the Communist party and will support the constitutions of the United States and this state.[33] The portion of the loyalty oath requiring disavowal of membership is in violation of the First and Fourteenth Amendments of the U.S. Constitution, and, according to the attorney general, should not be administered.[34] A check of the oath used in the swearing-in ceremonies for the 1993-94 biennium shows that the House continues to use the Communist party proviso, while the Senate has dropped it.[35]

Rather than administer these oaths of office separately, the General Assembly practice has been to combine and administer them as one (see p. 57).

Commission

Each member of the Georgia General Assembly is entitled to a commission after taking the oath of office. It is the secretary of state's duty to prepare and furnish to the legislator this commission which bears the great seal of the state. The commission recognizes that the person is a duly elected member of the General Assembly of Georgia for the term specified and notes any prior service that may have been performed in either house.[36]

ELECTIONS

Terms

Members of both the House and the Senate are elected at the general election held on Tuesday following the first Monday in November of even-numbered years. Both serve two-year terms of office, which begin on the second Monday in January following election (the time for convening the regular session) and end with the convening of the General Assembly following the second year of the term.[37] Neither house provides for staggered terms, and each member of the General Assembly must face reelection every two years.

Contested Elections

The Georgia Constitution vests in each house the authority to be judge of the eligibility and qualifications of its members.[38] (See pp. 57-58 for a discussion of resolving election contests by the House and Senate.) Nevertheless, there are some instances (e.g., voting fraud or error) where the results may be contested in state or federal court. To judicially contest an election, a petition is filed in superior court, where after notice to the defendant, the judge hears and decides the case alone (unless a jury is requested and the issues are such as could be determined by a jury). Such judgment may be appealed to a higher court within 10 days.[39]

Filling Vacancies

Georgia relies on the special election, rather than gubernatorial appointment, to fill vacancies that occur in the General Assembly.[40] Should a seat become vacant during a session of the General Assembly, or at a time when legislators would have to meet prior to the next general election, the governor issues within 10 days of such vacancy (or after the calling of a special session) a writ of election to the secretary of state.[41] An election to fill the vacancy then takes place as authorized by the writ, no less than 30 or more than 60 days after its issuance.

House and Senate Districts

The Senate consists of 56 members elected from single-member districts.[42] The House, which through 1992 consisted of single-and multi-member districts, now consists of 180 members elected from single-member districts.[43]

Reapportionment acts in 1972 brought a major change in the composition of the Georgia House and Senate by creating legislative districts which are no longer drawn strictly according to county lines. They may instead be composed of either a portion of a county, a whole county, several counties, or any combination of these. Appendixes 1 and 2 contain maps of current House and Senate districts.

According to the Georgia Constitution, the House and Senate must be reapportioned as necessary at the first session after each United States decennial census becomes official.[44] Federal courts insist that such reapportionments in both houses be conducted strictly on a basis of population, with minimum deviation among similar legislative districts.[45] While the U.S. Voting Rights Act continues in effect, all reapportionment plans (as well as other election changes) for the Georgia General Assembly must be submitted to the U.S. Attorney General for approval before becoming effective.[46]

SALARY, ALLOWANCES, AND BENEFITS

On January 1, 1987, members of the General Assembly began receiving an annual base salary of $10,000, paid in 12 monthly installments. Additionally, at the beginning of each fiscal year (July 1), lawmakers are entitled to a cost-of-living adjustment (COLA) equal to one-half the percentage increase given executive, legislative, and judicial employees.[47]

Ordinarily, a COLA is not considered a salary increase but rather an adjustment to help offset the impact of inflation. For it to work, the adjustment must be built into the base salary to which the next year's COLA will be applied. However, these annual inflation adjustments are not incorporated into the official legislative salary of $10,000 specified in O.C.G.A. §45-7-4(22). To statutorily change the official salary would trigger the provision in Georgia's constitution that prohibits legislative salary increases from going into effect during the biennium in which the increase is made. However, if you look at the statutory salary as representing $10,000 in 1987 dollars, then some mechanism for offsetting inflation becomes essential. That mechanism is the COLA—but because legislators get half the percentage other state employees receive, their COLA only partially offsets the impact of inflation.

Questions over whether legislative COLAs are de facto salary increases have not been addressed by the courts, but in an unofficial opinion, Georgia's attorney general has advised that they are legal. The COLA "does not elevate the salaries of the General Assembly but preserves those salaries in relation to inflation and in relation to their comparison with other state salaries. Not to have a COLA when others have one, in effect, would be a pay decrease."[48]

Since 1987, the annual legislative COLA has been 1.25 percent, except for one year when there were no COLAs and one year when legislators received 2.0 percent. Based on cost-of-living adjustments since 1987, the FY 1995 adjusted salary for legislators is $10,854.

There is no additional remuneration for any further service as a legislator—including special sessions—except for expense, mileage, travel, and office allowances as provided by law and noted below.

Salaries for Legislative Officers

In recognition of the greater demands placed on their offices, certain legislative leadership positions in the General Assembly are authorized to receive supplemental amounts over their basic $10,000 salaries. The speaker of the House of Representatives is paid an additional supplement, adjusted at the convening of each new term, so the salary will equal that of the lieutenant governor. The speaker pro tempore in the House and president pro tempore in the Senate each receive a $4,800 supplement. The majority leader, minority leader, administration floor leader, and the assistant administration floor leaders in both houses each receive additional amounts which are provided by resolution in each house, but shall not be greater than the amount provided for the speaker pro tempore of the House.[49]

In 1987, the salary of the lieutenant governor was set at $54,920, and that is the official salary provided for in the code.[50] Though serving as president of the Senate, he or she is a member of the executive branch, and thus entitled to the full cost-of-living adjustment granted state employees. Given those increases, the lieutenant governor's adjusted salary for FY 1995 is $64,113. He or she receives no additional compensation, though during sessions the president also receives the standard daily allowance of $59, plus reimbursement for actual transportation costs while traveling by public carrier, or 21 cents per mile for use of a personal automobile.[51]

The secretary of the Senate and clerk of the House receive such salary, expenses, and allowances as provided by resolution of their respective houses.[52] Additionally, both officials are entitled to the same expense, mileage, and travel allowances as legislators for each day of official services.

Expense Allowance

Legislators are entitled, by law, to a standard expense allowance of $59 per day for

1. each official legislative day of a regular or special session (which can include Saturdays and Sundays, unless both houses have adjourned by joint resolution for a weekend or other period of time);

2. each day's service as a member of a standing committee or an interim committee created by, or pursuant to, a resolution of one or both houses; and

3. each day's service as a member of a statutory or constitutional committee, board, bureau, commission, or other agency.[53]

During formally invoked adjournments—including the customary budget recess—legislators are not entitled to the expense allowance unless involved in committee work under the second provision.

Depending upon the housekeeping resolution adopted in each house, legislators may also be entitled to collect the $59 daily allowance during the interim between sessions while serving as a "committee of one" (see discussion on pp. 68-69).

For performing official duties out of state, legislators receive actual expenses (e.g., food, lodging, taxis, etc.) as an expense allowance—in lieu of the $59 daily rate—plus travel expenses outlined below. Members are also reimbursed for registration fees to attend approved legislative conferences or meetings, whether in or out of state.[54]

Prior to out-of-state travel at state expense, a senator or Senate staff member must have prior approval in writing by the Senate Administrative Affairs Committee (Senate Rule 189).

Mileage and Travel Allowances

Each member of the General Assembly is provided a mileage allowance of 21 cents per mile for one round trip each week, or portion of a week, during a regular or special session. The mileage is calculated between the member's home and the state capitol "by the most practical route." If the member travels by public carrier for any part of the round trip, the reimbursement for that part is the actual expense in lieu of the mileage allowance.[55]

For authorized legislative travel, a member may receive a mileage allowance of either 21 cents per mile or actual transportation costs if traveling by air, bus, or other public carrier.[56] Reimbursement for commercial airfare is limited to the amounts provided for in the statewide contract for airline travel incorporated in the state travel regulations established by the Department of Audits and Accounts and the Office of Planning and Budget.[57] (Certain exceptions are outlined in O.C.G.A. §28-1-8 [3].) These allowances or reimbursements will be paid upon submission of proper vouchers.[58]

Expense and Travel Vouchers

As noted above, during a regular or special session, legislators are automatically paid the daily $59 expense allowance and the round-trip mileage allowance to their home city once a week.

For any other expense, mileage, or travel reimbursements, a legislator must sign and submit a voucher to the legislative fiscal officer certifying (1) that he or she has personally performed the service and personally incurred the expense for mileage and travel covered by the voucher, and (2) that the information contained on the voucher is correct and true.[59] Penalties for knowing and willful submission of false information on a voucher by a legislator include a fine of not more than $1,000, imprisonment of not less than one or more than five years, or both.[60]

At least once every two months, the House Journals Committee and a special audit subcommittee designated by the Senate Rules Committee must examine and review legislative expenditures including all vouchers submitted by members of their respective houses.[61]

Office and Other Allowances

In addition to any other allowances authorized by law, each member of the General Assembly may receive reimbursement up to $4,800 each year for the following expenses: lodging, meals, office equipment, postage, personal services, printing and publications, rents, supplies, telecommunications, transportation, utilities, and per diem differential (defined in this section).[62] However, specifically excluded from reimbursement is postage for a "political newsletter."

Georgia's attorney general has issued an official opinion to the lieutenant governor that where funds from the $4,800 allowance are used to purchase items that are not fully consumed (e.g., office equipment, computers, and cellular telephones), the items become state property and cannot be retained as personal property by the legislator.[63]

Legislators whose homes are more than 50 miles from the state capitol may draw a "per diem differential" from their office allowance for each day of the session.[64] A per diem differential is the difference in the $59 daily per diem allowed by state law and the actual per diem amount needed to stay in Atlanta as calculated by the federal government. Currently, the U.S. General Services Administration estimates that food, lodging, transportation, and parking cost $119 per day in Atlanta, which is $60 more than what is allowed by state law. Thus, legislators who qualify can claim a $60 per diem differential, but this money must come out of their $4,800 office allowance.

Supporting documents are not required for the per diem differential. Other expenses will be reimbursed to the $4,800 limit upon submission to the Legislative Fiscal Office of sworn vouchers accompanied by supporting documents showing payment.

Sickness and Death

If a member becomes unable to attend a session of the General Assembly because of personal or family sickness, or if granted leave by his or her legislative house, the member is entitled to the same daily expense allowance as attending members.[65] Regardless of the length of sickness, a legislator continues to receive the salary of his or her office as long as it is held—even if forced to miss part or all of a session.

Should a member die during or after a session without having received all or any part of his or her daily expense allowance, the amount due for the entire session (minus any portion already paid) is paid to the surviving spouse, or if none, to the children; and if there are no children, to the estate of the deceased legislator. The legislator's salary for the full calendar month in which he or she died is paid in the same manner.[66]

Restrictions on Additional Compensation

Georgia law prohibits any member of the General Assembly from receiving any compensation, salary, per diem, contingent expense allowance, longevity pay, or allowance of any kind for service as a legislator other than that specified by law.[67] One exception is that legislators may be reimbursed by the executive or judicial branches for service on advisory or investigatory boards and committees. For such service, legislators can claim (1) actual expenses, or (2) actual travel expenses and the standard per diem allowance for legislators. However, no claims for reimbursement can be paid for days a legislator receives compensation or reimbursement from the legislative branch of government.[68]

Georgia's attorney general has issued an opinion that these restrictions do not apply to a legislator who continues to receive his or her regular salary and benefits during a legislative session from a full-time employer— as long as the paying of salary and benefits is not done for the purpose of influencing the legislator or the legislator's reelection campaign.[69]

As will be discussed in Chapter 3, the ban on additional compensation or allowances applies not only to receipt of public monies but private as well. The Georgia Supreme Court has held that, "Other than those emoluments of public office that are expressly authorized by law, *no* holder of public office is entitled to request or receive—from any source, directly or indirectly—anything of value in exchange for the performance of any act related to the functions of that office."[70]

INSURANCE AND RETIREMENT BENEFITS

Health Insurance

Legislators and the administrative and clerical personnel of the General Assembly, and their dependents, are authorized to participate in a group health insurance plan for state employees.[71] Administration of this plan is vested in the State Merit System. Payments into the health insurance fund are made by both employer and employee, with the legislative fiscal officer making employer payments for all legislators and legislative personnel.

Retirement

In 1967, the Georgia Legislative Retirement System (LRS) was established to provide retirement benefits for legislators, the secretary of the Senate, and the clerk of the House.[72] Five years later, membership eligibility was extended to the messenger and doorkeeper for each of the two houses.

In 1971, the state Employees' Retirement System (ERS) was extended to cover General Assembly members. Legislators who were members of LRS prior to May 1, 1971, could continue to claim benefits as outlined in the LRS, while all new members of the legislature received benefits as provided by ERS. The assumption was that, in time, LRS would be phased out, with ERS taking over administration of retirement benefits for legislators.

In 1979 and 1980, legislators elected since 1971 were given a chance to withdraw from ERS and join LRS. Any member of the General Assembly as of April 13, 1979, could elect to withdraw from ERS and join LRS or choose not to be a member of either system. This decision had to be made prior to the convening of the 1981 session of the General Assembly and once made was irrevocable.

General Assembly members elected after April 13, 1979, but before July 1, 1984, could join LRS or ERS, but they had to decide within 60 days from the date of becoming a member of the General Assembly. The decision once made was irrevocable. Since July 1, 1984, all persons elected to the General Assembly become members of LRS upon taking office.

Members of LRS may retire at age 62 with 8 years of *membership service* (service as a member of the General Assembly) or at age 65 with 8 years of *creditable service* (service as a member of the General Assembly plus service in the military during wartime and/or service in the General Assembly prior to January 1, 1954). Military service rendered prior to January 1, 1954, does not require a contribution; but military service after January 1, 1954, requires making the employee contribution plus 7 percent interest compounded annually. Up to 5 years of military service may be purchased at the rate of 1 year for every 5 years served in the legislature.

The monthly retirement allowance is calculated at $20 times the number of years of creditable service. Early retirement is available at age 60 with 8 years of membership service and with normal benefits reduced 5 percent for each year below age 62.

A 100 percent or 50 percent joint and survivor annuity is available for a named beneficiary, but LRS does not provide a disability retirement option. If an LRS member ceases to be a member of the General Assembly before reaching age 60, he or she may continue as a noncontributing member, retaining membership service credits. If contributions are withdrawn, membership credits are irrevocably lost and cannot be reestablished even if the person is reelected to the General Assembly.[73]

Under ERS, a member may retire at age 60 with 10 years' service, although members can continue working beyond this age and increase their benefits. Benefits are based on a member's age at retirement, years of service, and highest average monthly compensation over eight consecutive quarters.[74]

For legislators who belong to ERS, employee contributions to the system are paid by the legislative branch. For LRS members, the legislative branch contributes an amount equivalent to that paid for legislators in ERS, with the difference (employee contributions required by LRS are higher than ERS) deducted from each member's salary. Since 1986, LRS members contribute an additional 1 percent of salary.[75]

OFFICE SPACE, CLERICAL ASSISTANCE, TELEPHONES, LICENSE PLATES, AND PARKING

Office space. The General Assembly and other components of the legislative branch are housed in the state capitol and in the Legislative Office Building across the street from the capitol. Individual offices in the capitol are provided for the president and president pro tempore of the Senate, the speaker and speaker pro tempore of the House, and the majority leaders, and administration floor leaders, of both houses. All of the House committee chairs have capitol offices and so do a majority of Senate committee chairs. Remaining legislators have private offices in the Legislative Office Building.

Committee space. The Legislative Services Committee has designated certain rooms at the capitol and Legislative Office Building for committee use in each house. During a session, Senate committees rely on the secretary of the Senate to schedule a room for their meetings. In contrast, each House committee has a designated meeting room for the session. Between sessions, the legislative counsel's office attempts to coordinate meeting times and places for committees in both houses.

Clerical assistance. Legislative leaders and some committees are provided with individual secretarial and clerical help. Every member has access to a secretary who may work for four or more legislators.

Telephones. The GIST telephone system at the state capitol provides a number of long-distance lines for use by any legislator needing to contact a constituent, or for any other legislative matter. Additionally, each legislator's office has a telephone with GIST access.

The public information offices in each house maintain toll-free telephone numbers (House, 1-800-282-5800; Senate, 1-800-282-5803) for citizens outside the Atlanta telephone exchange to use to call and leave a message for a legislator to return the call or to find the status of legislation.

Long-distance calls and telephone service pertaining to legislative business and incurred away from the capitol qualify for reimbursement from each legislator's annual $4,800 office expense allowance (see p. 19).

Legislative license plates. Each member of the General Assembly is entitled to a custom license plate that shows a capitol dome, plus the member's district number. After taking the oath of office, a new member may apply to the director of the Motor Vehicle Division of the Georgia Department of Revenue for up to two custom plates. (The manufacturing fee is $25 for each license plate ordered.) A new member must bring proof of payment of ad valorem taxes from the tag agent of the member's home county for each car that will bear a legislative plate. Legislators must pay a $25 annual fee per tag as well as the standard $20 tag/decal fee.

Parking. Although there are plans for a new parking deck behind the Twin Towers office building, parking in the state capitol complex is usually at a premium. Legislators are assured of a space, but this is not always true for aides and constituents.

The parking lot east of the capitol on Capitol Avenue is known as Parking Lot #1. Here, for a fee of $10, each legislator is assigned a reserved space (marked with that legislator's name) for use during the session. The Georgia Building Authority, which has responsibility for the capitol complex parking lots, will issue the legislator a permit, which must be attached to the inside rearview mirror of the car and be on display at all times when the car is in Lot #1. If a legislator is not going to be using the reserved space on a particular day, he or she can allow someone else to borrow the permit and use the parking space for the day. As an alternative, the legislator can give written permission to the borrower to present to the Lot #1 parking attendant.

Between sessions, legislators can pay $20 for unlimited use of Lot #1 for official business, or they can pay the standard $3 parking fee each time they use the lot. During the interim, parking spaces are not reserved, and a legislator's parking permit is nontransferable—only the legislator can use it. Interim parking permits are only valid during normal office hours at the capitol and cannot be used for sporting events or at any of the other parking lots in the capitol complex area.

The parking situation for a legislator's aides and interns sometimes becomes difficult. On a space-available basis, the Building Authority will assign a Lot #1 permit for one aide for each legislator. However, less than 100 spaces are available for aides, and these are allocated on a first-come, first-served basis. Most aides have to find other arrangements, which are limited in the complex. Several public parking facilities (such as the lot at State Archives) are maintained, but generally these lots don't open until around 9 a.m. (to discourage state employees from filling up the spaces). These lots charge the standard $3 parking fee.

ENDNOTES

1. GA. CONST. art. 3, §2, ¶1(b).
2. GA. CONST. art. 3, §2, ¶1(a).
3. *The Book of the States: 1994-95* (Lexington, Ky.: Council of State Governments, 1994), Table 3.3, p. 113.
4. GA. CONST. art. 3, §2, ¶3.
5. GA. CONST. art. 3, §4, ¶5.
6. GA. CONST. art. 3, §2, ¶3.
7. GA. CONST. art. 2, §2, ¶3.
8. Ibid.; *see also* OFFICIAL CODE OF GEORGIA ANNOTATED (O.C.G.A.) §45-2-1(3).
9. 1983 Op. Att'y Gen. 83-33.
10. GA. CONST. art. 2, §2, ¶3. *See also* O.C.G.A. §45-2-1(2).
11. O.C.G.A. §45-2-1(5).
12. GA. CONST. art. 2, §1, ¶3(b).
13. O.C.G.A. §45-5-1.
14. Ibid.
15. O.C.G.A. §§21-2-111, 21-2-153.
16. O.C.G.A. ch. 21-2 provides most of these procedures.
17. O.C.G.A. §21-2-137.
18. O.C.G.A. §21-2-133.
19. GA. CONST. art. 3, §2, ¶4. *See also* O.C.G.A. §45-2-1(4).
20. Ibid.
21. McWilliams v. Neal, 130 Ga. 733, 61 S.E. 721 (1908).
22. O.C.G.A. §21-2-136.
23. *See also* 1977 Ops. Att'y Gen. U77-26, U77-40; 1985 Op. Att'y Gen. U85-33; O.C.G.A. §28-1-13.
24. *See, e.g.,* 1977 Op. Att'y Gen. 77-47; 1968 Op. Att'y Gen. U68-169.
25. GA. CONST. art. 1, §2, ¶3.
26. O.C.G.A. §16-10-9.
27. Greer v. State, 233 Ga. 667, 212 S.E.2d 836 (1975); Murphy v. State, 233 Ga. 681, 212 S.E.2d 839 (1975). *See also* 1974 Op. Att'y Gen. 74-109.
28. Galer v. Regents of the University System, 239 Ga. 268, 236 S.E.2d 617 (1977).
29. GA. CONST. art. 3, §2, ¶4(c).
30. Ibid. Also, in what appears to be the only appellate court decision considering these two prohibitions, the Georgia Supreme Court sustained the governor's appointment of the speaker of the House of Representatives to the State School Building Authority—an authority which the speaker, as a member of the General Assembly, had helped to create. The court based its holding upon the establishing act's express declaration that the authority members were to receive no compensation (thus no emolument was annexed), and upon its determination that the authority did not constitute a civil office because it did not perform "government functions." In making this latter determination, the court disregarded the act's express provision that governmental functions would be exercised by the authority. *See* Sheffield v. State School Building Authority, 208 Ga. 575, 68 S.E.2d 590 (1952). *See also* McLucas v. State Bridge Building Authority, 210 Ga. 1, 77 S.E.2d 531 (1953); Greer v. State, 233 Ga. 667, 212 S.E.2d 836 (1975); 1974 Op. Att'y Gen. 74-109.
31. O.C.G.A. §28-1-4.
32. O.C.G.A. §45-3-1.
33. O.C.G.A. §§45-3-11 through 45-3-14.

34. 1985 Op. Att'y Gen. 85-19.

35. Georgia *House Journal* 1993, reg. sess., 1–10; Georgia *Senate Journal* 1993, reg. sess., 1–17.

36. O.C.G.A. §28-1-5.

37. GA. CONST. art. 3, §2, ¶5; O.C.G.A. §21-2-502.

38. GA. CONST. art. 3, §4, ¶7.

39. O.C.G.A. §§21-2-520 through 21-2-529.

40. GA. CONST. art. 5, §2, ¶5; art. 3, §4, ¶5. *See also* 1969 Op. Att'y Gen. 69-59.

41. O.C.G.A. §21-2-544.

42. GA. CONST. art. 3, §2, ¶1; O.C.G.A. §§28-1-1, 28-2-2.

43. O.C.G.A. §§28-1-1, 28-2-1.

44. GA. CONST. art. 3, §2, ¶2. See Chapter 1 of this handbook for a brief history of reapportionment efforts in Georgia.

45. Toombs v. Fortson, 205 F. Supp. 248 (N.D. Ga., 1962); Gray v. Sanders, 372 U.S. 368 (1963); Reynolds v. Sims, 377 U.S. 533 (1964); Kilpatrick v. Preisler, 394 U.S. 526 (1969); Wells v. Rockefeller, 394 U.S. 542 (1969); Georgia v. United States, 411 U.S. 526 (1973). For a history of reapportionment in Georgia prior to 1970, see Brett W. Hawkins (ed.), *Reapportionment in Georgia* (Athens: Institute of Government, 1970). For a look at state redistricting—including court decisions and trends for the future—see Reapportionment Information Update Series (National Conference of State Legislatures, 1987).

46. 42 U.S.C.A. §§1971, 1973.

47. O.C.G.A. §45-7-4. *See also* O.C.G.A. §28-1-8.

48. 1992 Op. Att'y Gen. U92-19.

49. O.C.G.A. §28-1-8. These amounts are set in the "housekeeping resolution" adopted by each house at the beginning of a biennium.

50. O.C.G.A. §45-7-4(2).

51. O.C.G.A. §§45-7-20, 50-19-7.

52. O.C.G.A. §28-3-23.

53. O.C.G.A. §28-1-8.

54. Ibid.

55. Ibid.

56. Ibid.

57. O.C.G.A. §45-7-30.

58. O.C.G.A. §28-1-8.

59. Ibid.

60. Ibid.

61. Ibid.

62. O.C.G.A. §45-7-4.

63. 1992 Op. Att'y Gen. 92-33.

64. O.C.G.A. §45-7-4.

65. O.C.G.A. §28-1-8.

66. Ibid.

67. O.C.G.A. §45-7-3.

68. Ibid.

69. 1992 Op. Att'y Gen. 92-27.

70. State v. Agan, 259 Ga. 541, 544, 384 S.E. 2d 863 (1989).

71. O.C.G.A. §§45-18-1, 45-18-2.

72. O.C.G.A. §47-6-1.
73. O.C.G.A. ch. 47-6.
74. O.C.G.A. §§47-2-28, 47-2-110, 47-2-120, 47-2-121.
75. O.C.G.A. §47-6-60.

Standards of Legislative Conduct

A number of constitutional and statutory provisions, as well as House and Senate rules, apply to the behavior and ethics of members of the General Assembly. Some of these set privileges, immunities, or standards of conduct that only apply on the floor of a member's house, while other standards have a broader application.

PRIVILEGES AND IMMUNITIES

Georgia law extends several privileges and immunities to members of the General Assembly.

Freedom of speech. Georgia's constitution provides that no legislator is liable to answer in any other place for anything spoken on the floor or in committee in either house.[1] Apparently, this means that a legislator cannot be sued for slander for remarks made during floor debate or in committee. Freeing legislators from the threat of suit presumably fosters a climate of free and open debate in the General Assembly. Nevertheless, as will be noted, there are other limitations that do restrict what a legislator may say.

Immunity from arrest. The constitution of Georgia establishes an immunity for members of its General Assembly in providing that they shall be free from arrest while attending, going to, or returning from meetings of the legislature or legislative committees, except for treason, felony, or breach of the peace.[2]

Immunity in court proceedings. Members are also granted certain immunities in relation to state court proceedings that occur while they are attending sessions of the General Assembly. Any legislator summoned to serve as a witness or a juror in a case is excused from service while attending a session of the General Assembly.[3] In all civil cases, either party has the right to take interrogatories, as provided by the law, of any legislator needed as a witness in the case, when the times for the legislative session and the court session conflict.[4]

In all criminal cases, the presiding judge must, on motion of either the state or the defendant, "continue" (postpone) the case when it appears that a material witness is absent from the court by reason of his or her attendance at the General Assembly.[5] Further, if a legislator is a party or attorney in any civil or criminal trial, the judge must grant a continuance in the case during the legislative session and for a period of three weeks following any recess or adjournment, including adjournment *sine die*. In such instances, it is not necessary that the legislator/attorney be present in court for the call of the case. When several attorneys are involved in one case, this continuance is granted only on a showing that the absent counsel is necessary or desirable for the proper handling of the case. The right of continuance may be waived by the party or attorney announcing in court that he or she is ready for trial when the case is called.[6]

Questions of privilege. In both houses, members are permitted to make certain statements as a matter of privilege. These statements, observations, or discussions are called "questions of privilege" and are divided into two classes. These are

1. questions affecting the rights of the body collectively—its dignity, safety, and the integrity of its proceedings.
2. questions affecting the conduct of members individually, but in their representative capacity only.

Protests. Should a member of the Senate disagree with the action taken, a written protest against the action may be entered in the journal of the Senate. The protest must clearly set forth the grounds of disagreement and may not impugn the motive of the Senate or of any member.[7]

If it is filed with the clerk on the day of the vote, a member of the House may provide a written explanation (not more than 200 words) of his or her vote, and such explanation is printed in the journal.[8]

MISCONDUCT, CRIMES, AND ETHICS

There are some standards of conduct and ethics that apply to all branches of state government, some that apply only to members of the General Assembly and employees of the legislative branch, and some that apply only to members of the General Assembly.

Disorderly conduct. Under Georgia's constitution, each house of the General Assembly has the power to punish its members for disorderly behavior or misconduct.[9] Although this or something similar has been part of the state constitution since 1789, the question of what constitutes "disorderly behavior" or "misconduct" has never been defined, in part because this provision of the constitution has never been argued before Georgia's appellate courts. However, flagrant abuse of House or Senate rules and refusal to accept rulings of the chair or orders by the entire body would probably be considered examples of disorderly conduct. In terms of misconduct, Georgia's recall statute defines misconduct for recall purposes as "an unlawful act committed willfully by an elected public official or a willful violation of the code of ethics for government service contained in Code Section 45-10-1."[10]

Punishment for disorderly conduct can involve censure, a fine, imprisonment, or expulsion. A motion to expel a member requires approval of two-thirds of the entire house to which that member belongs. As a practical matter, these punishments are very seldom invoked.

Disruptions. Members of both houses are to refrain from private conversations and preserve silence until the member speaking has finished.[11] Although only the House has a specific rule, both houses prohibit applause or hisses in their chambers, galleries, or lobbies during any speech or legislative proceeding.[12] Additionally, members in the Senate are forbidden from passing between the presiding officer and a member who is speaking.[13]

Obtaining recognition to speak. No member can address either house (except in the case of appeals in the House of Representatives) or question a member who is speaking unless he or she does so through the presiding officer. If the member speaking declines to be interrupted, no questions can be asked.[14]

Addressing or referring to members by name. Senate rules instruct senators to avoid calling each other by name during floor proceedings. Instead, they are to refer to each other by district or position on the floor, saying, for instance, "the senator from the 44th district" or "the gentleman (lady) in the well."[15] House rules allow the use of "Mr.," "Mrs.," "Miss," or "Ms." plus the member's last name, or the member's title, position on the floor, or district, city, or county—for example, saying "Mr. Jones," "Mrs. Smith," "Miss Brown," "Ms. Black," "Mr. Majority Leader," "the gentleman from the 61st district," or "the lady from Fulton."[16] Although not mandated by rule in either house, the presiding officer is always designated "Mr. Speaker" or "Mr. President."

Privileged conversations. No senator or representative, when debating, can refer to any private conversation with another member.[17]

Disparaging remarks. When candidates are nominated for any office in the Senate, no member may make disparaging remarks concerning them.[18] Additionally, senators recording protests in the journal with respect to some action taken by their house may not impugn the motive of that house or of any member.[19]

Securing a quorum. When the presiding officer has ordered the doors of the chamber closed in order to keep or secure a quorum, no member may depart without first obtaining leave from the body. If necessary, the sergeant-at-arms (and messenger and doorkeeper in the House), on order of the presiding officer, may seek out and arrest absentees and bring them before the body to secure a quorum.[20] In the event that a member is arrested and brought before the body, the full house determines under what conditions he or she is to be discharged from arrest.[21]

Floor decorum. During floor sessions, rules in both houses direct members to act at all times with dignity and in a manner to ensure decorum. The presiding officer of each body is instructed to enforce decorum by calling to order members for such activities as eating at desks, reading newspapers and other materials not pertinent to legislation, unnecessary conversation, and inappropriate dress.[22] Additionally, Senate rules forbid the use of cellular phones in the chamber, and further prohibit eating, reading newspapers, or using cellular phones while any Senate committee is meeting.[23]

Should the presiding officer call a member to order, that member must sit down immediately unless permitted to explain his or her actions. If the member appeals the order of the presiding officer, the member's house decides whether the order was proper. If the member does not then submit to the decision of the body, he or she is reprimanded for the first offense. For the second offense, the member is fined a sum not exceeding $10 in the Senate and $100 in the House. If misconduct continues, the offending legislator may be expelled from the body by a two-thirds vote of the total members on a roll call vote.[24]

Smoking. Rules of the Senate prohibit smoking in the chamber while the Senate is in session, or in committee rooms during committee meetings.[25] In the House, smoking is prohibited in the chamber, in the anteroom on the north side of the chamber, in the restrooms on the north side of the chamber while the House is in session, or during any committee or subcommittee meeting.[26]

Intoxication. The House of Representatives has a specific rule forbidding members in an intoxicated condition or under the influence of drugs listed in the Georgia Controlled Substances Act from entering the floor. The messenger and doorkeeper are charged with rigid enforcement of this rule.[27] Though there is no parallel rule in the Senate, that house follows the same practice of not allowing intoxicated members on the floor.

Voting another member's machine. Because of the extensive use of electronic voting, rules in both houses that prohibit any member or other person from voting in the place of another member on any question or proposition are of particular importance.[28] Designed to protect the integrity of the voting process, these rules apply not only to the practice of voting for an absent colleague, but apparently to the practice of a legislator not in his or her seat signaling another legislator—usually a member in an adjacent seat—to press the voting switch in his or her behalf. Violation of the prohibition against voting in the place of another member can be punishable by censure, fine, imprisonment, or expulsion.[29] More commonly, the presiding officer will admonish members to vote their own machine.

Refusing to vote. If a quorum is present and a member of either house refuses to vote on a measure, that refusal, unless excused by the body, is deemed a contempt of that house.[30]

Bribery. Bribery is committed when someone gives anything of value, or offers to do so, to any person acting on behalf of the state for purposes of influencing that person in the performance of any act related to the functions of his or her office.[31] A legislator commits bribery when, directly or indirectly, he or she solicits, receives, accepts, or agrees to receive any thing of value by inducing the reasonable belief that the giving of the thing will influence his or her performance or failure to perform any official action.[32] State law, however, specifically exempts the following as things of value in terms of the bribery statute:

1. food or beverage consumed at a single meal or event;
2. legitimate salary, benefits, fees, commissions, or expenses associated with a recipient's nonpublic business, employment, trade, or profession;
3. an award, plaque, certificate, memento, or similar item given in recognition of the recipient's civic, charitable, political, professional, or public service;
4. food, beverages, and registration at group events to which all members of the Georgia House, Senate, and their committees or subcommittees are invited;
5. actual and reasonable expenses for food, beverages, travel, lodging, and registration for a meeting, which are provided to permit participation or being a speaker at the meeting;
6. a commercially reasonable loan made in the ordinary course of business;
7. any gift with a value less than $100;
8. promotional items generally distributed to the general public or to public officers;
9. a gift from a member of the legislator's immediate family; or
10. food, beverage, or expenses afforded legislators, members of their immediate families, or others, which are associated with normal and customary business or social functions or activities.

Additionally, the receipt, acceptance, or agreement to receive anything not specified in this list of exclusions shall not create the presumption that criminal bribery has been committed. However, if bribery is proven in a court of law, a legislator faces a fine up to $5,000, imprisonment from 1 to 20 years, or both.

Influencing the passage or defeat of legislation. Although very similar to bribery, legislators face a separate felony crime should they ask for or receive anything of value in return for agreeing to procure (or attempting to procure) the passage or defeat of legislation by the General Assembly, or for attempting to procure the signing or veto of legislation by the governor.[33] The penalty for conviction is imprisonment for one to five years.

Influencing state officials or employees. Legislators face another felony crime similar to bribery if they ask for or receive anything of value in return for attempting to influence official action by any state agency, official, or employee.[34] Upon conviction, a legislator would face imprisonment for one to five years.

Extortion. Extortion is committed when public officers unlawfully take, under color of office, from any person, any money or thing of value that is either not due to them or is more than is due.[35]

Conspiracy to defraud. A legislator commits conspiracy to defraud when agreeing with another to steal any property belonging to the state or under the control or possession of the legislator in his or her official capacity.[36]

Other crimes. It is also a crime (with punishment including fine, imprisonment, and/or removal from office) for a legislator to

1. willfully and intentionally violate the terms of office;[37]
2. enter into a contract, combination, conspiracy in restraint of trade or free and open competition in any transaction with the state or any agency thereof, whether for goods, materials, or services;[38]
3. willfully and knowingly submit a false expense, mileage, or travel voucher;[39]
4. accept any fee, money, gift, or any other thing of value in connection with any claim presented to the Claims Advisory Board.[40]
5. accept a monetary fee or honorarium over $101 for a speaking engagement, participation in a seminar or discussion panel, or other activities directly related to a legislator's official duties. (Exempted are actual and reasonable expenses for food, beverages, travel, lodging, and registration for a meeting to permit a legislator to speak or appear on a panel.)[41]

Conflict of interest. Few issues pose so difficult a problem as that of conflict of interest in so-called "citizen legislatures." One stance supports the belief that lawmakers should neither vote on issues in which they have a personal interest, nor should they be allowed to financially benefit by virtue of their office. An opposing view, however, recognizes that membership in a part-time legislature means that most lawmakers must pursue personal occupations or professions which will occasionally face business dealings with the state.

Georgia's constitution is silent on the issue of conflict of interest except to note that, "Public officers are the trustees and servants of the people and are at all times amenable to them."[42]

Each house of the General Assembly has adopted rules to discourage lawmakers from voting on issues in which they have a personal interest, but these have proven difficult to interpret and enforce. For instance, should a legislator who is a public school teacher be allowed to vote on the state appropriations act which, among other things, sets his or her salary? In the way of guidance, House rules provide that a representative may not vote on any question if "immediately and particularly interested" in its result, while Senate rules stipulate the standard of "direct pecuniary interest."[43]

What should a legislator do in case of an actual (or perceived) conflict of interest when voting on a particular bill? Ordinarily, the rules of parliamentary procedure dictate that the member should abstain from voting. But, rules of both houses in the General Assembly prohibit legislators from abstaining on a vote.[44] The proper procedure is that before the vote begins, the legislator should request permission of his or her house to be excused from voting, briefly stating the reasons why. No debate is permitted on the request, and the body decides whether to allow the excusal.

In 1968, the General Assembly enacted a Code of Ethics for Government Service as a guide for all state officials and employees.[45] According to this code, any person in government service should do as follows:

1. Put loyalty to the highest moral principles and to country above loyalty to persons, party, or government department.
2. Uphold the constitution, laws, and legal regulations of the United States and the state of Georgia and of all governments therein and never be a party to their evasion.
3. Give a full day's labor for a full day's pay and give to the performance of his duties his earnest effort and best thought.
4. Seek to find and employ more efficient and economical ways of getting tasks accomplished.
5. Never discriminate unfairly by the dispensing of special favors or privileges to anyone, whether for remuneration or not, and never accept, for himself or his family, favors or benefits under circumstances which might be construed by reasonable persons as influencing the performance of his governmental duties.

6. Make no private promises of any kind binding upon the duties of office, since a government employee has no private word which can be binding on public duty.
7. Engage in no business with the government, either directly or indirectly, which is inconsistent with the conscientious performance of his governmental duties.
8. Never use any information coming to him confidentially in the performance of governmental duties as a means for making private profit.
9. Expose corruption wherever discovered.
10. Uphold these principles, ever conscious that public office is a public trust.

Because it is couched in terms of "should"—rather than legally enforceable "shall" or "shall not"—and because there are no legal penalties attached for violation, enforcement of the code is presumably left to the conscience of each individual. However, passage of the Recall Act of 1989 gave at least some teeth to the code. Willful violation of the Code of Ethics by an elected official now constitutes "misconduct in office" and is grounds for that official being recalled from office.[46]

The clearest resolution of conflict of interest has come in the area of legislators' financial dealings with the state. Except for situations exempted by statute, legislators may not transact any business with any state agency for themselves or on behalf of any business. Likewise prohibited are financial transactions with state agencies by any business in which a legislator or family member has direct or indirect ownership of more than 25 percent of its assets or stock. Among exceptions to this general rule are (1) transactions made according to sealed competitive bids; (2) single transactions not exceeding $250 (providing the total per calendar year does not exceed $9,000); (3) lease of real property to or from any agency if the transaction has been approved by the State Properties Commission or space management division of the Department of Administrative Services; (4) transactions involving property or a service where the legislator is the only source in Georgia; and (5) emergency purchases.[47]

An additional elaboration on conflict of interest came with a 1982 Georgia Supreme Court decision that the Georgia Constitution's provision declaring public officials to be trustees of the people prohibits legislators (or any other officials) who are also attorneys from representing a client for financial gain in any *civil* transaction or matter in which the state or one of its agencies is an opposing party.[48] Following this decision, Georgia's attorney general issued several opinions clarifying the court's ruling: (1) legislators/lawyers are not prohibited from representing defendants in *criminal* cases; (2) legislators are not prohibited from contacting or appearing before a state agency on behalf of a constituent, without receiving a fee, to ensure that the constituent receives available rights or benefits; (3) legislators/lawyers are not precluded from appearing before a state agency for a client when the state is not a party; and (4) legislators/lawyers are not prevented from dealing with state agencies to protect their own personal interests or rights.[49] In 1985, the Supreme Court ruled a legislator/lawyer could represent clients before state agencies when no fee was charged for the services rendered.[50]

Senate ethics standards. In addition to state statutes, Georgia's Senate has adopted a specific rule that prescribes and governs enforcement of ethical standards for members and employees of the Senate.[51] These standards are as follows:

- Senators and staff must refrain from using government positions to attain financial gain.
- Senators and staff must not use public resources or personnel for the purpose of conducting personal or private business.
- Senators must not seek, accept, use, allocate, grant, or award public funds for any purpose other than as approved by law.
- No senator or staff may solicit a campaign contribution in a state office building, nor may he or she operate political campaigns or fund-raising campaigns from state office buildings unless such space has been leased or rented for this purpose.
- Senators may not withhold, or threaten to withhold, political action or constituent services because of a person's decision to provide or not to provide a political contribution, charitable contribution, or support.
- Senators and staff shall avoid financial conflicts of interest and close economic associations where official action or decisions are motivated not by public duty but by economic self-interest or association.
- No senator or staff, acting as an attorney or representative of another, may seek or accept any special treatment not otherwise approved by law or court order because of his or her legislative role.
- No senator or staff may accept anything of value when such thing is offered with the understanding that official action will be taken or withheld by the senator or staff in consideration of acceptance of that which is offered.
- No senator or staff may seek, accept, or retain employment which makes it unreasonably difficult to fulfill legislative obligations; requires the disclosure or use of nonpublic or confidential information acquired in the course of legislative service; requires improper use of government relationships or the prestige associated with legislative office; or will require the senator or staff to compromise any other ethical or legal duty.

- Unwelcome sexual advances, requests for sexual favors, and other verbal or physical conduct of a sexual nature shall constitute prohibited sexual harassment when (a) submission to such conduct is made explicitly or implicitly a term or condition of an individual's employment, or (b) submission to or rejection of such conduct by an individual is used as a basis for employment decisions affecting that individual, or (c) such conduct interferes with an individual's work performance or creates an intimidating, hostile, or offensive work environment.

- Senators and staff shall not knowingly engage in conduct that violates rights of others, nor shall they unlawfully discriminate against or abuse any person in the course of legislative activities. All contact with constituents, staff, lobbyists, representatives of the media, and others interested in the legislative process shall be conducted in a courteous, professional manner.

- No senator or staff may use improper schemes to circumvent the clear purpose of these rules outlining standards of conduct.

- Senators and staff may not subject any person who reports alleged violations of these rules or any state law to reprisal, harassment, discrimination, or ridicule.

Complaints alleging violations of these rules are to be reported to the secretary of the Senate, who in turn will refer the complaint to the chair of the Senate Ethics Committee. That committee investigates the complaint, using in-house staff and such outside counsel and investigators as necessary. If the committee finds that a violation has occurred or is occurring, it may attempt to negotiate a settlement with the senator or staff member to resolve the complaint. If no settlement is reached, the committee is required to hold an open hearing, at which attendance of witnesses and the production of materials can be required. The senator or staff member being investigated has the right to counsel of his or her own choosing and also has the right to call witnesses and present evidence. The burden of proof is on the committee, which must find "clear and convincing evidence" in order to conclude that a violation of these rules has occurred. If such evidence is found, the committee files a report of its findings and recommended penalties with the secretary of the Senate. If the committee has found evidence of a criminal violation, the matter is referred to the appropriate law enforcement agency for further action.

House ethics standards. The House of Representatives has a similar set of rules that prescribe and govern enforcement of ethical standards for its members and employees.[52] These rules are as follows:

- No House member or staff may unlawfully use his or her office or official position for personal financial gain.

- No House member or staff is entitled to compensation for official duties beyond the pay and allowances attached to that office or as may otherwise be provided by law.
- Unwelcomed sexual advances, unwelcomed requests for sexual favors, and other unwelcomed verbal or physical conduct of a sexual nature shall constitute prohibited sexual harassment when (a) submission to such conduct is made explicitly or implicitly a term or condition of an individual's employment, or (b) submission to or rejection of such conduct by an individual is used as a basis for employment decisions affecting an individual, or (c) such conduct interferes with an individual's work performance or creates an intimidating, hostile, or offensive work environment.
- No House member or staff may knowingly abuse the financial entitlements and privileges authorized by law or resolution.
- House members and staff may not knowingly violate any rule of the House.

Any House member or employee can file a written complaint alleging violations of these rules. The complaint can be presented to any member of the House Ethics Committee, who in turn must present it to the committee's chair. The committee is empowered to investigate the complaint, hold hearings, and compel the attendance of witnesses and production of documents relevant to the investigation. Any House member or employee being investigated has the right to full notice of the alleged charges, the right to counsel, the right to cross-examine committee witnesses, the right to present witnesses and evidence, and the same rights as the committee to call witnesses and present evidence.

Should the committee conclude that a violation of House ethics standards has occurred and that disciplinary action is warranted, it is directed to report these findings to the speaker of the House, clerk of the House, Legislative Services Committee, or any other officer or agency of the General Assembly. Should the Ethics Committee find strong evidence that a House member or employee has committed a criminal violation, such evidence is to be reported to the appropriate law enforcement agency.

Among other powers, the Ethics Committee can issue advisory opinions that address questions of ethical and proper conduct by House members and employees.

REGULATION OF LOBBYING

Prior to 1983, Georgia's constitution declared "lobbying" to be a crime— a prohibition dating back to 1877.[53] However, the constitution left it up to the General Assembly to define "lobbying" by statute and provide for its penalties. Because this meant that lobbying was totally regulated by statute, framers of the Constitution of 1983 deleted reference to lobbying from the new constitution.

Until 1992, Georgia statutes continued to declare "lobbying" to be a crime but defined it in terms of attempting to influence a legislator's vote by means "not addressed solely to the judgment" (e.g., bribery or coercion). State law required anyone who attempted to influence the legislative process to register with the secretary of state and pay a $5 annual fee. Legally, the lobbyist was then known as a "registered agent."

In passing the Public Officials Conduct and Lobbyist Disclosure Act of 1992, the General Assembly finally decided to erase the legal fiction that lobbying was a crime in Georgia. The law made important changes in the definition of lobbying and instituted new registration and disclosure procedures for lobbyists.[54]

Georgia law now defines "lobbying" as any effort by any natural person (including members of the executive or judicial branches) to promote or oppose passage of legislation in the General Assembly (including committees) or the approval or veto of legislation by the governor if (1) such effort is conducted for compensation (either individually or as an employee of someone else) or (2) more than $250 is spent on lobbying activities in a calendar year (not including that person's own travel, food, lodging, or the cost of informational material).[55]

On the issue of compensation, Georgia's attorney general has ruled in an unofficial opinion that it is not necessary that a person be employed for compensation solely for the purpose of lobbying in order to fall within the requirements for registration. "As long as an individual is compensated to represent the general business or purpose of a corporation, association, or agency, and that individual contacts a member of the General Assembly for the purpose of promoting or opposing the passage of legislation on behalf of such group, then that individual must register as a lobbyist and comply with the provision of Article 4 of O.C.G.A. Chapter 21-5."[56] At issue in the opinion was whether compensated officers of unions and business organizations who attempt to influence legislation on behalf of their organization come under the lobbyist registration requirements, which the opinion held that they did.

The State Ethics Commission has given some guidance on determining whether someone who as "an employee of another person" is lobbying "for compensation" and thus comes under the registration requirements. Foremost, there must be a connection between the promoting or opposing of legislation and the job for which the employee is paid. In making that determination, the following are among the factors that should be considered:

- whether the subject matter of the legislation would affect the business of the employer;

- whether the lobbying effort is undertaken during hours for which the employee is being paid;
- whether the employer reimburses or pays directly any expenses incurred by the employee during the lobbying effort;
- whether any equipment, property, or facilities of the employer are used in the lobbying effort;
- whether the lobbying effort is known to the employer;
- whether the lobbying effort is approved by the employer;
- whether the employee routinely, or when needed, handles lobbying or "governmental relations" functions for the employer;
- whether the lobbying effort is encouraged by the employer;
- whether the lobbying effort is directed by the employer;
- whether the employer has a policy as to who is and is not authorized to lobby on behalf of the employer;
- the nature and extent of the activity (For example, is it a pure "appeal to reason" through a letter or telephone conversation discussing the merits of legislation? Is it the cultivation of goodwill through some social event or through some other form of payment designed to encourage or influence? Is it a gift of anything of value?);
- whether the parties had some previous relationship outside the lobbying context;
- the ability of the individual by virtue of his or her position or other factors to influence a legislative decision;
- the number of times of contact or activity;
- the number of persons contacted or involved in an activity; and
- how the contact or activity was initiated.[57]

In determining what expenditures are and are not counted against the $250 threshold for nonpaid lobbyists, the following types do count:

- any purchase, payment, distribution, load, advance, deposit, or conveyance of money or anything of value made for the purpose of influencing the actions of any public officer or employee;
- any form of payment when such can be reasonably construed as designed to encourage or influence a public officer;
- any gratuitous transfer, payment, subscription, advance, or deposit of money, services, or anything of value, unless consideration of equal or greater value is received; and
- food or beverage consumed at a single meal or event by a public officer or employee or a member of the immediate family of such public officer or employee.[58]

Not counted against the $250 threshold are

- the value of personal services performed voluntarily and without compensation;
- gifts received from a member of a public officer's immediate family;
- legal compensation or expense reimbursement provided public officers and employees in the performance of their duties;
- promotional items generally distributed to the general public or to public officers;
- foods and beverages produced in Georgia;
- awards, plaques, certificates, mementos, or similar items given in recognition of the recipient's record of service;
- legitimate salary, benefits, fees, commissions, or expenses associated with a recipient's nonpublic business, employment, trade, or profession;
- food, beverages, and registration at group events to which all members of a state or local agency—including the House, Senate, and the committees and subcommittees of either house—have been invited;
- campaign contributions or expenditures reported as required by Article 2 of Chapter 5 of Title 2; or
- commercially reasonable loans made in the ordinary course of business.[59]

Registration of lobbyists. No person may engage in lobbying as defined by law unless first registered with the State Ethics Commission. All lobbyists must register annually, at which time they must provide information about themselves and the person, firm, association, or agency they represent. Lobbyists must pay an annual registration fee of $200, $10 for each supplemental registration, and $5 for an identification card. Persons who represent state or local government agencies or authorities do not have to pay any fees, while persons who represent any organization exempt from federal income taxation must pay only an initial registration fee of $25.[60]

Once registered, the lobbyist receives an identification badge with the word "LOBBYIST" and the name of the lobbyist. If the lobbyist represents a single client, the name of that client is also listed on the badge. In the case of multiple clients, client names are omitted.

Lobbyists must display their identification badges in a readily visible manner whenever they are lobbying in the state capitol or any governmental facility.[61]

Exemption from registration requirements. State law exempts the following persons from having to register as lobbyists:

- any individual who on his or her own behalf expresses personal views to any public official;

- any person not otherwise required to register as a lobbyist who appears before a government agency, committee, or hearing to testify;
- any public employee who appears before a government agency or committee at that entity's request;
- any licensed attorney appearing on behalf of a client in any adversarial proceeding before a state agency;
- any person employed or appointed by a registered lobbyist whose duties and activities do not include lobbying;
- elected public officials performing their official duties; and
- any public employee who performs services at the discretion of a member of the General Assembly, including such services as bill drafting, taking testimony, collecting facts, preparing arguments and submitting them to legislative committees or other legislators, and "other services of like character intended to reach the reason of legislators."[62]

Lobbyist disclosure reports. Each registered lobbyist must file a monthly disclosure report, current through end of the preceding month, on or before the fifth day of any month in which the General Assembly is in session. A disclosure report current through the end of the six-month period ending July 31 must be filed by August 5, and a similar report for the six-month period ending December 31 must be filed by the following January 5.

Disclosure reports must include a description of all expenditures made by a lobbyist or his or her employees, including the name and title of the officer for which the expenditure was made; the amount, date, and description of the expenditure; and if applicable, the number of the bill or resolution for which the lobbying expenditure was made. Additionally, the lobbyist must disclose the names of any members of the immediate family of a public officer who are employed by, or whose professional services were paid for, by the lobbyist during the reporting period.[63]

Other regulations. No person, firm, corporation, or association may retain or employ an attorney-at-law or an agent to aid or oppose legislation for a compensation which is contingent, in whole or in part, upon the passage of any legislative measure.[64]

State law prohibits any registered lobbyist, or any other unauthorized person, from going upon the floor of either house of the General Assembly while it is in session to discuss privately measures then pending in the legislature.[65]

Lobbyists and the legislative process. Many states have what is termed a "professional legislature," which implies long sessions, aides for each legislator, and professional staffing for each committee. In contrast,

Georgia's General Assembly historically has functioned more as a "citizen legislature" with brief sessions, few aides and committee staff, and extremely limited office space. Over the last two decades (particularly since the acquisition of the Legislative Office Building in the 1980s), this has been changing. Each house now has a small research office, and the two houses share 30 or so college interns. But, except for these and the Office of Legislative Counsel and the Legislative Budget Office, most legislators and committees still must function without aides or professional staff.

Given the fact that the General Assembly may consider 3,000 or more bills and resolutions in a single session, many Georgia legislators have come to depend on lobbyists for information on measures before that body. Interestingly, even as the General Assembly has taken strides to improve legislative staffing, the number of registered lobbyists has grown steadily, jumping from 280 in 1971, to 571 in 1983, to 917 by mid-1994.[66] However, many of those now registered as lobbyists are state employees, who since 1992 have had to register if they are involved in lobbying.

Ambiguities in what is allowed. Georgia law appears to provide some clear black-and-white answers about what types of expenditures lobbyists can make in attempting to influence legislation. But, unfortunately, there are many shady areas about what a lobbyist can offer and what a legislator can accept.

The bribery and bribery-related crimes discussed earlier seem to set unambiguous standards. According to exceptions spelled out in Georgia statutes, it is *not* bribery for a lobbyist to buy a meal for a legislator, to give a legislator a gift (such as tickets to a sporting event) that does not exceed $100 in value, or to pay all expenses for a legislator to attend a conference or meeting at which the legislator will participate or speak. However, while such expenditures may be legal in the abstract, there are some circumstances where they might be ruled illegal.

For example, what if the legislator is receiving an all-expenses-paid trip to attend a "conference" at one of Hawaii's finest hotels, most of the "business" will take place on the golf course, the legislator being feted is the chair of the committee considering a major bill sought by one of Georgia's industries, the lobbyist represents that industry, and a divided committee is scheduled to vote on the bill the following week? The *timing* and overall *context* in which an otherwise legal gift is offered by a lobbyist and accepted by a legislator could combine to make it illegal.

The State Ethics Commission publishes a manual for lobbyists, that deals with registration and reporting requirements.[67] Unfortunately for both lobbyist and legislator alike, there is no comprehensive compilation of do's and don'ts covering every possible situation that might arise. That is because state law does not specify exactly what is and is not permissible, as so much depends on the total circumstances of the offer/acceptance.

As a final caution, even if the acceptance of a gift or expenditure proves to be entirely legal, legislators should remember that state law requires the lobbyist to report it to the State Ethics Commission, at which time the expenditures become a matter of public record available to the press and political opponents. This means keeping in mind that both *legal* and *political* ramifications can potentially arise when a legislator accepts a gift.

FINANCIAL REGULATIONS

Campaign contribution requirements. Contributions for any candidate seeking office in the General Assembly must be made directly to the candidate or to the candidate's campaign committee. Every campaign committee must have a chair and a treasurer, although the candidate may serve in these two roles.[68]

Before the candidate or campaign committee can accept any contributions, the name and address of the chair and treasurer must be filed with the secretary of state, and no contributions may be accepted if there is a vacancy in either office. Once elected to the General Assembly, a legislator's campaign committee does not have to be re-registered unless the legislator creates a new committee.[69]

Contributions of money must be deposited in a separate campaign depository account opened and maintained by the candidate or campaign committee for use in the campaign for election or reelection. Such account may earn interest, but that interest is counted as a contribution and can only be used for purposes of the campaign committee.[70]

Should separate contributions of less than $101 be received from a common source (such as the same family, firm, partnership, or employees of the same person), those contributions are to be aggregated for reporting purposes. Excluded from this requirement is the purchase of tickets for a fundraising event that do not exceed $25 each.[71]

Acceptance of anonymous contributions is prohibited, and a candidate is required to turn such monies over to the state and to report the gift to the State Ethics Commission.[72] Also, neither candidate nor campaign committee can accept any direct or indirect campaign contribution from any state or local government agency.[73]

Each candidate or campaign committee treasurer must keep detailed accounts, current within not more than five business days after receipt of a contribution or making an expenditure, of all contributions received and all expenditures made. Also required are detailed accounts of all deposits and withdrawals made to the separate campaign depository and of all interest earned on such deposits. Such records must be kept for three years after the race.[74]

Funds from a campaign account may only be used for ordinary and necessary expenses associated with a campaign for election or reelection, which may include any loan from a candidate to the campaign committee. Any monies left over in the account after the election may only be used to donate to charitable organizations or to any committee of any political party or candidate; to reimburse donors up to the amount of their contributions; and for repayment of any prior campaign obligations incurred as a candidate. Additionally, any unspent funds may be used in future campaigns, but only if for the elective office for which they were originally given.[75] Thus, a legislator campaigning for reelection could use unspent funds collected in a previous race for the legislature, but could not spend them in a campaign for any other office. Apparently, this would prohibit a member of the one house of the General Assembly from using leftover funds from a previous race in a future race for a seat in the other house.

Any candidate for a seat in the General Assembly, or officer of his or her campaign committee, must file with the election superintendent of the county in which the candidate resides (along with a copy to the secretary of state) a contribution disclosure report listing

- the name, mailing address, occupation, amount, and date of receipt of each contribution of $101.00 or more;
- a list of separate contributions of less than $101.00 (which would require identification of the donor should additional contributions push the total to $101.00 or more);
- the name, mailing address, and occupation or place of employment of any person to whom an expenditure of $101.00 or more is made, including the amount and general purpose of the expenditure;
- name of lending institution or party when the contribution consists of a loan, advance, or other extension of credit, and the names, mailing addresses, occupations, and places of employment of all persons having any liability for repayment of such contribution; and the fiduciary relationship (if any) of the person making the contribution to the lending institution or party advancing or extending credit;
- the corporate, labor union, or other affiliation of any political action committee making a contribution of $101.00 or more.

This report must be filed 45 days and again 15 days before the primary, 10 days after the primary, and 15 days prior to the general election. A final campaign contribution disclosure report must be filed not later than December 31 of the election year.[76]

Contributions prohibited during legislative session. No member of the General Assembly or that member's campaign committee is allowed to accept any contribution during a legislative session. This restriction, however, does not apply to the receipt of a contribution during a session arising from a dinner, luncheon, rally, or similar fundraising event held prior to the session.[77]

Financial disclosure statements. Between January 1 and July 1 of each odd-numbered year, each member of the General Assembly is required to file with the secretary of state a financial disclosure statement for the preceding calendar year that identifies

1. each monetary fee or honorarium of $101.00 or less accepted by the legislator for speaking engagements, participation in seminars, discussion panels, or other activities which directly relate to the legislator's official duties, with a statement identifying the amount of the fee or honorarium and from whom it was accepted;
2. all fiduciary positions held by the legislator, the title of each such position, the name and address of the business entity, and the principal activity of the business entity;
3. name, address, and principal activity of any business entity and the office held by the legislator, the duties of the legislator in the business entity as of December 31 of the covered year in which the legislator has a direct ownership interest which (1) is more than 10 percent of the total interests in such business, or (2) has a net fair market value of more than $20,000;
4. each tract of real property in which the legislator has a direct ownership interest as of December 31 of the covered year when that interest has a net fair market value in excess of $20,000, and the county, state, and general location where the property is located;
5. all annual payments in excess of $20,000 received by the legislator or any business entity identified in paragraph (3) above from the state, or any agency or authority created by the state, and authorized and exempted from disclosure under O.C.G.A. §45-10-25, and the agency making the payment, and the general nature of why the payment is being made.[78]

SUSPENSION AND REMOVAL FROM OFFICE

In addition to being subject to censure, fine, imprisonment, expulsion, and impeachment, legislators may be suspended under certain circumstances. By virtue of constitutional amendments in 1984 and 1986, lawmakers and other state officials face suspension if indicted for certain offenses.

For a legislator, suspension works in the following manner. If indicted for a felony by a state or federal grand jury, the legislator's indictment is reviewed by a special committee consisting of the attorney general and one member from each house. (If the attorney general has prosecuted the indictment, the governor names a retired supreme court justice or court of appeals judge to sit on the committee instead.) The committee has 14 days to conduct its investigation and hold a hearing. If it determines that the indictment relates to and adversely affects the legislator's duties, and that the interests of the public are adversely affected, it so informs the governor, who shall immediately suspend the legislator (with pay). If the suspended lawmaker is subsequently convicted in a trial court, the pay is stopped. If the conviction is overturned on appeal, the suspension is lifted and the withheld pay returned. If not overturned, or if no appeal is filed, the office is declared vacant immediately.[79]

RECALL

State legislators (as well as every other public official who holds elected office in Georgia) are subject to recall from office by the registered voters of their respective districts.[80] Following are the statutory grounds for recall:

1. While in office, an elected official conducts himself or herself in a manner which relates to and adversely affects the administration of that office and adversely affects the rights and interests of the public.

2. The elected official (a) has committed one or more acts of malfeasance while in office; (b) has violated his or her oath of office; (c) has committed an act of misconduct in office [which is defined by statute as an unlawful act committed willfully by an elected public official or a willful violation of the code of ethics for government service contained in O.C.G.A. §45-10-1]; (d) is guilty of a failure to perform duties prescribed by law; or (e) has willfully misused, converted, or misappropriated, without authority, public property or public funds entrusted to or associated with the elective office. However, discretionary performance of a lawful act or a prescribed duty shall not constitute a ground for recall.

To recall a state legislator, a petition must first be filed identifying the official sponsors and chair of the recall drive and the specific statutory grounds for the legislator's recall. The petition must be signed by at least 30 percent of the number of registered voters in the legislator's district at the last general election. No petition may be filed during the first 180 days or the last 180 days of a legislator's term of office.

If these conditions are met, the legislator can ask a superior court judge to review the legal sufficiency of the recall grounds and the legal sufficiency of the alleged facts upon which such grounds are based. If the judge rules that the grounds and facts are sufficient, the recall proceedings can continue.

Within 10 days of receiving a certification of sufficiency, the governor must call a recall election, to be held not less than 30 or more than 45 days after the call. At that election, if more than 50 percent of the votes cast are in favor of recall, the legislator's office shall immediately be declared vacant and a special election to fill the office called within 10 days, the date of such election to be at least 30 days and not more than 45 days from the date of vacancy. The legislator who was recalled is eligible to run in that election.

ENDNOTES

1. GA. CONST. art. 3, §4, ¶9.
2. Ibid.
3. OFFICIAL CODE OF GEORGIA ANNOTATED (O.C.G.A.) §§9-10-159, 17-8-28, 15-12-2.
4. O.C.G.A. §§9-10-159, 17-8-28.
5. O.C.G.A. §17-8-28.
6. O.C.G.A. §§9-10-150, 17-8-26.
7. Senate Rule 61.
8. House Rule 137.
9. GA. CONST. art. 3, §4, ¶7.
10. O.C.G.A. §21-4-3 (8).
11. Senate Rule 57; House Rule 13.
12. House Rule 14.
13. Senate Rule 58.
14. Senate Rule 53; House Rule 83.
15. Senate Rule 55.
16. House Rule 85.
17. Senate Rule 54; House Rule 84.
18. Senate Rule 192.
19. Senate Rule 61.
20. Senate Rule 47; House Rule 43.
21. Senate Rule 48; House Rule 44.
22. Senate Rule 50, House Rule 13.
23. Senate Rule 50.
24. Senate Rule 50; House Rule 81.
25. Senate Rule 50.
26. House Rule 13.
27. House Rule 12.
28. Senate Rule 168; House Rule 136.
29. Ibid. GA. CONST. art. 3, §4, ¶7, provides for punishment for disorderly behavior and misconduct.
30. Senate Rule 170; House Rule 132.
31. O.C.G.A. §16-10-2.
32. Ibid.
33. O.C.G.A. §16-10-4.
34. O.C.G.A. §16-10-5.

35. O.C.G.A. §45-11-5.

36. O.C.G.A. §16-10-21.

37. O.C.G.A. §16-10-1.

38. O.C.G.A. §16-10-22.

39. O.C.G.A. §28-1-8.

40. O.C.G.A. §28-5-62.

41. O.C.G.A. §21-5-11.

42. GA. CONST. art. 1, §2, ¶1.

43. Senate Rule 175; House Rule 134.

44. Senate Rule 174; House Rule 134.

45. O.C.G.A. §45-10-1.

46. O.C.G.A. §21-4-3(8).

47. O.C.G.A. §§45-10-24, 45-10-25.

48. Ga. Dept. of Human Resources v. Sistrunk, 249 Ga. 543, 291, S.E. 2d 524 (1982).

49. 1982 Ops. Att'y Gen. 82-82, U82-44.

50. Ga. State Board of Pharmacy v. Lovvorn, 255 Ga. 259, 336 S.E.2d 238 (1985).

51. Senate Rule 185A.

52. House Rules 164-71.

53. GA. CONST. art. 3, §4, ¶7.

54. O.C.G.A. §§21-5-70 through 21-5-73.

55. O.C.G.A. §21-5-70 (6). "Lobbying" is also defined to include attempts to influence the passage of ordinances and resolutions by local governments or the approval or veto of such measures (where applicable).

56. 1993 Op. Att'y Gen. U92-2.

57. *Information Concerning Lobbyist Registration and Reporting* (Atlanta: State Ethics Commission, 1993), pp. 3-4.

58. O.C.G.A. §21-5-70 (1). In §21-5-70 (1) (E) (x), the law includes a provision exempting "[f]ood, beverage, or expenses afforded public offficers, members of their immediate families, or others that are associated with normal and customary business or social functions or activities" from the definition of "expenditure." However, this apparent exemption is overriden by §21-5-70 (1) (D), which states, "Notwithstanding division (x) of subparagraph (E) of this paragraph, includes food or beverage consumed at a single meal or event by a public officer or public employee or a member of the immediate family of such public officer or public employee." The position of the State Ethics Commission is that food and beverage expenses do count when calculating whether a person qualifies as a lobbyist by virtue of having spent more than $250 in attempting to influence legislation. Also, by virtue of §21-5-73 (d) (1) (C), food and beverage expenditures must be listed in the disclosure forms that lobbyists must file with the commission.

59. Ibid.

60. O.C.G.A. §21-5-71.

61. Ibid.

62. Ibid.

63. O.C.G.A. §21-5-73.

64. O.C.G.A. §28-7-3.

65. O.C.G.A. §28-7-4. Similarly, Senate Rule 17 and House Rule 12 prohibit any person engaged in lobbying or otherwise attempting to influence legislation from going on the floor of either house.

66. Figures compiled by the Office of Secretary of State and the State Ethics Commission.

67. *Information Concerning Lobbyist Registration and Reporting* (Atlanta: State Ethics Commission, 1993).

68. O.C.G.A. §21-5-30 (a).

69. O.C.G.A. §21-5-30 (b).

70. O.C.G.A. §21-5-30 (c).

71. O.C.G.A. §21-5-30 (d).

72. O.C.G.A. §21-5-30 (e).

73. O.C.G.A. §21-5-30.2 (c).

74. O.C.G.A. §21-5-32.

75. O.C.G.A. §21-5-33.

76. O.C.G.A. §21-5-34.

77. O.C.G.A. §21-5-35.

78. O.C.G.A. §21-5-50.

79. GA. CONST. art. 2, §3, ¶1-2.

80. O.C.G.A. ch. 21-4.

4 Convening and Organizing

SESSIONS OF THE GENERAL ASSEMBLY

Regular Sessions

Members of Georgia's House and Senate are elected for a two-year term of office—a period known as a *biennium*. During their term, regular sessions are held annually, with lawmakers convening on the second Monday in January. The first session is held in odd-numbered years, and the concluding session of the biennium in even years. Legislative matters pending at the end of the first session can be carried over to the second. Any business still pending at the end of the second session, however, dies.

By concurrent resolution, the General Assembly may adjourn a regular session at any time and set a later time to reconvene, but in the aggregate a regular session may not extend more than 40 days each year.[1]

Between 1963 and 1976, the constitution provided for a split session in each odd-numbered year, whereby the legislature convened in January for no longer than 12 days, during which time it organized, began consideration of legislation, and received the governor's proposed appropriations bill. Thereafter, the General Assembly adjourned for a "budget recess" to study the appropriations bill. On the second Monday in February, it reconvened in regular session for no more than 33 additional days, permitting sessions of 45 days in odd years.[2] In even years, there was no provision for a budget recess, and the regular session was limited to 40 days.

This difference in session length traces to the practice of biennial appropriations acts that were adopted in odd-numbered years. Before a 1972 constitutional amendment formalized annual appropriations, the General Assembly appropriated money on an annual basis by passing a biennial budget in odd years and amending that budget in even years. The 45-day split session, however, was abandoned by the Constitution of 1976, and now all sessions extend for 40 days in the aggregate.

Legislative sessions are measured by *legislative* days, which are synonymous with *calendar* days, unless both houses adopt a joint resolution to adjourn, in which event the count of legislative days is suspended during the adjournment. Such formal adjournments are common, meaning that annual sessions of the General Assembly always exceed 40 calendar days.[3]

Unless both houses formally adjourn, Saturdays and Sundays count in the 40-day limit for a session—regardless of whether the legislature is actually in session. State law and House and Senate rules provide that daily sessions convene at 10:00 a.m. and make no exclusion for Sunday (although Senate rules exempt Sunday unless otherwise ordered by the Senate).[4] Saturday sessions, although not common, do sometimes occur, while Sunday sessions rarely—if ever—happen.

Adjournment by concurrent resolution. Early in a session, each house typically concludes legislative activity Friday afternoon and adjourns separately until Monday morning. In the absence of concurrent resolution to formally stop the count of days, Saturdays and Sundays are counted against the total session length. As the legislative workload escalates later in the session, both houses will often agree through concurrent resolution to adjourn and stop the count of days over a weekend. Occasionally, particularly when a legislative impasse has arisen, a formal adjournment (usually from several days to a week or two) will be invoked.

Simple adjournment. At the conclusion of legislative activities during a day—or at any time—either house may terminate or suspend its proceedings through a simple motion "to adjourn" or "to adjourn to a time definite." A motion to adjourn—which takes precedence over all other motions in either house—terminates proceedings for that day, with reconvening at 10:00 a.m. the next morning.[5] A motion "to adjourn to a time definite" is used to suspend proceedings until a later time during the same day, to terminate proceedings but designate a specific time for reconvening the next day, to adjourn over the weekend, or to adjourn for not more than three days.

It should be noted that these motions—unless jointly undertaken through concurrent resolutions—do *not* have the effect of suspending the count of days authorized for a session.

The constitution prohibits either house from adjourning for more than three days or meeting at any other place without the approval of the other house. (During special sessions, neither house may adjourn more than twice, and each adjournment may not exceed seven days.)[6]

After the 30th day of any session, if one house adopts a resolution to adjourn for a specified period of time, and the other house has not concurred by the end of the day set for such adjournment, the governor may adjourn both houses for not more than 10 days.[7]

Adjournment sine die. At the conclusion of a session, the final adjournment is accomplished through a concurrent resolution for *adjourn-*

ment sine die, which literally means "adjournment without a day [for reconvening]." The House and Senate chambers are located on opposite sides of the state capitol. Traditionally, when the time for final adjournment comes, the presiding officers of both houses order the doors to their chambers opened. Looking across to the other chamber, the two presiding officers attempt to gavel adjournment *sine die* simultaneously.

Carry-over legislation. All business pending in either house at the adjournment of the first session of a biennium is carried over to the second session of the same General Assembly and taken up again at whatever point the measure had progressed at the close of the previous session. But bills and resolutions (or other business) pending at the adjournment of the second regular session of a biennium die and cannot be carried over to the newly elected legislature that meets the following January, unless reintroduced and routed through the proper channels.

Special Sessions

Should important matters arise between regular sessions, Georgia's governor may call the General Assembly back into special session (once termed "extraordinary session"). Since 1900, 25 separate special sessions have been convened, most recently in 1981, 1982, 1989, and 1991. In recent years, most have been called to deal with legislative and congressional reapportionment or with state budget crises.

To convene a special session, the governor issues an executive proclamation stating the subjects to be considered. The decision to call a special session is not reviewable by the courts, nor is there a limit as to how many subjects may be included in the proclamation.[8]

Any time prior to the opening of the special session, the governor may amend the call to add or delete subjects; however, once the session is under way, the governor may amend the call only with approval of three-fifths of the members of each house.[9]

No law may be enacted at a special session that does not relate to the purposes stated in the governor's proclamation.[10] While in some states the subjects to be dealt with must be stated *specifically* in the governor's call, Georgia courts have ruled that the state constitution only requires that enactments *relate* to subject matter set forth in the call.[11] Should the General Assembly pass a law at a special session not related to these matters, the governor's subsequent signing of the bill will not make it valid.[12]

Statutes have been held invalid when the court thought that they clearly did not meet this requirement. For example, a statute purporting to require the equipping of automobiles with brakes, horns, headlights, and the like, and regulating the speed at which drivers could approach bridges, was held not to relate to the governor's call of a special session for the purposes of amending the automobile license tax.[13]

Self-convening sessions. Since 1937, the legislature has been empowered to convene itself in special session. This authority resulted from the refusal of a governor to call a special session after the regular session had failed to approve an appropriations bill for the state.

Now, a governor must convene a special session within three days (excluding Sundays) of receipt of a petition signed by three-fifths of the members of each house stating that in their opinion an emergency exists in the affairs of the state.[14] If the governor refuses, the legislature may convene itself.

Length of special sessions. However called, special sessions are limited to 40 days, unless a resolution to extend the length is approved by three-fifths of each house and the governor. Should an impeachment trial be under way at the expiration of 40 days, the House must adjourn, leaving the Senate in session until the impeachment trial has been completed.[15]

Emergency Sessions

In the event of an emergency or disaster resulting from man-made or natural causes or enemy attack upon Georgia, the legislature may meet in an emergency session. The emergency meeting would be held at the new location of state government as designated by the governor. It could take place either upon the call of the governor, or, if no call is issued, by initiative of the legislators themselves following the emergency or disaster. At this emergency meeting, the General Assembly is not controlled by constitutional limitations upon length of sessions, and it can suspend operations of constitutional rules governing the procedures of both houses.[16]

ORGANIZING THE TWO HOUSES

At 10:00 a.m. on the second Monday in January of odd-numbered years, newly elected and reelected members of the General Assembly gather in their respective chambers for swearing-in ceremonies.[17] The first task after the oaths are taken is organization of the two houses.

Organizing officials. State law provides that the task of organizing the two houses is to be performed by the secretary of the Senate and the clerk of the House of Representatives.[18] In actual practice, however, the lieutenant governor, as president of the Senate, presides and calls the Senate to order, while the clerk of the previous House of Representatives presides there until a speaker is elected.

Oath. Before taking a seat, each senator and representative must take an oath or affirmation. The oath used in the House of Representatives states:

> I do hereby solemnly swear or affirm that I will support the Constitution of this State and of the United States, and on all questions and

measures which may come before me, I will so conduct myself, as will, in my judgment, be most conducive to the interests and prosperity of this State.

I further swear or affirm that I am not the holder of any public money due this State, unaccounted for, that I am not the holder of any office of trust under the government of the United States, nor of any one of the several States, nor of any foreign state, that I am otherwise qualified to hold said office according to the Constitution and laws of Georgia and that I am not a member of the Communist Party.[19]

The oath in the Senate is identical, except that reference to membership in the Communist party has been deleted, while "So help me God" has been added to the end.[20]

The oath may be administered to legislators by any supreme court justice or by any court of appeals, superior court, or state court judge. Arrangements for the justice or judge are made by the officer organizing each branch.[21] All members take the oath as a group.

Assignment of seats. Assignment of seats to members in the House is the express duty of the speaker, although House rules provide that representatives during the last preceding regular session may sit in the seats they occupied at that time.[22] In the Senate, choice of seats goes first to the president pro tempore, majority leader, minority leader, senators with over 20 years continuous service, administration floor leader, majority whip, one assistant floor leader, and the chair of the Rules Committee, in that order, with all other senators seated by district number in ascending numerical order beginning with the lowest permanently numbered available seat.[23]

Contested elections. The state constitution empowers each house to be judge of the election, returns, and qualifications of its members.[24] Georgia appellate courts have ruled that the power to judge the eligibility of members exclusively belongs to each house, and these courts have refused to take jurisdiction of controversies involving these matters.[25] However, as noted on page 15, election contests can be based on other issues and thus be properly handled by the courts.[26]

While Senate rules are silent, House rules specify the procedure for handling election contests in that body. A contest may only be filed by a person certified as having won an election to the House or by the challenger(s) for that contested seat. The contest is filed with the clerk, who reports the matter to the speaker, who in turn refers it to the Rules Committee. As soon as possible, that committee must notify the person whose seat is being challenged that he or she will have the right to speak, have counsel, and compel the production of evidence. Then, a hearing is held by the committee, followed by its decision on the contest. If the hearing is held prior to the session, the full House votes on the first day of the session whether to sustain or reverse the committee's decision, or take other action. If the hearing is held during the session, the House votes on the next legislative day.[27] Rules of both houses require the member being challenged and the challenger to leave the chamber before a vote by the full body is taken.[28]

ELECTION OF OFFICERS IN THE TWO HOUSES AND THEIR POWERS AND DUTIES

After the members have been sworn and have taken their seats, the houses of the General Assembly elect their respective officers for the session.

Georgia's constitution provides for a speaker, a speaker pro tempore, and a clerk in the House of Representatives, and for a president, a president pro tempore, and a secretary in the Senate, plus such assistants as each house may provide for.[29]

Elected officers of each house are formally selected by recorded vote in each house at the first session following election of a new General Assembly. As a practical matter, however, the speaker, speaker pro tempore, and president pro tempore are selected at caucuses of the majority party of the House and Senate prior to the session.

President of the Senate

Georgia's lieutenant governor, a member of the executive branch, serves ex officio as the presiding officer of the Senate, and in this capacity is designated president.[30] While this would appear to violate the constitutional scheme of separation of powers, it is an exception allowed under the concept of checks and balances. Although the lieutenant governor sits on several boards in the executive branch, it is primarily in the legislative branch that his or her power lies.

Once the Senate is in session, the president assumes important powers and responsibilities, including appointing new members, reassigning members who so request, and designating officers to all standing committees and subcommittees in the Senate.[31] He or she refers every bill or resolution introduced in the Senate, or sent from the House, to the proper standing committee without debate, unless otherwise ordered by the Senate.[32] Also, should the Senate authorize a conference committee with the House, it is the lieutenant governor who names Senate members to the committee.[33]

Among the president's other powers are (1) recognizing senators who wish to ask a question from their desk either to the presiding officer or another senator speaking from the well; (2) deciding which senator may next address the full body from the Senate well; (3) commanding silence in the chamber; and (4) clearing the Senate galleries and lobbies, if necessary.[34]

The lieutenant governor may order Senate doors closed, have the roll called to determine if a quorum is present, and compel the attendance of senators in order to obtain or keep a quorum.[35]

All questions on priority of Senate business are decided by the president without debate, unless Senate rules provide otherwise.[36] Not only may irrelevant debate be suspended in the chamber, but the president may rule out amendments not germane to the measure before the body.[37] The presiding officer may require the third reading of a bill in its entirety rather than by title alone, and may order a roll call vote on any matter before the Senate.[38] The lieutenant governor, however, cannot vote on any matter or under any circumstance in the Senate. The president does sign all acts and resolutions passed by the Senate, as well as all writs, warrants, and subpoenas issued by its order.[39]

During a day's session, the president may name any senator to perform the duties of the chair during any part of that day's session (but for no longer).[40]

Speaker of the House

While a nonlegislator (the lieutenant governor) serves as president of the Senate, the presiding officer in the House (called "speaker of the House") is a member of that body, nominated and elected by the entire membership. From this distinction come several differences in the powers of the two presiding officers, though both generally possess similar powers and duties over their respective chambers.

The speaker of the House has full power to recognize which representative will be accorded the right to the floor,[41] to suspend irrelevant debate and command silence,[42] and to call to order any member violating the rules of the House (in which event the offending member must immediately sit down).[43] Additionally, the speaker may compel the attendance of members to keep or obtain a quorum, and if necessary, order the arrest of absentees by the messenger or doorkeeper.[44]

All questions on the priority of business before the House are decided by the speaker,[45] who is also customarily authorized by the Rules Committee to call bills and resolutions on the rules calendar in any order desired during the last 21 days of a session. The speaker may direct that the third reading of general bills be in their entirety rather than by title only.[46] Amendments and motions may be ruled out of order by the speaker if not considered germane to the subject under consideration.[47] Also, the speaker may order a roll call vote at any time on any question, unless otherwise ordered by the House.[48]

Another power expressly delegated to the speaker is that of determining which persons are to be allowed to sit in the House gallery. No person can enter the gallery without displaying an appropriate card issued by the speaker, to the doorkeeper. If necessary, the speaker may clear the galleries and lobbies and order the messenger or doorkeeper to arrest any person for disturbance or misconduct, directing that such person be brought before the House for contempt.[49]

Like his counterpart in the Senate, the speaker refers all bills and resolutions introduced in the House or sent from the Senate to the appropriate standing committee without debate.[50] The speaker is required to sign all acts and joint resolutions passed by the House, as well as any writs, warrants, and subpoenas ordered by that body.[51]

The speaker also appoints House members to conference committees.[52] Should the House resolve itself into the Committee of the Whole, the speaker appoints a chair to preside, but, in contrast to the president of the Senate's role, the speaker may take part in the proceedings and must vote, unless excused.[53]

In addition, the speaker exercises several other important powers. For example, the assignment of new representatives to standing committees and seating locations in the House is at the speaker's discretion.[54] The speaker also appoints all subcommittees, as well as officers for standing committees and subcommittees.[55] Although only possessing a vote on the Rules Committee, the speaker serves as an ex officio member of all standing committees.[56]

Unlike the lieutenant governor, who cannot vote in any Senate proceedings, the speaker can vote in four instances: (1) when the House is equally divided; (2) when a fixed constitutional vote is required to pass some bill or measure, and one more vote is needed for passage; (3) when the speaker's vote, if given to the minority, would make an equal division of the House on a particular question, thereby defeating it; and (4) when the House is conducting an election.[57] Also, as previously noted, the speaker may vote when the House is acting as a Committee of the Whole.[58]

During a day's session, the speaker or speaker pro tempore, if presiding, may name any representative to perform the duties of the chair for any part of that day's session. Whenever the speaker is not presiding, the speaker may be recognized at any desk.[59]

Speaker Pro Tempore and President Pro Tempore

Each house elects a member of that body to preside in the absence of the speaker or president. Termed the president pro tempore in the Senate, and speaker pro tempore in the House, these two officers have the same powers as the president and speaker, respectively, and perform their duties in their absences.[60]

Clerk of the House and Secretary of the Senate

The clerk and secretary are the chief ministerial officers for their houses, serving as full-time officers with responsibility for many important functions during and between sessions. Despite the differences in titles, they have similar duties, contributing much to the orderly process of business in the respective houses.

Each is elected by a recorded vote of the majority of the members of his or her respective house. Their terms of office are the same as those of the members of the General Assembly, and they serve until a successor is elected. In the event of a vacancy in the office of clerk, the speaker appoints a qualified person to serve for the remainder of the term. In case of a vacancy or permanent disability in the office of the secretary of the Senate during a session, the Senate shall elect a successor for the remainder of the unexpired term. If the Senate is not in session, the president pro tempore shall appoint a qualified person to serve until the next session. Any question as to permanent disability shall be determined by the president of the Senate with the concurrence of a majority of standing committee chairs.[61]

Any bill or resolution introduced in the General Assembly must be filed through its offices, where it is assigned a number and printed in multiple copies for distribution to members of both houses, and, upon request, to the public. The secretary and clerk prepare other materials vital to the legislative process, including the daily and composite status sheets, the general calendars, and first readers.

In each house, these officers see that bills are read before the body, tally all votes, retain copies of all recorded votes, and function in effect as on-the-spot parliamentarians, assisting the presiding officers, on request, with the procedural questions which arise. The clerk and secretary also must note in the journal the names of members absent when the roll is called, as well as members not voting when the yeas and nays (a recorded vote) are ordered on a question.[62]

All writs, warrants, and subpoenas issued by order of the House or Senate must be attested by the clerk or secretary. These officers must also certify all engrossed and enrolled copies of bills for their houses.[63]

Should both the president and president pro tempore be absent in the Senate, or the speaker and speaker pro tempore in the House, the secretary or clerk must call their particular house to order and preside until a temporary replacement can be elected.[64] When there is a joint meeting of both houses, the secretary joins with the clerk to perform the duties required at the meeting.[65]

Within 10 days after a session adjourns, the secretary and clerk must file all papers and documents of their houses and deliver them to the secretary of state. After each session, the clerk and secretary also oversee compilation of the *House Journal* and *Senate Journal*, which constitute the official record of the session's legislative action.

The "housekeeping resolution" adopted by each house at the beginning of a biennium also authorizes the secretary and clerk to select and appoint the assistants necessary to carry out all clerical work, including the clerks for special or standing committees in each house.[66] The clerk and secretary each commonly employ an assistant, a reading clerk, a journal clerk, a calendar clerk, and other staff assistants and employees.

The clerk and secretary, before assuming their duties, must take an oath to discharge their duties faithfully and to the best of their skill and knowledge. Both also must post bond and security in the amount of $5,000, payable to the governor and his or her successors in office and conditioned on the faithful discharge of their duties.[67]

The courts seem to view the secretary and clerk as the chief staff officers of their respective houses, answerable for their actions only to those bodies under their rules and regulations. Thus, the Georgia Court of Appeals has stated that these two officially owe no duty to citizens in general,[68] and the Georgia Supreme Court has held that a constitutional direction to the "General Assembly" that certain actions be taken, in itself, imposed no duty upon the clerk or secretary.[69]

Doorkeepers, Messengers, and Sergeants-at-Arms

In the House, a doorkeeper and a messenger are elected by a majority vote of the members. Together, they perform such duties as required.[70] The messenger is under the direction of the speaker to enforce orders during a session and to execute the demands of the House. The position of House sergeant-at-arms has been abolished, and House rules provide that any officer of the Department of Public Safety assigned to the speaker for special duty or personal security has full authority to maintain order in the House chamber and to exercise any authority previously granted to the sergeant-at-arms.[71]

The Senate elects a sergeant-at-arms to attend to the wants of the Senate while in session. The sergeant-at-arms aids in enforcing order under the direction of the president and the Decorum Committee.[72] Any messages sent to the Senate are announced at the door by the sergeant-at-arms.[73]

Both houses utilize assistant doorkeepers at the doors of their chambers and galleries to ensure that unauthorized persons do not enter.

Pages

Members of both houses are served by pages. On the desk of each legislator is a switch for use when the services of a page are desired. When the switch is pressed, a light flashes on a board in the corridor, showing the available page which legislator needs his or her services. An enactment of the General Assembly directs that schools grant excused absences to students who serve as pages and that the days spent away from school be counted as present.[74]

By their rules, the Senate and House require pages to be at least 12 years of age. The rules of the Senate further provide that each senator may name up to 10 pages during a session, plus an additional 10 honorary pages (to be paid by the senator). Any senator not utilizing all of his or her pages or page days may assign these to another senator. The lieutenant governor can name additional pages without limitation as to number. To name a page, a senator must file the name of the page and date of proposed service with the director of pages at least three days prior to the date requested. However, senators should be cautioned that Senate rules limit the number of pages that can serve on any single day to 30 (excluding those named by the lieutenant governor), and these 30 are selected by the director of pages in the order in which senators submit their requests.[75]

The rules of the House provide that each member is allowed a maximum of 10 "page days" during the session and may use these either on one or on separate legislative days. A "page day" is the service of one page on one day. A member must make a reservation for each page at least one week before his or her selected "page day."[76]

House and Senate Party Organization

A recognized party organization for both Democrats and Republicans exists in the House and Senate of the General Assembly.

Democratic Caucus. A Democratic Caucus was established in the House in 1967 and in the Senate in 1970. Both the House and the Senate consider all members who are elected as Democrats to their respective houses as eligible caucus members, even though participation is voluntary. The House Democratic Caucus meets no earlier than 5 and no later than 15 days after the general election. The Senate Democratic Caucus convenes within 15 days after the general election.

In the Senate, the Democratic Caucus elects a caucus chair, caucus vice-chair, party leader, party whip, and caucus secretary. Except that there is no position of caucus vice-chair, the offices are the same for the House Democratic Caucus. Caucus positions are for two-year terms. The party leader and party whip of the majority party are designated as majority leader and majority whip in both houses. The Senate Democratic Caucus elects a nominee for president pro tempore, and the House Democratic Caucus elects nominees for speaker and speaker pro tempore. Caucus members are honor bound to support their caucus nominees in the election of the officers of their respective houses.

The rules for the Democratic Caucus in the House and the bylaws for the Democratic Caucus in the Senate establish a permanent policy committee composed of the caucus nominees for chamber offices, party leaders, caucus leaders, and several caucus members. The committees deal with organizational measures for each body. In addition, the committees may recommend party positions which the party leader and party whip communicate to the membership.

Republican Caucus. The House and Senate Republican members are also organized as a caucus in each chamber. The House Republican Caucus was organized in 1966 and the caucus in the Senate formed in 1969. All members elected as Republicans are considered members of the caucus, but participation is voluntary. Both the House and Senate Republican Caucus meet before the convening of the General Assembly following a general election. Caucus officers and party leaders are elected for two-year terms in each chamber. The officers chosen in both the House and Senate are the party leader and party whip (designated as minority leader and minority whip when the party is in the minority), the caucus chair, vice-chair, and secretary. The caucus leadership establishes policy for the caucus.

COMMITTEES IN THE LEGISLATURE

After the session officers have been elected, the next important step in organizing the two houses is the appointment of House and Senate members to their respective standing committees. The standing committees of both houses are established by House and Senate rules adopted at the beginning of each session.[77] It is through these committees, listed in tables 4 and 5, that most of the work of the General Assembly is carried on.

Senate rules provide that the Senate president (lieutenant governor) appoint all standing committee members, while House rules give this authority to the speaker. It is interesting to note that in almost all state legislatures, the speaker appoints House committee members, while practices in state senates are more varied.[78]

At present, there are 26 standing committees in the Senate and 31 in the House. Unlike the U.S. Congress, there is no requirement in either house of the General Assembly for minority representation on each standing committee.

Standing Committees

House. House rules provide that the speaker shall appoint the members of all standing committees.[79] The speaker also appoints the chair, vice-chair, and secretary for all standing committees and for all subcommittees created by the speaker.[80]

Each House member must serve on at least two, but not more than three, standing committees, except that membership on the Ethics, Interstate Cooperation, and Intragovernmental Coordination committees does not count against this limit.[81]

Unlike the Senate, House rules do not specify the number of members to serve on each standing committee. During the 1993-94 biennium, the largest committee was Appropriations, with 54 members, and the smallest was Interstate Cooperation, with 3 members.

Table 4: *Standing Committees in the Georgia House of Representatives*

Agriculture and Consumer Affairs	Journals
Appropriations	Judiciary
Banks and Banking	Legislative and Congressional Reapportionment
Children and Youth	
Defense and Veterans Affairs	Motor Vehicles
Education	Natural Resources and Environment
Ethics	Public Safety
Game, Fish, and Parks	Regulated Beverages
Governmental Affairs	Retirement
Health and Ecology	Rules
Human Relations and Aging	Special Judiciary
Industrial Relations	State Institutions and Property
Industry	State Planning and Community Affairs
Insurance	Transportation
Interstate Cooperation	University System of Georgia
Intragovernmental Coordination	Ways and Means

House rules dictate a few mandatory committee assignments—the majority and minority leaders are ex-officio members of the Rules Committee; the chairs and vice-chairs of the Appropriations and the Ways and Means committees are ex-officio voting members of each other's committees; and the speaker is an ex-officio member of all House committees (though with voting privileges only on the Rules Committee).[82]

Except for the Committee on Rules and the Committee on Interstate Cooperation, a member has the right to remain on the committee to which appointed as long as he or she is a member of the House. After members have been appointed to the various standing committees and the appointments have been announced, no other members can be placed on them. An exception to this rule is provided for members elected to fill vacancies in the House. The speaker may also fill any vacancy in the offices of chair, vice-chair, or secretary of a committee.[83]

The standing rules of the House of Representatives expressly give the speaker the power to create subcommittees and to appoint their chairs, vice-chairs, and secretaries.[84] In recent years, a large number of subcommittees have been created, usually with 5 or 6 members each. Subcommittee actions are subject to review by parent standing committees, and no bill can be reported to the House until it has been acted upon by the full standing committee to which it was referred.[85]

Senate. Senate rules currently provide for 26 standing committees and direct that their members and officers be appointed by the president of the Senate.[86] This authority, however, does not extend to reassigning incumbent senators, since once appointed, a senator cannot be removed from a standing committee while remaining a member of the Senate, except upon his or her request.[87]

In contrast to the House, where the size of a committee is at the discretion of the speaker, Senate rules specify the number of members on each committee.[88] At present, the size of Senate standing committees ranges from 4 to 31 members, with Appropriations the largest committee.

Each senator is appointed to 4 standing committees, and no more, except that membership on Reapportionment, Ethics, and Interstate Cooperation does not count against this limitation.[89]

The president of the Senate has the discretion to create subcommittees within any standing committees, to appoint their members, and to designate their officers.[90] During the 1993-94 biennium, a total of 27 subcommittees existed within the 26 standing committees, with a majority of these subcommittees consisting of 3 to 6 members.

Like the House, Senate rules prohibit the placement of other members after the announcement of the standing committees has been made, except that the president of the Senate may assign newly elected members to committees with vacancies. The president may also fill vacancies of committee officers.[91]

Committee operations. In the Senate, a number of uniform rules of procedure have been adopted for the standing committees. In the House, rules are adopted within each committee, leaving each free to decide, for instance, how many members constitute a quorum for the purposes of meeting and transacting business.

Committee seniority. Ranking status or seniority, gained through continued service on a standing committee, is not recognized in the rules

Table 5: *Standing Committees in the Georgia Senate*

Agriculture	Insurance and Labor
Appropriations	Interstate Cooperation
Banking and Financial Institutions	Judiciary
Consumer Affairs	Natural Resources
Corrections	Public Safety
Defense and Veterans Affairs	Reapportionment
Economic Development, Tourism, and Cultural Affairs	Retirement
Education	Rules
Ethics	Science, Technology, and Industry
Finance and Public Utilities	Special Judiciary
Governmental Operations	Transportation
Health and Human Services	Urban and County Affairs
Higher Education	Youth, Aging, and Human Ecology

of either house of the General Assembly. Nor is it necessarily observed in practice, for, although notice may be taken of that committee member with longest tenure when selecting officers, neither the speaker in the House nor the president of the Senate is bound by seniority or any other consideration in appointing committee chairs and other officers. Furthermore, these assignments are not protected by tenure, and committee officers may be reappointed at any time at the presiding officer's discretion.

Committee tenure. Although selection of committee officers is entirely within the discretion of the presiding officers of each house, committee tenure does protect members of standing committees in both houses from reassignment, except upon their own request. House rules require that, except for the Committee on Interstate Cooperation and the Committee on Rules, a member has the right to remain on the committee to which appointed as long as he or she is a member of the House. If a representative desires reassignment—and almost all do seek advancement to such committees as appropriations and rules—a request is made to the speaker. If a vacancy exists on the desired committee and the speaker approves of the transfer, a reassignment is then made.[92] Senate rules simply provide that once appointed to a standing committee, a senator may not be removed as long as he or she remains a member of the Senate, unless reassignment is requested.[93] The effect of this tenure system is that once a legislator is appointed to a standing committee, that assignment is secure as long as there is uninterrupted service in that house. Should a legislator resign or fail to win reelection, but later be elected to the former post, he or she has no assurance of regaining former committee assignments.

Ethics committees. Special mention should be made of two standing committees—the House Committee on Ethics and the Senate Committee on Ethics. While each functions as a standing committee to which bills and resolutions are referred, the two committees serve the additional function of implementing ethics rules in their respective houses. Both conduct investigations when charges of unethical or improper conduct are filed; hold hearings, at which witnesses and documents can be compelled; and recommend punishment to the full house. Each committee can also issue advisory opinion with respect to ethical and proper conduct.[94]

Joint standing committees. Each year, the Senate and House Appropriations committees hold joint hearings to consider the governor's proposed budget for the next fiscal year, as well as the proposed amended budget for the current fiscal year. From time to time, other standing committees in the House and Senate hold joint meetings or hearings, but there is no provision in state law or legislative rules to encourage or require similar committees in both houses to attempt to hold joint hearings and meetings when possible.

Special or Interim Committees

Special or interim committees undertake studies and investigate matters about which one or both houses desire further information during the interim between sessions. They are created by motion or resolution of one or both houses. In addition, the so-called "housekeeping resolutions" in each house grant the presiding officers authority to create special or interim committees as needed. Thus, there are joint interim committees representing both houses created by joint resolution, as well as special committees of either house.

Interim committees have no official power (other than to study a problem), cannot introduce legislation, and are dissolved upon the completion of their task. Additionally, members of these committees are not necessarily on the related standing committee which would be assigned legislation resulting from the committee's study. Despite these limitations, use of interim study committees does permit the legislature to respond overtly to matters of public concern, and such committees can provide valuable reports based upon serious investigation and study. Still, both houses rely more on the interim study of legislative matters by the appropriate standing committee.

Other Types of Committees

Several other types of committees are utilized by the legislature. The presiding officers of both houses may appoint *conference committees* to meet jointly and resolve differences between the two houses on a given piece of legislation. To facilitate deliberations, or upon occasion as required by House or Senate rules, each house may resolve itself into a Committee of the Whole, whereby the total membership sits in a body as a committee. To oversee operations of the General Assembly, a Legislative Services Committee has been established, consisting of the leadership from both houses, while a special Fiscal Affairs Subcommittee periodically sits to authorize budget transfers proposed by the governor. As the name implies, the Budgetary Responsibility Oversight Committee attempts to enhance the legislature's capacity to oversee state budgeting and planning.

Rules of one or both houses provide for several special-function committees, such as the Senate's Decorum Committee and Committee on Senate Administrative Affairs. Custom dictates others, such as the Committee of Escort. In recent years, the General Assembly has established *overview committees* through joint resolutions to provide legislative review and evaluation of selected projects such as MARTA and the World Congress Center.[95]

Through housekeeping resolutions, both houses currently authorize a unique type of committee—*the committee of one*. This is a special status that allows a single legislator to engage in official legislative business in Georgia—other than attending standing or interim committee meetings—and receive the standard per diem allowance. In the House, the speaker, speaker pro tempore, majority leader, minority leader, and administration floor leader may serve as needed, while all other representatives may serve up to 7 days a year.[96] In the Senate, the president pro tempore, majority leader, minority leader, and administration floor leader serve as needed, with other senators permitted up to 15 days service each year.[97]

These committees, as well as the rules regarding committee procedure, are discussed in subsequent chapters.

ENDNOTES

1. GA. CONST. art. 3, §4, ¶1.

2. GA. CONST. of 1945, art. 3, §4, ¶3, *as amended* (*see* Ga. Laws 1962, p. 750).

3. A comparison of the time and length of regular sessions among 50 state legislatures shows that Georgia is one of 31 states which operate within constitutionally mandated limits (two of these, Colorado and Kansas, limit only the second year) and six states (Arizona, Iowa, Nevada, Rhode Island, Tennessee, and Vermont) have statutory or indirect limitations based on cutoffs in legislative salaries or per diem expense payments. January prevails as the month for convening regular sessions. The length of regular sessions ranges from a low of 20 legislative days to no restrictions at all. See *The Book of the States, 1994-95* (Lexington, Ky.: Council of State Governments, 1994), p. 99.

4. Senate Rule 42; House Rule 39; OFFICIAL CODE OF GEORGIA ANOTATED (O.C.G.A.) §28-1-2.

5. Senate Rules 42, 62, 68-72; House Rules 39, 86, 152-56.

6. GA. CONST. art. 3, §4, ¶1.

7. Ibid.

8. Bunger v. State, 146 Ga. 672, 92 S.E. 72 (1917).

9. GA. CONST. art. 5, §2, ¶7(a).

10. Ibid.

11. Mayes v. Daniel, 186 Ga. 345, 198 S.E. 535 (1938). Moreover, matters germane and incident to purposes broadly stated in the proclamation will permit passage of ancillary legislation at a special session. In determining "germaneness," the entire proclamation will be considered by the courts. Carroll v. Wright, 131 Ga. 728, 63 S.E. 260 (1908).

12. Jones v. State, 151 Ga. 502, 107 S.E. 565 (1921).

13. Bibb County v. Williams, 152 Ga. 489, 110 S.E. 273 (1921).

14. GA. CONST. art. 5, §2, ¶7(b).

15. GA. CONST. art. 5, §2, ¶7(c).

16. O.C.G.A. §§38-3-52 through 38-3-53. *See also* GA. CONST. art. 3, §6, ¶2(a)(4).

17. O.C.G.A. §28-1-2.

18. O.C.G.A. §28-1-3.

19. This oath is a composite of the oath contained in O.C.G.A. §28-1-4, as well as the oaths required in O.C.G.A. §§45-3-1 and 45-3-11 through 45-3-14.

20. Georgia *Senate Journal* 1993, reg. sess., 1–17.

21. O.C.G.A. §28-1-4.

22. House Rule 21.

23. Senate Rule 8.

24. GA. CONST. art. 3, §4, ¶7.

25. *See* Rainey v. Taylor, 166 Ga. 476, 143 S.E. 383 (1928); Fowler v. Bostick, 99 Ga. App. 428, 108 S.E. 2d 720 (1950); Beatty v. Myrick, 218 Ga. 629, 129 S.E. 2d 764 (1963); *But see*, Bond v. Floyd, 251 F. Supp. 333 (1966), *rev'd*, 385 U.S. 166 (1966), where the U.S. Supreme Court affirmed that even though a state constitution may declare that each house of the state legislature shall be the judge of the election and qualifications of its own members, such provision does not deprive federal courts of jurisdiction where a legislature's action or decision as to the qualifications of a member involves substantial federally protected rights. *See also* Powell v. McCormack, 395 U.S. 486 (1969).

26. O.C.G.A. §§21-2-520 through 21-2-529. Although contested elections for the General Assembly are infrequent, it is reported that when they occur, they are variously dealt with by the appropriate house or by the courts, depending on the grounds upon which the election is being challenged.

27. House Rule 159.

28. Senate Rule 175; House Rule 134.

29. GA. CONST. art. 3, §3, ¶¶1 through 3.

30. GA. CONST. art. 5, §1, ¶3.

31. Senate Rules 25, 185.

32. Senate Rule 115.

33. Senate Rule 156.

34. Senate Rules 53, 21, 26.

35. Senate Rule 47.

36. Senate Rule 19.

37. Senate Rules 21, 152.

38. GA. CONST. art. 3, §5, ¶¶6 and 7.

39. Senate Rule 101.

40. Senate Rule 23.

41. House Rule 18.

42. House Rule 19.

43. House Rule 81.

44. House Rule 43.

45. House Rule 17.

46. GA. CONST. art. 3, §5, ¶7.

47. House Rules 110, 118.

48. GA. CONST. art. 3, §5, ¶6.

49. House Rules 15, 14.

50. House Rule 53.

51. House Rule 151.

52. House Rule 146.

53. House Rules, 62, 66.

54. House Rules 5, 6, 21.

55. House Rules 5, 6.

56. House Rule 6.

57. House Rule 16.

58. House Rule 66.

59. House Rule 23.

60. O.C.G.A. §28-1-6.

61. O.C.G.A. §28-3-20.

62. Senate Rules 49, 171; House Rules 44, 45.

63. Senate Rule 101; House Rule 151; and O.C.G.A. §28-1-11.

64. Senate Rule 24; House Rule 24.

65. O.C.G.A. §28-3-22.

66. *See, e.g.,* House Resolution 3 and Senate Resolution 3 for the 1988 "housekeeping resolutions."

67. O.C.G.A. §§28-3-25, 28-3-21.

68. Richter v. Harris, 62 Ga. App. 64, 7 S.E. 2d 432 (1940).

69. Horrigan v. Rivers, 183 Ga. 141, 187 S.E. 836 (1936).

70. O.C.G.A. §28-3-1; House Rule 2.

71. House Rule 2.

72. O.C.G.A. §28-3-1; Senate Rule 15.

73. Senate Rule 38.

74. O.C.G.A. §20-2-692.

75. Senate Rule 16.

76. House Rule 160.

77. One exception is that Georgia statutes (O.C.G.A. §28-6-1) provide for a "standing committee" in each house to be known as the Committee on Interstate Cooperation, with members and officers to be appointed "in the same manner" as that for other standing committees. In practice, however, these committees consider few—if any—bills during a legislative session.

78. See *The Book of the States*, Table 3.3, pp. 157-58.

79. House Rule 6.

80. Ibid..

81. Ibid.

82. Ibid.

83. Ibid.

84. Ibid.

85. House Rule 7.

86. Senate Rule 185.

87. Ibid.

88. Ibid.

89. Ibid.

90. Ibid.

91. Senate Rule 186.

92. House Rule 6.

93. Senate Rule 185.

94. Senate Rule 185A; House Rules 164-71.

95. The Georgia Supreme Court has ruled that a state authority overseeing construction of an undertaking such as the World Congress Center is performing an "executive function," and thus legislative membership on its governing board would violate the constitutional separation of powers prescription. Greer v. Georgia, 233 Ga. 667 (1975). To provide a measure of legislative review of this type of project, the General Assembly has created several legislative overview committees to periodically review the operations of the overseeing authority, to evaluate the success of the authority in accomplishing its statutory duties and functions, and to report their findings and recommendations at least annually back to the General Assembly.

96. House Resolution 3, approved January 11, 1993.

97. Senate Resolution 3, approved January 11, 1993.

 *Powers and Limitations*

SEPARATION OF POWERS

The Georgia Constitution commands that

> [t]he legislative, judicial, and executive powers shall forever remain separate and distinct; and no person discharging the duties of one shall at the same time exercise the functions of either of the others except as herein provided.[1]

This is the celebrated "separation of powers" clause, and an understanding of its impact on the General Assembly is important to the legislator.

Generally speaking, the doctrine of separation of powers has been interpreted to mean that no branch—legislative, executive, or judicial—is subordinate to the others, but all are to be recognized as coordinate, independent, and coequal branches.[2] Without an express constitutional provision, no branch may infringe upon the power, jurisdiction, or ordinary functions of the others.[3] Furthermore, on numerous occasions, the court has demonstrated its commitment to protecting each branch from invasion by the others.[4]

Yet, "this separation is not, and, from the nature of things, cannot be total."[5] First, under the concept of *checks and balances*, each branch has been given certain constitutional powers to limit the other branches, such as executive veto of legislation. Second, in a legal sense, the legislative branch is a first among equals by virtue of its broad lawmaking and funding powers over the other branches (except where constitutionally limited).[6] Third, it is impossible to draw a precise line to distinguish every governmental action as either *executive*, *legislative*, or *judicial*.[7]

Regarding the third point, the Georgia Supreme Court occasionally has incorporated some variant of Chief Justice John Marshall's separation of powers maxim: "the legislature makes, the executive executes, and the judiciary construes the law."[8] Unfortunately, this offers little help in understanding the exact domain of each branch.

Defining when a particular function is "executive" in nature, and thus outside the limits of legislative exercise, has been particularly troublesome.[9] Courts have tended simply to conclude that if a particular activity is not "judicial" or "legislative" in the strictest sense, then it apparently falls within the executive branch.[10]

Several decisions of the Georgia Supreme Court help to more clearly define separation of powers. In 1975, the court looked at legislative membership on two statutory agencies—the World Congress Center Authority and the State Properties Commission—and ruled in both cases that since the agencies performed executive functions, legislative membership on these bodies violated the constitution's separation of powers mandate.[11] To allow the legislature to create an agency to implement specific legislation and then place legislators on that agency's governing body allowed the legislature to retain some control over implementation, the court added. This arrangement, if carried to the extreme, could allow the legislature to enact specific legislation and then appoint an ad hoc committee of its own members to implement it.[12]

In these decisions, it should be noted, the court did not rule out legislative participation in the executive branch in all situations. For example, it seems that no constitutional harm is incurred by legislative participation on "executive" boards and councils which perform advisory functions only, and which in no way become involved in the executive or implementing process. Also, Georgia's supreme court has affirmed the right of members of the legislative branch—in this case, the speaker—to appoint nonlegislators to an executive commission without violating the separation of powers clause.[13]

In 1976, the court was faced with the question of whether the state auditor—who is elected by, funded through, and responsible to the General Assembly—was a member of the executive or legislative branch of government. The justices ruled that the auditor was part of the executive, "for he has no lawmaking powers."[14] The auditor's election by the legislative branch was, to the court, "simply a reflection of the system of checks and balances among the three branches of government."[15]

Thus, rather than being a rigid principle, "separation of powers" has and does assume a degree of flexibility to permit practical arrangements in a complex government.[16]

DELEGATION OF LAWMAKING POWERS

If the separation of powers clause prevents one branch from encroaching on the functions of the others, it also prohibits any branch from delegating its essential functions to another. Georgia's constitution specifically vests the legislative power of the state in the General Assembly.[17] The supreme court has interpreted this to mean that what the legislature has been granted cannot be delegated to anyone else—the so-called "non-delegation doctrine."[18] On numerous occasions, the court has used this theory to strike down laws which attempted to delegate legislative powers to another branch, local government, or nonpublic body.[19] For example, the Georgia General Assembly cannot confer on any person or any other body the power to determine what the law shall be in this state.[20] A statute will be declared unconstitutional as an improper delegation of legislative power if it is incomplete as legislation and allows an executive agency to decide what is and what is not an infringement of the law.[21] Following this principle, the supreme court has invalidated a statute which, in delegating certain powers to a state board, gave that board authority to determine which acts (for example, possession of depressant and stimulant drugs) would constitute a crime.[22]

Nevertheless, the legislature may confer upon administrative agencies "quasi-legislative functions which it itself might perform, but could not so adequately perform directly as it could by delegating them."[23]

> Thus, while it is necessary that a law, when it comes from the law-making power shall be complete, still there are many matters as to methods or details which the legislature may refer to some designated ministerial officer or board. [Cit.] The constitutional prohibition, therefore, does not deny to the lawmaking body "the necessary resources of flexibility and practicality, which will enable it to perform its function in laying down policies and establishing standards, while leaving to selected instrumentalities the making of subordinate rules within prescribed limits and the determination of facts to which the policy as declared by the legislature is to apply." [Cit.][24]

While repeatedly upholding the nondelegation doctrine, Georgia's supreme court has also recognized that in a complex society, the General Assembly cannot be aware of all facts and anticipate all situations that will arise in implementing legislative policy. Consequently, the court has approved numerous delegations of legislative authority in situations where the General Assembly has spelled out sufficient guidelines for the delegatee.[25]

Related to the nondelegation doctrine are questions about two devices used in some states to circumvent the concept that full lawmaking authority belongs to the legislature. One of these, *popular initiative*, allows the public directly to change state law without legislative involvement. While specifics vary in the 18 states which currently allow popular initiative, if a specified percentage of the voters (usually 5-10 percent of the votes cast in the last general election) sign a petition, a proposed measure is placed on a state ballot.[26] In all states, a majority of the popular vote is necessary to enact the proposal into law. Georgia's constitution does not provide for popular initiative, and in view of art. III, sec. I, para. I, would undoubtedly require a constitutional amendment to authorize the procedure.

The second device related to delegation of legislative power is the *referendum*. With this procedure, the legislature passes a law, but voters then have to approve the law before it can go into effect. Almost 40 states have some type of referendum, though in many cases it is limited to certain types of laws (e.g., debt authorization).[27] Georgia's constitution specifically authorizes a public referendum on general laws in only one case—any law to exempt property from ad valorem taxes must be approved by two-thirds of each house of the General Assembly and by a majority of the qualified voters voting in a referendum on the exemption.[28] The constitution also directs that local referenda be held in conjunction with several types of local acts, such as those (1) changing the homestead exemption in any county; (2) exempting from ad valorem taxes inventories of goods in the process of manufacture or production, and inventories of finished goods; and (3) consolidating or reorganizing local governments.[29] From time to time, the General Assembly enacts other types of local acts which call for voters of the affected city or county to give their consent.

Clearly, there is no issue of delegation of legislative power when the state constitution specifically authorizes voter approval for designated laws. The constitutionality of referenda on other types of acts, however, could raise the delegation of legislative power question. Almost exclusively, referenda are associated with local legislation, and the supreme court has upheld the right of the General Assembly to require local approval for legislation affecting a named city or county. In fact, in several cases in which a local referendum was challenged as violating the delegation of legislative power provision of the constitution, the court has seemed sympathetic with the general concept of the referendum. For example, in a 1931 decision, the court observed: "This state has been committed for many years to the doctrine that the legislature may submit to the electorate the question whether legislation framed and approved by the General Assembly shall become operative." Similarly, a 1953 decision noted: "Such [a referendum] is not a delegation of legislative power, but is simply an exercise of that power, guided by the will of the people to be affected." At issue in each case was a local act in which the people of the community affected were called on to decide whether the act would become effective.[30]

The constitutionality of a statewide referendum on a general statute (other than one granting an exemption from ad valorem taxes) is not so clear—and one the supreme court has carefully shied away from. Excluding laws creating agricultural commodity commissions (which only affect growers of particular commodities) and ad valorem tax exemptions, the General Assembly has called for a statewide referendum in only a few cases, with only one—a 1935 referendum on repealing prohibition—actually held.[31] In every instance where the constitutionality of a referendum on a general statute has been before the supreme court (including the prohibition referendum), the justices have avoided ruling on the issue.[32]

LAWMAKING POWERS

The Georgia Constitution confers broad lawmaking powers on the legislature, stating that "[t]he General Assembly shall have the power to make all laws not inconsistent with this Constitution, and not repugnant to the Constitution of the United States, which it shall deem necessary and proper for the welfare of the state."[33]

Nor are the powers of the General Assembly limited only to those expressly enumerated in the constitution. The Georgia Supreme Court has held that there are no restrictions on the General Assembly's power to legislate, so long as its laws do not violate the U.S. or Georgia constitutions.[34] The courts will assume that the General Assembly is authorized to enact a given law unless there is a stated or implied constitutional denial of legislative authority involved.

In addition to granting broad power to make laws, Georgia's constitution explicitly entrusts many lawmaking powers into the hands of the General Assembly, such as those to

1. tax for any purpose authorized by law (and for purposes that existed as of June 30, 1983, the day before the Constitution of 1983 became effective);[35]
2. appropriate public funds for the operation of all state agencies and to meet the expenses of the state (no state fund can be drawn from the treasury except by appropriation act);[36]
3. establish the jurisdiction of courts (except where otherwise provided within the constitution), as well as authorize administrative agencies to exercise quasi-judicial powers;[37]
4. create, abolish, or change superior court circuits, courts, and judgeships (so long as no circuit consists of less than one county);[38]
5. prescribe the duties, authority, and salaries of the executive officers of the state (unless otherwise provided by the constitution);[39]
6. provide for the state militia (National Guard);[40]
7. provide grants, scholarships, loans, and assistance for educational purposes;[41]
8. provide for the recall of elected public officials;[42]
9. provide for the regulation of insurance within the state;[43] and
10. waive or qualify the state's sovereign immunity from suit.[44]

The General Assembly has broad authority to legislate with regard to the powers, duties, and functions of city and county government in the state.[45] Also, exclusive power is given the General Assembly to propose amendments to the existing constitution or to propose a new constitution (or provide for a convention or commission to propose a new constitution), though such proposals must be submitted to the voters of the state for ratification.[46]

No general obligation debt may be incurred by the state until the General Assembly has enacted legislation stating the purposes for which such debt is to be incurred, specifying the maximum principal amount of such issue and appropriating an amount at least sufficient to pay the highest annual debt service requirements for the issue. Similarly, guaranteed revenue debt may not be incurred until the General Assembly has authorized by legislation the guarantee of the specific issue, specifying the maximum principal amount of such issue and appropriating an amount at least equal to the highest annual debt service requirements for such issue.[47]

Except as provided by the constitution, the General Assembly has broad powers over public officers and employees in the executive branch. These powers cover matters of eligibility and qualifications for office; oaths; bonds; vacancies and resignations; inspection of books, papers, and reports; salaries; fees; counsel for state employees; open meetings; insurance; strikes; retirement; crimes; and various other matters.[48]

In addition to these specific powers, the constitution, in providing for many of the executive officers, boards, and departments, directs that their powers, authority, and duties shall be provided by the General Assembly. Thus, there are a variety of "constitutional boards," or "constitutional agencies," whose memberships, terms of office, and appointments are constitutionally stipulated, but whose powers and duties are directed by statute. Currently, there are no executive agencies so constitutionally insulated as to be totally immune from at least some aspect of legislative control; certainly this is true regarding appropriations.

As will be discussed later, however, the constitution contains numerous restrictions on the General Assembly's lawmaking powers.

NONLAWMAKING POWERS AND FUNCTIONS

In addition to enacting laws and appropriating funds, the Georgia legislature performs a variety of other important functions.

Appointment of State Officers

Any state officer whose selection is not otherwise provided for is elected by the General Assembly in the same manner and at the same time it elects other officers.[49] (Currently, there are no state officials whose selection is unprovided for.) Under present law, the General Assembly selects the state auditor, who is elected by the House and confirmed by the Senate for an indefinite term (until his or her successor is elected in a like manner).[50] Also, the senators and representatives in each of the state's 11 congressional districts caucus to elect the member of the State Transportation Board from their district.[51]

Confirming Appointments of the Governor

All appointments by the governor to boards, commissions, and bureaus created by the General Assembly are subject to confirmation by the Senate.[52] If they are not confirmed, they may not hold office, and the name of another appointee must be submitted immediately by the governor. With regard to this Senate power, the Georgia Supreme Court has observed that the Senate does not acquire the power to discharge officials once confirmed, and that the power of approving appointees does not include the power to later discharge that appointee.[53] Once the Senate has rejected an appointment of the governor to any office, such person may not be reappointed by the governor to the same office for a period of one year from the date of rejection.[54]

Appointments by the governor to boards and commissions established by executive order are not subject to Senate confirmation.

Elections

In a chiefly ministerial function, designated legislative officers sit as the Constitutional Officers Election Board to open and publish the returns of the races for elected officials in the executive branch.[55]

The General Assembly may provide by general law procedures and grounds for the recall of any elected public official in the state.[56]

Special Oversight Powers

In addition to its other powers, the General Assembly possesses some special authority to oversee the executive branch. First, all books kept by any public officer under Georgia laws are subject to the inspection of any legislator (as well as any citizen),[57] and the minutes of any meeting of any state agency at which official actions are taken must be recorded and open for similar inspection.[58] By law, the General Assembly is granted authority as complete and absolute as that granted to the attorney general to conduct investigations at any time into the affairs of the state, any agency, or of any person or organization to the extent that the person or organization has dealings with the state.[59] For purposes of conducting these investigations, the General Assembly may subpoena witnesses, require them to testify under oath, and require the production of books, records, and papers.[60]

Either the House or Senate Appropriations Committee (or the governor) may require the state auditor to make a special examination and audit of all books, records, accounts, vouchers, warrants, bills, and other papers and records, and the financial transactions and management of any agency at any time.[61] Additionally, the auditor is directed to cooperate with either appropriations committee and to furnish any information requested for its use.[62] Officers and employees of all state agencies are directed to produce and turn over to the auditor or his or her assistants for examination and audit—upon demand—all of their books, records, accounts, vouchers, warrants, bills, and other papers dealing with or reflecting upon the financial transactions and management of such agency, officer, or employee.[63]

Georgia's constitution directs the governor to give the General Assembly information on the state of the state at the beginning of each session, and to recommend for its consideration such measures as deemed necessary.[64] In addition, state law requires the governor to furnish a written report to each legislator by the fifth day of each session outlining the governor's policies and goals on the major program areas of state government, as well as any other subject matters.[65] State law also requires the governor, through the Office of Planning and Budget, to prepare an annual state strategic plan that addresses statewide goals and policies and to transmit this to the General Assembly at the beginning of each session.[66]

Legislative capacity to oversee the executive branch—particularly with respect to budgeting and planning—was greatly expanded when the General Assembly passed the Budget Accountability and Planning Act of 1993. This legislation created a Budgetary Responsibility Oversight Committee consisting of five members from each house with broad authority to review executive agencies and make recommendations to the General Assembly with respect to the budget.[67] To assist it in its responsibilities, the committee has a full-time director and staff. (For a discussion of the committee's oversight powers, see pp. 211-13.)

Though not all agencies are so required, many executive departments and agencies are directed by statute to submit annual or other periodic reports to the General Assembly and governor, detailing accomplishments and activities, as well as recommendations for additional legislation.

Another oversight power of the legislature is that over rules and regulations adopted by executive agencies subject to the Administrative Procedures Act (see O.C.G.A. ch. 50-13). Because of legislative concern that executive agencies were adopting rules and regulations that either exceeded or violated legislative intent, a legislative review process was instituted in 1978. That process requires that any proposed rule or rule change subject to the APA must be sent to the legislative counsel at least 30 days prior to its adoption. (See Fig. 1, "Georgia's Administrative Rule-Making Process.") Within 3 days of receipt, the legislative counsel forwards it to the presiding officer of each house, who assigns the rule to the appropriate standing committee (and to any committee member who has

Figure 1: *Georgia's Administrative Rule-Making Process*

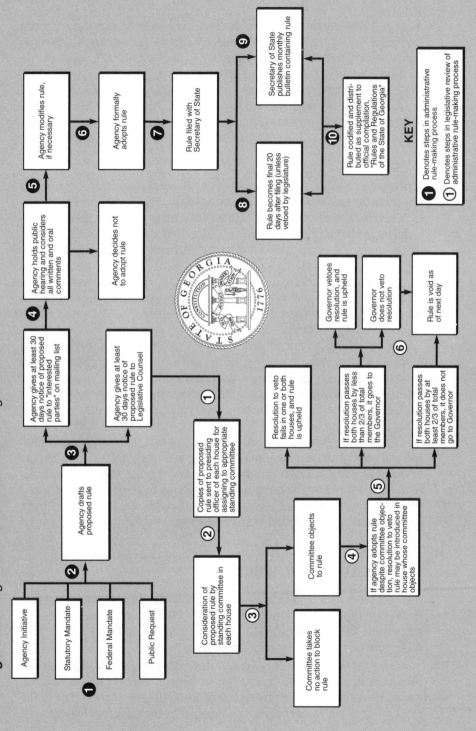

requested notification) for review. If the committee objects to the proposed rule prior to its adoption, and the agency adopts the rule anyway, a resolution to void the rule may be introduced in that committee's house within the first 30 days of the next regular session. If that resolution is adopted, it is sent to the other house. If passed in both houses by a two-thirds vote, the resolution does not go to the governor, and the rule is voided after the second house passes the resolution. If less than a two-thirds vote is received, the resolution may be vetoed or sustained by the governor.[68]

Impeachment

Still another nonlawmaking power of the General Assembly is the power of impeachment. The Georgia Constitution specifically invests this power in the General Assembly. Impeachment has been generally defined as "a criminal proceeding against a public officer, before a *quasi* political court, instituted by a written accusation called 'articles of impeachment.' "[69]

In Georgia, the House of Representatives is given the sole power to vote impeachment charges against any person who has been, or is, in office.[70] After the members of the House have voted the "articles of impeachment" against a particular official, the Senate is vested with the sole power of trying the case.[71]

When sitting for the purpose of trying impeachments, the members of the Senate are on oath or affirmation, and are presided over by the chief justice of the Georgia Supreme Court. If the chief justice should be disqualified, the presiding justice conducts the trial. Should the presiding justice be disqualified, the Senate selects for its presiding officer another supreme court justice.[72]

To convict a defendant in an impeachment case, two-thirds of the total membership of the Senate must vote to do so.[73] Judgments of the Senate in such cases can extend no further than removal from office and disqualification from holding and enjoying any office of honor, trust, or profit within this state. However, the convicted official is still liable and subject to indictment, trial, judgment, and punishment by the appropriate courts of the state.[74]

LIMITATIONS ON POWERS

It would seem appropriate to consider some of the limitations and restrictions placed upon the powers exercised by the General Assembly. The limitations vary widely in nature and importance, and only some of the more general ones will be mentioned here.

General limitation. The General Assembly cannot validly pass any act that is in violation of the Georgia or United States constitutions.[75] It can enact no law that curtails or restrains the liberty of speech or of the press.[76] The social status of citizens can never be the subject of legislation.[77]

The legislature is prohibited from passing any bill of attainder, ex post facto law, retroactive law, or law impairing the obligation of contract. It is forbidden to make any irrevocable grant of special privileges or immunities.[78]

Monopolies. Contracts or agreements which tend to lessen competition or encourage monopoly are expressly illegal in Georgia, and the legislature is forbidden to authorize them.[79]

Taxation. The power of the General Assembly is limited in that it cannot irrevocably give, grant, limit, or restrain the right of taxation except as provided by the constitution.[80]

Donations and gratuities. Except as specifically authorized in the constitution, lawmakers are prohibited from (1) making any donation or granting any gratuity, (2) forgiving any debt owed the state, or (3) granting extra compensation to any public officer, agent, or contractor after a contract has been signed or a service rendered.[81] Several exceptions to this rule, allowed by the constitution, include educational scholarships[82] and indemnification for law enforcement officers, prison guards, and emergency medical technicians killed or permanently disabled in the line of duty.[83]

Appropriations. The General Assembly may not appropriate funds for any fiscal year which exceed the current surplus plus anticipated revenue.[84] In other words, deficit budgets are prohibited by the constitution. The appropriation of money to aid any church, sect, or denomination, or any sectarian institution, is also prohibited.[85]

Separation of powers. In addition to these types of limitations, the General Assembly is constrained by the separation of powers clause in the constitution from encroaching on the functions of the executive and judicial branches, as well as voluntarily yielding legislative powers to these branches (see "Delegation of Lawmaking Powers"). Thus, not only is the legislature prohibited from assuming or exercising executive powers, but its members may not sit on state boards entrusted with executive functions.[86]

Similarly, the General Assembly may not dictate to the judiciary how to write its opinions or what form the decisions must take,[87] nor may it alter judgments of such courts.[88] The legislature cannot circumscribe the power of the supreme court by adopting rules and regulations governing the bar and practice of law in the state.[89]

Binding future legislatures. Another important limitation on the General Assembly is that one legislature cannot bind or tie the hands of its successors, or impose upon them conditions with reference to subjects upon which they have an equal power to legislate.[90] However, an act of one legislature—such as setting salaries—will be binding upon future legislatures, unless they choose to repeal or amend it. The important point is that no one statute can preclude or bind future statutes on the same subject. Similarly, one legislature has no power to declare the intent of a prior General Assembly in enacting a law, as this would be a legislative attempt to construe a law—a judicial function under Georgia's constitution.[91]

Powers of cities and counties. In a variety of designated areas—such as police and fire protection, garbage and solid waste collection, public health facilities and services, parks and recreational programs, water treatment and distribution, public housing, and public transportation—the General Assembly, by general legislation, may regulate, restrict, or limit the exercise of powers by local governments. But it cannot withdraw such powers.[92]

Other. Additional limitations on the General Assembly are discussed in the following chapter, particularly those that relate to requirements for legislation.

ENDNOTES

1. GA. CONST. art. 1, §2, ¶3.
2. *See* 16 *American Jurisprudence* 2d, §211, p. 450.
3. Parks v. State, 212 Ga. 433, 93 S.E. 2d 663 (1956); Fortson v. Weeks, 232 Ga. 472, 208 S.E. 2d 68 (1974).
4. McCutcheon v. Smith, 199 Ga. 685, 35 S.E. 2d 144 (1945); Parks v. State, 212 Ga. 433, 93 S.E. 2d 663 (1956). *See also* Galer v. Board of Regents, 239 Ga. 268, 236 S.E. 2d 617 (1977).
5. Beall v. Beall, 8 Ga. 210 (1850); Mayor & Council of Americus v. Perry, 114 Ga. 871, 40 S.E. 1004 (1902); Department of Transportation v. Atlanta, 260 Ga. 699, 398 S.E. 2d 567 (1990).
6. Myers v. U.S., 272 U.S. 52 (1926). As Georgia's high court noted on one occasion:

   While, in theory, the other departments, judicial and executive, may be co-ordinate, yet it is a fact authenticated by history, that the people attach themselves to the Legislature as the fountain of power, whose right it is to direct the action and enlarge or limit the powers exercised by the others. [Walker v. Whitehead, 43 Ga. 538 (1871).]

7. Southern Railway v. Melton, 133 Ga. 277, 65 S.E. 665 (1909); Stephens v. State, 207 Ga. App. 645, 428 S.E. 2d 661 (1993).
8. Wayman v. Southard, 23 U.S. 1 (1825).
9. *Black's Law Dictionary* (6th ed., 1990) suggests the executive function relates to management, control, and supervision of programs or activities, with accompanying authority to outline duties and direct the work of subordinate employees. According to this same source, "executive officers" are those officials in government who have been entrusted with the power to administer laws, and are charged with the duty to ensure that enactments of the legislature are implemented and obeyed (p. 569).
10. Springer v. Philippine Islands, 277 U.S. 189 (1928); Rich v. State, 237 Ga. 291, 227 S.E. 2d 761 (1976). Framers of Georgia's Constitution of 1945 were aware of this problem but unable to resolve precisely what constitutes the executive branch. See Albert B. Saye, ed., *Records of the Commission of 1943-44 to Revise the Constitution of Georgia*, vol. I, p. 197 (1946).
11. Greer v. State, 233 Ga. 667, 212 S.E. 2d 836 (1975); Murphy v. State, 233 Ga. 681, 212 S.E. 2d 839 (1975).

12. Greer v. State, 233 Ga. 667, 212 S.E. 2d 836 (1975).

13. Caldwell v. Bateman, 252 Ga. 144, 312 S.E. 2d 320 (1984).

14. Rich v. State, 237 Ga. 291, 227 S.E. 2d (1976).

15. Ibid.

16. Greer v. State, 233 Ga. 667, 212 S.E. 2d 836 (1975); Rich v. State, 237 Ga. 291, 227 S.E. 2d 761 (1976); Parks v. State, 212 Ga. 433, 93 S.E. 2d 663 (1956).

17. GA. CONST. art. 3, §1, ¶1.

18. According to the court, "The nondelegation doctrine is rooted in the principle of separation of powers, in that the integrity of our tripartite system of government mandates that the General Assembly not divest itself of the legislative power granted to it by Art. III, Sec. I, Par. I, of our Constitution, see generally, Mistretta v. United States, 488 U.S. 361, 109 S. Ct. 647, 654, 102 L.Ed. 2d. 714 (1989)." Department of Transportation v. Atlanta, 260 Ga. 699, 398 S.E. 2d 567 (1990).

19. Georgia Railroad v. Smith, 70 Ga. 694 (1883); Southern Railway v. Melton, 133 Ga. 277, 65 S.E. 665 (1909); Moseley v. Garrett, 182 Ga. 810, 187 S.E. 20 (1936); Long v. State, 202 Ga. 235, 42 S.E. 2d 729 (1947); Phillips v. Atlanta, 210 Ga. 72, 77 S.E. 2d 723 (1953).

20. Bohannon v. Duncan, 185 Ga. 840, 196 S.E. 897 (1938). Somewhat related to this principle—though dealing with the broader issue of delegation of *governmental* power—is a supreme court ruling that the legislature cannot delegate the power to appoint members of a public agency or board to a private organization. *See* Rogers v. Medical Ass'n of Ga., 244 Ga. 151, 259 S.E. 2d 85 (1979); *Atlanta Journal* v. Hill, 257 Ga. 398, 359 S.E. 2d 913 (1987).

21. Sundberg v. State, 234 Ga. 482, 216 S.E. 2d 332 (1975); Johnston v. State, 227 Ga. 387, 181 S.E. 2d 42 (1971); Department of Transportation v. Atlanta, 260 Ga. 699, 398 S.E. 2d 567 (1990).

22. Sundberg v. State, 234 Ga. 482, 216 S.E. 2d 332 (1975).

23. Abbot v. Commissioners, 160 Ga. 657, 129 S.E. 381 (1925); Campbell v. Farmer, 223 Ga. 605, 157 S.E. 2d 276 (1967); Scoggins v. Whitfield Finance Co., 242 Ga. 416, 249 S.E. 2d 222 (1978); Department of Transportation v. Del-Cook Timber Co., 248 Ga. 734, 285 S.E. 2d 913 (1982). For a discussion of delegation of legislative power to local governments in Georgia, see R. Perry Sentell, Jr., "Delegation in Georgia Local Government Law," 7 *Georgia State Bar Journal* 9 (August 1970).

24. Bohannon v. Duncan, 185 Ga. 840, 843, 196 S.E. 897, 899 (1938). *See also* Department of Transportation, 260 Ga. 699, 398 S.E. 2d 567 (1990).

25. Southern Railway v. Melton, 133 Ga. 277, 65 S.E. 665 (1909); Russell v. Venable, 216 Ga. 137, 115 S.E.2d 103 (1960); Scoggins v. Whitfield Finance Co., 242 Ga. 416, 249 S.E. 2d 222 (1978); Department of Transportation v. Atlanta, 260 Ga. 699, 398 S.E. 2d 567 (1990).

26. *The Book of the States, 1994-95* (Lexington, Ky.: Council of State Governments, 1994), Table 5.15, p. 294.

27. Ibid.

28. GA. CONST. art. VII, §2, ¶2(a)(1).

29. Ibid. art. VII, §2, ¶2(a)(2); art. VII, §2,¶3(a); art. IX, §3, ¶2.

30. Hines v. Etheridge, 173 Ga. 870, 872, 162 S.E. 113, 115 (1931); Phillips v. Atlanta, 210 Ga. 72, 77 S.E. 2d 723 (1953).

31. Ga. Laws 1935, p. 327.

32. Mayor and Council of Brunswick v. Finney, 54 Ga. 317, 324 (1875); Reynolds v. State, 181 Ga. 547, 182 S.E. 917 (1935); Holcombe v. Georgia Milk Producers Confederation, 188 Ga. 358, 3 S.E. 2d 705 (1939).

33. GA. CONST. art. 3, §6, ¶1.

34. Nicholas v. Hovenor, 42 Ga. 514 (1870); Plumb v. Christie, 103 Ga. 686, 30 S.E. 759 (1898); Green v. Harper, 177 Ga. 680, 170 S.E. 872 (1933); Petty v. Hospital Authority of Douglas County, 233 Ga. 109, 210 S.E. 2d 317 (1974); Sears v. State, 232 Ga. 547, 208 S.E. 93 (1974).

35. GA. CONST. art. 7, §3, ¶1.

36. GA. CONST. art. 3, §9, ¶1.

37. GA. CONST. art. 6, §1, ¶1; art. 3, §3, ¶1; art. 6, §6, ¶3.

38. GA. CONST. art. 6, §1, ¶7.

39. GA. CONST. art. 5, §3, ¶3.

40. GA. CONST. art. 3, §6, ¶2(a)(2).

41. GA. CONST. art. 8, §7, ¶1.

42. GA. CONST. art. 2, §2, ¶4.

43. GA. CONST. art. 3, §8, ¶1.

44. GA. CONST. art. 1, §2, ¶9.

45. *See*, for example, GA. CONST. art. 9, §§1–6; art. 7, §§1–2; and art. 8, §5.

46. GA. CONST. art. 10, §1.

47. GA. CONST. art. 7, §4.

48. *See* OFFICIAL CODE OF GEORGIA ANNOTATED (O.C.G.A.) Title 45 in particular.

49. O.C.G.A. §28-1-12.

50. O.C.G.A. §50-6-1.

51. GA. CONST. art. 4, §4, ¶1; O.C.G.A. §32-2-20.

52. O.C.G.A. §45-12-54. *See also* 1966 Op. Att'y Gen. 66-231 for elaboration on confirming authority of Senate. Sec. 45-12-54 appears inconsistent with §45-12-53, which was passed two years earlier and states, "No appointment by the governor shall be subject to confirmation by the Senate unless the statute under which such appointment is made requires confirmation or confirmation is otherwise required by law."

53. Richmond County v. Jackson, 234 Ga. 717, 218 S.E. 2d 11 (1975).

54. GA. CONST. art. 5, §2, ¶9.

55. O.C.G.A. §21-2-498.

56. GA. CONST. art. 2, §2, ¶4.

57. O.C.G.A. §45-6-6.

58. O.C.G.A. §50-14-1.

59. O.C.G.A. §45-15-19.

60. O.C.G.A. §45-15-17.

61. O.C.G.A. §50-6-4.

62. O.C.G.A. §50-6-23.

63. O.C.G.A. §50-6-7.

64. GA. CONST. art. 5, §2, ¶6.

65. O.C.G.A. §45-12-39.

66. O.C.G.A. §45-12-177.

67. O.C.G.A. §28-5-5.

68. O.C.G.A. §50-13-4.

69. *Black's Law Dictionary* (6th ed., 1990), p. 753.

70. GA. CONST. art. 3, §7, ¶1.

71. GA. CONST. art. 3, §7, ¶2.

72. Ibid.

73. Ibid.

74. GA. CONST. art. 3, §7, ¶3.

75. GA. CONST. art. 1, §2, ¶5.

76. GA. CONST. art. 1, §1, ¶5.

77. GA. CONST. art. 1, §1, ¶25; art. 3, §6, ¶4(c).

78. GA. CONST. art. 1, §1, ¶10.

79. GA. CONST. art. 3, §6, ¶5(c). *See, e.g.*, Harrison Co. v. Code Revision Comm., 244 Ga. 325, 260 S.E. 2d 30 (1979).

80. GA. CONST. art. 7, §1, ¶1.

81. GA. CONST. art. 3, §6, ¶6.

82. GA. CONST. art. 8, §7, ¶1.

83. GA. CONST. art. 3, §6, ¶6.

84. GA. CONST. art. 3, §9, ¶4(b).

85. GA. CONST. art. 1, §2, ¶7.

86. Greer v. State, 233 Ga. 667, 212 S.E. 2d 836 (1975); Murphy v. State, 233 Ga. 681, 212 S.E. 2d 839 (1975).

87. Taylor v. Columbia County Planning Commission, 232 Ga. 155, 205 S.E. 2d 287 (1974).

88. Jenkins v. Jenkins, 233 Ga. 902, 214 S.E. 2d 368 (1975); Northside Manor v. Vann, 219 Ga. 298, 133 S.E. 2d 32 (1963).

89. Sams v. Olah, 225 Ga. 497, 169 S.E. 2d 790 (1969); Attwell v. Nichols, 466 F. Supp. 206 (1979).

90. State Highway Dep't v. Hatcher, 218 Ga. 299, 127 S.E. 2d 803 (1962); Shaw v. Mayor & Council of Macon, 21 Ga. 280 (1857).

91. Undercofler v. Swint, 111 Ga. App. 117, 140 S.E. 2d 894 (1965).

92. GA. CONST. art. 9, §2, ¶3(c).

 **Bills and Resolutions**

Before considering the procedure for introduction and passage of legislation, lawmakers should be aware of the various classifications of legislation. Knowledge of these is necessary to understanding some of the legal and procedural matters associated with the legislative process.

Bills and Resolutions

All legislation introduced in the Georgia General Assembly is classified as either a "bill" or a "resolution." The word "bill" refers to proposed legislation, from the initial draft as introduced in one of the houses, through the various committee and floor stages, until finally enacted into law. A "resolution" is similar to a bill, but may or may not have the force of law, depending on the subject matter and intent of the legislature. Although resolutions represent a formal expression of legislative opinion on a given subject, they may be used for other purposes, as noted later.

One important distinction between the two types of legislation is that bills are used to propose changes or additions to existing statutes, while resolutions are not. There are a few exceptions. For instance, annual appropriations measures—usually not considered to be statutes—are introduced as bills. Also, proposed constitutional amendments, which may affect or even override existing statutes, are introduced as resolutions.

A bill becomes what is known as an "act," "law," or "statute" when it passes both houses in identical form and is signed by the governor, becomes law without the governor's signature, or is passed over the governor's veto. Though these three terms tend to be used interchangeably, there is a slight distinction among them, depending on the context in which each is used.

"Statute" refers to formal enactments of the legislature of a more permanent nature (as distinguished from legislation of a temporary character, e.g., appropriation acts). "Statute" also is used to designate *written* law, as distinguished from unwritten law. "Law" is a general term, often used to refer not only to formal legislative enactments, but also to include the whole body of rules enacted by government, including constitutional provisions, judicial interpretation, etc. "Act" is any bill which has passed both houses in identical form and has been signed by the governor (or has become law without that signature, or has been repassed after a governor's veto).

Official Code of Georgia Annotated

A "code" is a compilation of all statutes currently in force within a political jurisdiction (regardless of when enacted) and is the most important single source for finding existing statutory law on any subject. A code typically is divided into major subject areas (e.g., education, elections, health) called "titles." Titles are further subdivided into component "chapters," which, in turn, are further divided into the code's basic entry, "the section." It is the section that contains the actual language of the law (see Fig. 2).

In 1977, the General Assembly created a Code Revision Committee to initiate work on a new code for Georgia (the last official code having been adopted in 1933). The committee began reorganizing Georgia's general statutes, making grammatical and typographical changes, omitting obsolete sections, deleting material that had previously been repealed by implication, and resolving conflicts within existing laws. The next year, the legislature contracted with the Michie Company, a legal publishing firm, to work with the state in preparing a new official code. During a special session in 1981, the General Assembly adopted the results of this effort—the Official Code of Georgia Annotated (O.C.G.A.)—marking the first comprehensive and official code for Georgia in nearly 50 years. It became effective November 1, 1982, simultaneously repealing all prior codes and most general laws.

The resulting 44-volume code includes all general statutes (organized into 53 titles), a 2-volume index to these statutes, the U.S. and Georgia constitutions, and a 1-volume index to local acts. (Local acts have not been codified, but citations are given to the location in the annual session laws where each act may be found.) Georgia and federal court decisions construing Georgia statutes and the Georgia and U.S. Constitution have been annotated along with summaries of attorney general opinions and research references to notes or articles in legal encyclopedias and journals.

GENERAL LEGISLATION

Bills considered by the General Assembly are classified as either (1) general or (2) local or special in their application.

Figure 2: *Official Code of Georgia Annotated*

45-2-5. Municipal or county governments not to require residence as condition of employment.

No municipal or county government in this state shall require as a condition of employment by such government that applicants for employment as officers or employees, or such officers or employees now or hereafter employed, must reside within the boundaries of the municipality or county. (Ga. L. 1975, p. 1576, § 1.)

Law reviews. — For article discussing effect of City of Atlanta v. Myers, 240 Ga. 261, 240 S.E.2d 60 (1977), on limits of municipal government autonomy, see 12 Ga. L. Rev. 805 (1978). For article, The United States Supreme Court as Home Rule Wrecker, see 34 Mercer L. Rev. 363 (1982).

JUDICIAL DECISIONS

Ordinance restricting residence held unconstitutional. — Ordinance of the City of Atlanta providing residential requirements for officers and employees of the police and fire bureaus contrary to this section is unconstitutional and void under Ga. Const. 1976, Art. I, Sec. II, Para. VII (see Ga. Const. 1983, Art. III, Sec. VI, Para. IV). City of Atlanta v. Myers, 240 Ga. 261, 240 S.E.2d 60 (1977).

OPINIONS OF THE ATTORNEY GENERAL

Qualifications of voter registrars and deputy registrars established by § 21-2-213 are unaffected by this section, prohibiting counties and municipalities from requiring employees to reside within. 1975 Op. Att'y Gen. No. 75-111.

City of Commerce may not require that city manager be elector of municipality. — 1986 Op. Att'y Gen. No. U86-12.

RESEARCH REFERENCES

Am. Jur. 2d. — 63A Am. Jur. 2d, Public Officers and Employees, §§ 60-62.

C.J.S. — 67 C.J.S., Officers and Public Employees, § 26.

45-2-6. Municipal or county governments not to use residence as advantage or disadvantage in administering employee merit system.

A municipal or county government of this state, in using any merit system examination or other type of examination or evaluation of personnel in connection with application for employment, demotion, or discharge of employees or promotion of employees, shall not apply additional points, credits, or other benefits to residents of the municipality or county to give such residents an advantage for the purpose of employment or promotion, or a disadvantage for the purpose of demotion or discharge, over the nonresidents solely on the basis of residency. This Code section and Code Section 45-2-5 shall not be construed to prohibit the choice of a resident over a nonresident when both applicants for

General laws are those enacted by the General Assembly that have statewide application. (Fig. 3 presents an example of a general act.) A law may be categorized as general by virtue of its uniform territorial application (e.g., a law affecting all counties), its uniform subject matter application (e.g., a law affecting observance of holidays), or by a combination of both.

Georgia's constitution provides that all general laws shall have uniform operation throughout the state, and no local or special law may be passed in subject areas covered by a general law.[1] One exception is that the General Assembly may, by general law, authorize local governments to enact local ordinances and resolutions based on their police powers, so long as they do not conflict with general laws.[2]

Georgia courts, however, have held that the constitutional prescription that a general law shall have uniform operation throughout the state does not mean that it necessarily applies to every citizen of the state, or even produces a uniform effect on every person or entity subject to the act.[3] The Fourteenth Amendment's "equal protection" clause does not prohibit the General Assembly from drawing lines that treat one class of individuals or entities differently from others, so long as

1. the legislative purpose is legitimate, and the classification has a reasonable relation to furthering that purpose;
2. the classification is rational and not arbitrary nor invidious;
3. the classification employed furnishes a legitimate ground of differentiation; and
4. the law will operate uniformly on all persons or classes who will be subject to its application.[4]

Any general law currently in force may be amended or repealed by any future legislature. As noted previously, no legislature may bind future bodies with respect to statutory law.

To change an existing law, a new statute is enacted which specifically cites the code section to be amended or stricken, plus any new language to be inserted in its place. Georgia courts acknowledge—but discourage—a second way to change general law—repeals by implication.[5] This occurs when legislators enact a new law which contains provisions inconsistent with statutes currently in force, but include no specific directions in the new act relative to amending or repealing existing law in conflict. If a court challenge is filed, and there appears to be no way to reconcile both new and existing law, a judge may be forced to rule that lawmakers repealed the former law by implication.

General laws inconsistent with federal or state constitutions or federal statutes may be ruled inoperative by state or federal judges. However, formal amendment or repeal of such laws must be enacted by the General Assembly before such action is officially incorporated into the state code.

Figure 3: *General Act*

MOTOR VEHICLES AND TRAFFIC — DRIVERS'
LICENSES; FEES; REDUCTION FOR APPLICANTS
MAKING ANATOMICAL GIFTS.

Code Section 40-5-25 Amended.

No. 1200 (House Bill No. 1547).

AN ACT

To amend Code Section 40-5-25 of the Official Code of
Georgia Annotated, relating to applications and fees for drivers'
licenses, so as to provide for reduced drivers' license fees for certain applicants who execute anatomical gifts; to provide for an
effective date; to repeal conflicting laws; and for other purposes.

BE IT ENACTED BY THE GENERAL ASSEMBLY OF
GEORGIA:

Section 1.   Code Section 40-5-25 of the Official Code of
Georgia Annotated, relating to applications and fees for drivers'
licenses, is amended by adding a new subsection at the end
thereof, to be designated subsection (d) to read as follows:

"(d)   (1)   The General Assembly finds that it is in the
best interest of the state to encourage improved public
education and awareness regarding anatomical gifts of
human organs and tissues and to address the ever
increasing need for donations of anatomical gifts for the
benefit of the citizens of Georgia.

(2)   Notwithstanding the provisions of paragraph (2)
or (3) of subsection (a) of this Code section, each appli-
cant for the issuance, reissuance, or renewal of a Class C,
M, A, or B drivers' license under paragraph (2) or (3) of
subsection (a) of this Code section shall accompany such
application with a license fee of $8.00 if such applicant
executes an anatomical gift pursuant to Code Section 40-
5-6."

Section 1.5.   This Act shall become effective July 1,
1995.

Population Acts

Because of the constitutional prohibition against passing a local law in a subject area covered by general law, lawmakers historically relied on a device known as the "population act" to allow their city or county to get around provisions of existing general law. (See Fig. 4.)

As used until July 1, 1983, the population act was a hybrid variety of general law. It was drafted to affect only localities falling within certain population brackets according to a definite census as specified in the act (e.g., a law providing that property titles may be recorded on microfilm in any county of the state having a population of not less than 185,000 or more than 190,000 according to the 1970 or any future census). Typically, only one city or county in the state fell within the brackets selected by the bill's drafter, resulting in what was technically a "general law" but clearly one of local application.

Criticism that population acts were eroding the constitutional supremacy of general law by allowing the exemption of cities and counties from uniform state policy led framers of the Constitution of 1983 to restrict their use by providing: "No population bill, as the General Assembly shall define by general law, shall be passed."[6] In 1983, the legislature enacted a law defining population bills. Subsequently, effective January 1, 1989, an amendment was adopted that expanded the definition in order to further restrict their passage. The amended law states that a population bill is one which uses a classification by population as a means for determining the applicability of a bill or law to any political subdivision or groups of political subdivisions. A political subdivision is defined as any county, municipality, county school district, independent school district, judicial circuit, militia district, or any other geographical area less than the entire area of the state. The general law defines the following bills as *not* being population bills:

1. A bill applicable to one specified type of political subdivision and containing a combination of population classifications which includes the population of and affects all political subdivisions of the type specified, including but not limited to statewide minimum salary bills for county officers. (Example: A statewide minimum salary bill for county officers whose salaries are tied to population of the county.)

2. A bill classifying political subdivisions having less than a specified population and affecting three or more such political subdivisions. This does not affect the legality of any bills classifying political subdivisions having less than a specified population enacted prior to or becoming effective on July 1, 1988. (Example: All counties with populations under 5,000....)

Figure 4: *Population Act*

LOCAL GOVERNMENT — AUDITS; GOVERNMENT AUDITING STANDARDS; LOCAL UNITS OF MORE THAN 1,500 PERSONS OR EXPENDITURES OF $175,000.00 OR MORE; LOCAL UNITS WITH LESSER EXPENDITURES; REPORT OF AGREED UPON PROCEDURES; CONTRACTS WITH STATE AUDITOR; CORRECTIVE ACTION; STATE GRANTS WITHHELD.

Code Sections 36-60-8 and 36-81-7 Amended.

No. 1161 (House Bill No. 1415).

AN ACT

To amend Title 36 of the Official Code of Georgia Annotated, relating to local governments, so as to change the standards under which audits of the financial affairs and transactions of certain local governments are conducted; to change the expenditure level with respect to the requirement of such audits; to provide for corrective action plans; to provide for withholding of grants for failure to comply; to repeal conflicting laws; and for other purposes.

BE IT ENACTED BY THE GENERAL ASSEMBLY OF GEORGIA:

Section 1. Title 36 of the Official Code of Georgia Annotated, relating to local governments, is amended by striking Code Section 36-60-8, relating to the contents of certain local government audit reports and the standards under which said audits are conducted, in its entirety and inserting in lieu thereof the following:

"36-60-8. Whenever an audit of the financial affairs of a county or municipal corporation or of an officer, board, department, unit, or other political subdivision of a county or municipal corporation is made pursuant to a requirement or to an authorization otherwise provided by law, the audit report shall include the auditor's unqualified opinion upon the presentation of the financial position and the result of the operations of the governmental unit or office which is audited. If the auditor is unable to express an unqualified

3. A bill classifying political subdivisions having more than a specified population and affecting three or more such political subdivisions. The legality of any bills classifying political subdivisions having more than a specified population enacted prior to or becoming effective on July 1, 1988, is not affected. Neither are amendments to those bills affected. (Example: All municipalities with populations over 20,000....)

4. A bill classifying political subdivisions on the basis of the population of standard metropolitan statistical areas and affecting three or more such political subdivisions. The legality of any bills classifying on the basis of population of standard metropolitan statistical areas enacted prior to or becoming effective on July 1, 1988, is not affected. (Example: All standard metropolitan statistical areas with populations over 200,000....)

5. A bill amending a population act for purposes of changing the population classification defined by general law in order for it to remain applicable to the political subdivisions it affected immediately prior to the time the most recent census figures applied to those political subdivisions.

6. A bill repealing a population law.[7]

In order to be permissible under the foregoing exceptions, a bill must fit within only one of the exceptions; and any bill which uses two or more of the foregoing classification devices is a prohibited population bill.[8]

In implementing its constitutional mandate to define population acts, the General Assembly has thus provided exceptions which mean that population in certain limited circumstances can still be a factor conditioning the applicability of a general law. In recognition of this, and in recognition of the many earlier Georgia court decisions which established standards regarding the permissible use of population within acts, the general statute defining population acts also provides that its provisions are not meant to invalidate established court requirements.

Because these standards will continue to apply to population acts that were in effect when the new constitution was passed and will most likely be applied to future acts embodying population classifications, an understanding of the court's prior stance is important.

The general position of the Georgia Supreme Court has been to view properly drafted population acts employing legitimate population classifications as valid general laws. The tests developed by the court have included the following:

1. Did the population classification in the act (a) constitute a legitimate ground for differentiation and (b) have a reasonable relation to the subject matter of the act?

2. Were the minimum and maximum population figures in the act so narrowly drawn that "it would be a matter of wildest chance if any other county...in the next census...or any subsequent census (would) have a population exactly within the prescribed limitations?"[9]

3. Was the act so framed as to allow all cities and counties coming within the population classification to be covered by its provisions, while all counties outside of this classification would be excluded?

4. Were provisions of the act "open-ended," so that following future censuses, cities and counties could pass out of, as well as into, population classifications set forth in the act?[10]

5. Did the population classification apply to only one county in the state, particularly where there are other counties with populations greater or less than those contained in the act?

For an act that classified by population to be considered general in application, the classification embodied was to be reasonably related to the subject matter of the law and furnish a legitimate ground of differentiation. On this basis, the court struck down one population act which attempted to prohibit noncommercial fishing on Sunday in three counties of unrelated populations.[11]

In apparently the last major supreme court decision regarding population acts before the Constitution of 1983, Georgia's high court dismissed as unconstitutional a population act which allowed tax commissioners in counties whose population was between 90,000 and 140,000 to retain as a fee 1 percent of all school taxes collected by that office, while general law provided a commission of 2.5 percent to county tax commissioners. In this instance, the court concluded that no rational relationship existed between the population bracket and the tax commissioner's fee. Moreover, the justices established a rule that in cases where a population act conflicts with general law, the burden of proving that the population classification is reasonably related to the subject matter of the law and that population furnishes a legitimate ground for differentiation falls upon the party who seeks to uphold the population act.[12]

A population act had to apply uniformly to all localities within its population brackets and could not be drafted where its provisions—for one reason or another—would not extend to all counties within the classification.[13]

In some of these acts, population brackets were so tightly drawn that the upper and lower population limits differed by as little as 10. In striking down one such act, the court noted that the limits made it apparent that the intent of the act was to apply to the one county in the state which fell within them. It suggested that it was improbable that any county in the future—including the county the act was designed for—would have a census population precisely between 4,340 and 4,350, the brackets for that act.[14] In another case, the high court noted that it would consider as suspect any population act which applies to only one county, particularly where other counties have populations greater or less than those of the county to which the particular act applies.[15]

Another court-formulated test required that the population range specified by the act be left open-ended so that following future censuses, localities would become subject to or exempt from the law as they gained or lost population. If the range was closed so that it could apply only to a locality or localities having the stated population at the time of the law's enactment, then clearly the law was not a general one.

In applying this test, the court upheld a population act applying to counties within a specified population range, according to a particular census "or" any future census, on the ground that the provisions were open-ended. In contrast, a law applying to counties within a range according to a particular census "and" any future census was held special and unconstitutional.[16] In the latter instance, the court explained, although counties gaining in population could become subject to the terms of the law, those to which the law applied when it was enacted would not pass out of the classification if they should lose population. Thus, one end of the classification was closed.

Several problems resulting from the past use of population acts should be noted. First, though classified as general legislation, the population act frequently was an obvious device to exempt a city or county from existing general law and thus amounted to a type of local legislation. Indeed, not infrequently, these acts were successfully overruled by the courts.[17]

Secondly, the population acts bearing on the powers and officers of cities and counties no longer applied to that locality when its population in the next census moved out of the brackets of the original act. Following a new census, many Georgia cities and counties found that the statutory bases for many of their powers were invalid. They had passed out of the brackets of their population acts, and new or amended acts were necessary. For instance, one county's new official population necessitated the passage of 30 new population acts.

Clearly, the Constitution of 1983 authorized the legislature to curtail the passage of population acts. This was accomplished when population bills were first defined. Their passage was further restricted when the original law was amended several years later. Thus, the legislature has made it increasingly difficult to pass a population bill.

LOCAL LEGISLATION

Local or special legislation is generally defined as that which applies to special or particular places or persons, as distinguished from legislation relating to classes of persons or subjects.[18] Although similar in many ways, there are differences as well between local and special legislation.

A local act is a legislative measure that applies to a specific city, county, or special district named in the act. Such acts are commonly used to create or abolish cities, change city boundaries, alter forms of local government, create local authorities or special districts, and make other changes that apply only to the political subdivision named in the act. As will be seen below, special procedures are spelled out by state constitution and statute for consideration of local legislation in the General Assembly, such as requirements for advertising in local newspapers before introduction.

Another type of nongeneral legislation is the special act. At one time, these were fairly common in Georgia and were used to provide special benefits or privileges to private individuals or companies named in the act. For instance, private acts were used early in the state's history to grant divorces. Later, special acts incorporated railroads, banks, and other companies; provided relief from judgments and tax penalties; and authorized individuals to peddle without obtaining a state license. Today, it is rare for the General Assembly to utilize special legislation, but the Georgia Supreme Court has upheld its right to do so if (1) it has not previously legislated in the area by general law, and (2) if the classification of those affected is reasonable and does not violate standards of equal protection.[19] An additional qualification is that the state constitution forbids passage of any special act relating to the rights or status of private persons.[20]

Local acts not inconsistent with the state or federal constitutions or with federal law have the force of statutory law. However, a provision in the Georgia Constitution stipulates that no local or special law can be enacted in any case for which provision has been made by an existing general law.[21] A review of the extensive number of appellate court decisions applying to this section cited in the annotations to this provision in the Official Code of Georgia Annotated suggests that the courts have had little reluctance to enforce this constitutional mandate.

The court's attitude has been that if a general act has been passed relative to a given subject matter, no local law can later be enacted which would repeal some portion of the general law.[22] Moreover, a local act can neither expand nor contract the meaning of a general statute, even if passed in the guise of an amendment to the general law.[23] Also disallowed are purported general acts which apply to all counties or cities in the state, but then exclude one city or county by name.[24]

When no general act has preempted an area for legislation, a local act is permissible. Should a general act later be passed covering a subject area already touched by one or more local acts, the local act will be allowed to stand unless the language of the general law makes it clear that the legislature contemplated or intended a repeal, or unless provisions of the two acts are clearly repugnant and irreconcilable.[25] Where both can stand, they should be construed accordingly; but where there is inconsistency, the general statute repeals the local act.[26]

As discussed in Chapter 5, many local acts (especially those involving annexation) incorporate referendum requirements, where voters of the city, county, or area to be affected decide whether that act shall become effective.

The use of local legislation to lengthen, shorten, or abolish the term of office of a local official during the time for which he or she has been elected is prohibited unless the legislation is approved in a referendum by the people of the jurisdiction affected.[27]

As a final observation, historically the majority of bills enacted by the Georgia General Assembly have been local in nature. However, as Table 6 shows, general bills now seem to predominate in terms of bills passed. Rather than the number of general bills going up, the recent trend has been a slight decline in local bills.

ENACTMENT OF LOCAL BILLS IN THE GENERAL ASSEMBLY

The large number of local acts in the General Assembly is generally accounted for by the limited amount and utilization of "home rule" authority by cities and counties.[28] "Home rule" refers to the ability of local governments to frame, adopt, and amend their own charters, powers, and laws. Because local governments are created by the state—and do not possess sovereignty as such—major changes often have to go before the legislature, rather than local governing authorities. (Fig. 5 presents an example of a local act.)

Introduction of Local Legislation

The constitution authorizes the General Assembly to enact procedures for considering local legislation. In addition, rules of the House and Senate prescribe special requirements for consideration of local legislation by the respective committees.

Notice of Intention

According to the constitution, the General Assembly must provide by law for advertising a notice of intention to introduce a local act. Before the bill is introduced in the legislature, such notice must be advertised once in the newspaper in which the sheriff's advertisements for the affected locality are published. It cannot be advertised more than 60 days prior to the convening date of the session at which it will be introduced. When the advertisement has been published prior to the convening date, the bill may be introduced at any time during that session. If, however, the advertisement is published during the session, the bill may not be introduced before Monday of the calendar week following the week in which the ad-

Table 6: *Enactment of Local and General Bills in the General Assembly*

Year	Total Bills Introduced[a]	Total Bills Passed[a]	Bills Passed		Local Acts as % of Total Acts Passed
			General	Local	
1970	1,002	634	246	388	61.2
1971	1,447	830	270	560	67.5
1972	1,339	779	321	458	58.8
1973	1,662	800	319	481	60.1
1974	1,171	677	289	388	57.3
1975	1,636	780	357	423	54.2
1976	1,928	709	360	349	49.2
1977	1,593	767	320	447	58.5
1978	1,898	760	391	369	48.6
1979	1,393	677	292	385	56.9
1980	1,817	766	419	347	45.3
1981	1,598	839	353	486	57.9
1982	1,891	753	358	395	52.4
1983	1,199	583	310	273	46.8
1984	1,658	783	385	398	50.8
1985	1,429	774	344	430	55.5
1986	1,893	913	381	532	58.2
1987	1,574	808	352	456	56.4
1988	1,781	693	427	266	38.3
1989	1,542	714	404	310	43.4
1990	2,133	769	435	334	43.4
1991	1,556	608	374	234	38.5
1992	2,429	870	507	363	41.7
1993	1,559	632	327	305	48.3
1994	2,157	654	354	300	45.9

[a]General and local.

vertisement was published. A copy of the advertised notice and an affidavit stating that the notice has been published as provided must be attached to the bill and become a part of the bill. The affidavit shall be made by the author of the bill.[29]

In the past, the Georgia Supreme Court has rather strictly interpreted this requirement. For example, the court has invalidated local laws on the sole ground that, during the process of their enactment, the enrolled bills did not embody a copy of the publication notice accompanied by the publisher's certification or the author's affidavit.[30] Further, it has held that the author of the local act be solely responsible that the enrolled bill contain the notice and certification of publication, regardless of the fact that their omission may have been due to the fault or neglect of the clerk.[31]

Figure 5: *Local Act*

CHATHAM COUNTY — INTERGOVERNMENTAL COUNCIL
OF CHATHAM COUNTY; ACT REPEALED.

No. 684 (House Bill No. 1133).

AN ACT

To repeal an Act creating the Intergovernmental Council
of Chatham County, approved March 20, 1990 (Ga. L. 1990, p.
3928); to provide for related matters; to repeal conflicting laws;
and for other purposes.

BE IT ENACTED BY THE GENERAL ASSEMBLY OF
GEORGIA:

Section 1. An Act creating the Intergovernmental
Council of Chatham County, approved March 20, 1990 (Ga. L.
1990, p. 3928), is repealed in its entirety.

Section 2. All laws and parts of laws in conflict with
this Act are repealed.

Notice of Intention to Introduce Local Legislation

Notice is hereby given that there will be introduced at the regular 1993 session of the General Assembly of Georgia a bill to
repeal an Act creating the intergovernmental COUNCIL of
Chatham County, approved March 20, 1990, (Ga. L. 1990, p.
3928); and for other purposes.

This 4th day of January, 1993.

Sonny Dixon Representative
Old District 128
New District 150

GEORGIA, FULTON COUNTY

Personally appeared before me, the undersigned authority, duly authorized to administer oaths, Sonny Dixon, who, on
oath, deposes and says that he is Representative from the 150th
District, and that the attached copy of Notice of Intention to

On the other hand, the court has been rather liberal on the actual content of the notice. For example, it ruled that no more information need be included than in the title of the bill, and that a rather broadly worded notice was sufficient.[32]

Local Bills Proposing Annexation

A copy of any local bill which proposes to allow a municipality to annex unincorporated land must be provided to the governing authority of the affected county. This action must take place when the notice to introduce local legislation is published. Failure to provide the county commission with a copy of the proposed annexation bill will void the annexation even if the bill is enacted by the General Assembly. However, should the bill be amended in the legislative process, its validity will not be affected if county commissioners were provided a copy of the initial bill before introduction.[33]

Readings

The constitution requires that a local act be read at least once—by title—before being voted upon.[34] A House member may ask unanimous consent that a local bill or resolution be taken up out of the normal order of business for its reading and passage, but this must be done within the first 30 minutes after the confirmation of the journal. In the Senate, the president cannot recognize any senator for the purpose of asking unanimous consent to vote on the passage of any local bill or resolution.[35]

Voting

When the time arrives for the body to vote on a local bill, the member who introduced it will normally address the group, stating that the bill deals with a purely local matter and requesting support as a matter of legislative courtesy. In actual practice, to conserve time, both houses often permit a number of local bills to be voted on at once. This practice is carried on by the use of a separate local bill calendar upon which uncontested local legislation may be placed.

Most local bills that have the support of two-thirds or more of the representatives and senators whose districts encompass any city or county affected by the local act are passed in each house without opposition under the tradition of "local courtesy." The idea behind local courtesy is that when a legislative delegation from a city or county agrees on the need for a legislative enactment to affect that city or county only, the other house members will defer to their judgment and support the bill. Of course, other legislators expect the same courtesy when their local bills are under consideration. It should be noted, however, that local courtesy is a custom of the General Assembly and is not provided for by the rules of either house. Hence, it cannot be enforced should legislators decide to challenge a local act (as is often the case for local acts affecting Atlanta and Fulton County).

Both houses allow the legislative delegation from a city or county to set its own majority requirement—simple, two-thirds, three-fourths, etc.— of members who must sign the bill before it will be favorably reported out from committee. If a delegation has not agreed upon this matter, a majority rule applies in the Senate, and a unanimity rule in the House.[36]

RESOLUTIONS

A resolution is another device that formally expresses the actions of either house or both houses concurrently. Resolutions are either (1) *simple* (requiring passage by only one house) or (2) *joint* (requiring passage by both houses). A joint resolution is identified by the phrase, "Be it resolved by the General Assembly."

Simple Resolutions

Simple resolutions are typically of several types. These are

1. privileged resolutions which express sympathy, appreciation, congratulations, or commendation;
2. resolutions expressing the opinion of the body on a particular issue;
3. resolutions authorizing creation of special study committees;
4. resolutions electing members or citizens to various boards and commissions to which that house is entitled appointing authority;
5. resolutions inviting some individual to speak to that body;
6. housekeeping resolutions authorizing appointment, employment, and compensation of aides and staff for officials and committees of that body;
7. resolutions adopting or amending the rules of the particular house in which they are introduced; and
8. resolutions formally notifying the other house relative to the convening of that body.

Simple resolutions do not have the effect of law and are typically read only once before adoption by the particular house. Privileged resolutions that commend, congratulate, extend condolences, or are of a similar nature are not referred to committee; House rules, however, provide that other privileged resolutions shall be assigned to committee.[37] House members are limited by rule to introducing no more than 10 privileged resolutions per session. Members must pay the full cost for additional resolutions.[38] Although initial adoption of the rules of procedure for each house at a session's beginning requires only a majority of a quorum, any subsequent resolutions that propose changes in the rules must be assigned to the Rules Committee of that house and be adopted by two-thirds of the members voting if the two-thirds amounts to a majority of the members elected to that house.[39] While practice varies between the two houses, certain other simple resolutions are customarily referred to committee, including those to establish interim study committees and many of those expressing an opinion held by a house.

Housekeeping Resolutions

Of special note is the housekeeping resolution, as it is commonly termed, adopted by each house at the beginning of every biennium (see Fig. 6). This resolution is introduced the first day of the session, without reference to committee and without the concurrence of the other house. It details and prescribes the number of aides, assistants, secretaries, and other legislative staff to be appointed for that house, its officers, party leaders, and committees, along with specifying the compensation for these staff members.

Typically, the housekeeping resolution provides authorization for (1) designated committees to meet following adjournment of the session to perform necessary administrative functions; (2) the presiding officer to appoint interim legislative study committees and prescribe the time during which they may function; (3) the presiding officer to designate standing committees or subcommittees to function during the interim between sessions; (4) designated legislative officers to keep their offices open and retain the staff and personnel deemed necessary during any period of adjournment during or following a session, and further entitling these officers to function as a *committee of one* for each day spent on official business; and (5) legislators to serve as a *committee of one* for a limited number of days in the interim. Unless subsequently amended, provisions of a housekeeping resolution apply to a house throughout the two-year life of the legislature.

Joint Resolutions

Joint resolutions, sometimes termed concurrent resolutions, require passage by both houses, and, depending on the intent of the legislature and the procedure used in passage, may or may not have the effect of law. Unlike the practice in Congress and some other states, no distinction is made between a joint and a concurrent resolution by Georgia law or legislative rules of either house. Thus the two terms can be—and are—used interchangeably.

The decision to employ the format of a joint resolution rather than a bill is dictated in some instances by custom or by the inclination of the author. The General Assembly is required to use a joint resolution when proposing constitutional amendments,[40] awarding compensation,[41] accepting bids for sale or lease of public properties under the custody of the State Properties Commission,[42] convening a joint session of the General As-

Figure 6: *Housekeeping Resolution*

```
                                            LC 14 5968
H. R. No. 3
By:  Representatives Murphy of the 18th, Connell of the
115th, Walker of the 141st, Groover of the 125th and Lee of
the 94th
```

A RESOLUTION

1   Relative to officials, employees, and committees in   27

2   the House of Representatives; and for other purposes.   28

3   BE IT RESOLVED BY THE HOUSE OF REPRESENTATIVES that   31

4   the following provisions shall be in effect during the   1993   32

5   regular session of the General Assembly of Georgia and until   33

6   otherwise provided for by resolution of the House: 34

7   Part 1.   37

8   Section 1-1. Subject to the availability of funds   40

9   appropriated or otherwise available for the House of   41

10   Representatives and House Research Office, the Speaker of   42

11   the House is authorized to employ on behalf of the House of   43

12   Representatives: a   sergeant-at-arms, a postmaster or   44

13   postmistress,   assistant   postmasters   or   assistant   44

14   postmistresses, assistant doorkeepers, pages, aides,   45

15   secretaries, stenographers, typists, clerks, porters, court   46

16   reporters, consultants, and other necessary personnel; and   47

17   the Speaker is authorized to provide for a House Research

18   Office and to employ personnel for said office. The numbers   48

19   and compensation of personnel so employed pursuant to this   49

20   section shall be fixed by the Speaker within the limitations   50

21   of funds appropriated or otherwise available for the   51

22   operation of the House of Representatives and the House

23   Research Office.   Personnel employed pursuant to this   52

24   section may be employed on a permanent or temporary basis   53

25   and on a part-time or full-time basis, as may be determined   54

26   by the Speaker.   The assignment and duties of personnel   55

27   employed pursuant to this section shall be as determined by

```
                         H. R. No. 3
                          - 1 -
```

sembly,[43] amending joint session rules,[44] and taking certain other actions.[45] Additionally, should a resolution be used by the General Assembly to appropriate money, it must be in the form of a joint resolution enacted in the same manner as a bill.[46]

Though occasionally used for quasi-statutory matters, joint resolutions primarily

1. propose amendments to the state constitution;
2. authorize payment to persons for claims against the state (compensation resolutions);
3. authorize land conveyances, leases, and easements in the name of the state;
4. create legislative overview committees, joint interim study committees, and other special agencies;
5. name or rename state parks, buildings, memorial highways, roads, bridges, or other public entities (in the Senate, these are termed "commemorative resolutions");
6. ratify, approve, and confirm executive orders of the governor which temporarily suspend collection of certain taxes;[*]
7. authorize the Department of Revenue to write off uncollectable sales and use tax accounts; and
8. authorize or direct a state agency or official to perform a certain task.[47]

Since these kinds of joint resolutions have the effect of law, they must be assigned to a standing committee and receive three readings in both houses before passage.[48] Once adopted by the two houses, they are submitted to the governor and given an act number if signed by the governor or if enacted without his or her signature. As with bills, joint resolutions that will have the force of law may be vetoed by the governor, except those proposing constitutional amendments, which do not require the governor's signature, and, in any event, cannot be vetoed.[49] (For specific information on a governor's veto power over resolutions, as well as additional exemptions, see pp. 170-76.)

Joint resolutions are also used for other purposes, such as (1) expressing the sympathy, appreciation, or recognition of both houses; (2) express-

---

[*]Pursuant to O.C.G.A. §45-12-22, the governor is authorized to suspend the collection of all or part of any taxes due the state, but only until the next meeting of the General Assembly, at which session the action is reviewed by the legislature and either ratified or rejected. The vehicle by which such ratification occurs is a joint resolution embodying the governor's executive order along with formal ratification, approval, and confirmation of that order. Because this action touches on the raising of revenue, the joint resolution must be introduced in the House.

ing an opinion shared by the two houses; (3) notifying the governor that the General Assembly has convened; (4) providing for a joint session of the General Assembly; (5) amending the rules of the legislature for meeting in joint session; and (6) setting a time and date for adjournment of the General Assembly. For these purposes, the joint resolution generally does not carry the weight of law, and thus assignment to committee, three readings, and submission to the governor are not necessary. In actual practice, some of these joint resolutions are assigned to committee in one or both houses, and some are not; and some receive only one reading, while others are read on two or three occasions before passage.

As with a bill, a joint resolution may be introduced in either house, unless it pertains to raising revenue or appropriating money when it must originate in the House.[50]

Joint resolutions of general application, which have the effect of law, are compiled and printed in volume one of the annual session laws, while those of local or special application are found in volume two. Simple resolutions are not included in either volume, but sometimes are included in the published House or Senate journals for the session at which introduced.

Compensation Resolutions

Compensation resolutions are used to allow the General Assembly to compensate citizens who, through no fault of their own, have been injured or have suffered damages because of negligence or certain other actions by state officials and employees, and who have no other recourse to recover for damages. (See Fig. 7.)

Under the Georgia Constitution, the state is immune from being sued except for cases involving a breach of written contract by the state and cases where the state has specifically waived its immunity within the Georgia Tort Claims Act.[51] Otherwise, Georgia state government is not subject to suit for negligent or other tortious acts by its personnel and, Georgia courts have held, the injured party must seek redress for such wrongs from the legislature, not from the courts.[52] Furthermore, payment of compensation in these cases is "purely a matter of legislative grace based upon a strong moral obligation and equitable duty and not upon the assumption of legal liability.[53]

To assist the General Assembly in the adoption of compensation resolutions, a Claims Advisory Board has been established, consisting of the secretary of state and the commissioners of human resources, corrections, and transportation.[54] This board receives notice of claims against the state, conducts investigations, holds hearings, prepares statements of its findings, and presents its recommendations regarding the merits of each case and such compensation as should be awarded the injured party. Its policy has been to recommend reimbursement for actual and substantiated out-

Figure 7: *Compensation Resolution*

LC 10 0753

H. R. No. 906
By: Representative Scoggins of the 24th

A RESOLUTION

1   Compensating Mr. Nelson O. Scoggins; and for other   27

2 purposes.   28

3   WHEREAS, Mr. Nelson O. Scoggins, a Senior Mechanic   31

4 with the Department of Transportation, works out of the   32

5 Athens-Clarke County Routing Maintenance Headquarters at 450   33

6 Old Hull Road in Athens, Georgia; and   34

7   WHEREAS, on July 30, 1992, at the end of the   37

8 business day, Mr. Scoggins left his tools locked in the tool   38

9 compartment of the Department of Transportation truck No.   39

10 451-0760 which was parked in the maintenance building that   40

11 was locked at the end of the business day; and   41

12   WHEREAS, during the night of July 30-31, 1992, an   44

13 assortment of tools which Mr. Scoggins had accumulated over   45

14 a period of 30 years were stolen from such truck locked in   46

15 the maintenance building; and   47

16   WHEREAS, Mr. Scoggins has suffered property loss   50

17 totaling $6,169.30; and   51

18   WHEREAS, the loss occurred through no fault or   54

19 negligence on the part of Mr. Scoggins and it is only   55

20 fitting and proper that he be compensated for his loss.   56

21   NOW, THEREFORE, BE IT RESOLVED BY THE GENERAL   59

22 ASSEMBLY OF GEORGIA that the Department of Transportation is   60

23 authorized and directed to pay the sum of $6,169.30 to Mr.   61

H. R. No. 906
- 1 -

of-pocket expenses only. Such recommendations, however, are advisory only and are not binding on the legislature.[55]

In 1982, the General Assembly acted to reduce the need for compensation resolutions by providing a procedure for claims not exceeding $500 to be settled without going before the legislature. In fact, the legislature stipulated that compensation resolutions could not be used for any claim involving $500 or less.[56]

In addition, the board can make recommendations to the legislature concerning payment of compensation, under certain conditions, to innocent persons who sustain injury or property damage, and to the dependents of innocent persons killed while attempting to aid prevention of a crime against another person or to aid a law officer at his or her request.[57]

Any resolution seeking compensation or reimbursement from the state of Georgia, or any of its agencies, for a person injured or property damaged, must be introduced in the House of Representatives within the first 25 days of a regular session.[58] However, before the preceding November 15, a notice of the claim *must* have been filed with the Claims Advisory Board. Should the event giving rise to the claim not occur until after November 5, the notice must then be filed with the board within 10 days after the occurrence.[59] Additionally, in the case of claims for compensation for damages resulting from attempts to prevent crimes, notice of the claim must have been filed with the board within 18 months of the personal injury or death, and the incident or offense resulting in the injury or death reported to a law enforcement officer within 5 days of its occurrence, or if the incident or offense could not reasonably have been reported within such period, within 5 days of the time when a report could reasonably have been made.[60]

After a claim has been filed, the board must then specify in writing to the claimant what information it must have for investigatory purposes, including accident reports, affidavits, statements, or receipts. All such information must be provided to the board before any action of the legislature on the claim.[61]

Thereafter, any member of the House of Representatives may introduce a compensation resolution in that body. The speaker is required to refer it to the Appropriations Committee, and the clerk is required to send a certified copy to the chair of the Claims Advisory Board. The board investigates the claim, holding a hearing if necessary, and then meets to take final action. The board must transmit its statement to the chair of the Appropriations Committee by the 30th day of the session. The representative who introduced the resolution is also notified of the board's actions and, if dissatisfied, can demand a hearing if one was not previously held.[62] Although the board's recommendations are advisory and not binding, the Appropriations Committee and the House of Representatives usually accept the board's recommendations.

GENERAL REQUIREMENTS FOR LEGISLATION

In January 1795, the most controversial law in the history of Georgia—the infamous "Yazoo Act"—was enacted under this caption:

> An Act supplementary to an Act, entitled an Act for appropriating a part of the unlocated territory of this State, for the payment of the late State troops, and for other purposes therein mentioned, declaring the right of this State to the unappropriated territory thereof, for the protection of the frontiers, and for other purposes.[63]

Under the patriotic language of this summary title, the body of the act proceeded to sell the greater part of the territory now comprising Alabama and Mississippi to four land companies for the incredible sum of $490,000, with most legislators being given shares in one or more of the companies. A new legislature immediately repealed this action and the Yazoo Land Fraud precipitated a constitutional requirement for enacting legislation: no law can be passed which contains matter different from that expressed in the title.[64] A second constitutional prohibition—that no law can be passed which refers to more than one subject matter—is also frequently attributed to the Yazoo scandal, although in fact it was not included until the Constitution of 1861.[65]

Legislators should be cautioned that these two prohibitions—regarding multiple subject matter and the title—have constituted the bases for numerous contests regarding the validity of various statutes passed by the General Assembly, and that the Georgia Supreme Court has ruled these requirements to be mandatory and not merely directory.[66]

Multiple-Subject-Matter Prohibition

The constitutional requirement against multiple subject matter is designed to prevent "omnibus" bills which combine many unrelated provisions, none of which could succeed upon its own merits, with the intent of combining the votes of advocates of each.[67]

The "subject of an act" is regarded as the thing or matter forming the groundwork of the act and is not synonymous with "provision."[68] The courts tend to give a broad meaning to the term "subject matter," so as to allow the legislature to include in one act all matters having a logical or natural connection.[69] Whether an act violates the multiple-subject-matter prohibition depends on whether all the bill's provisions seek to accomplish a single objective.[70]

To contain multiple subject matter, then, an act must embrace two or more dissimilar and discordant subjects that in no reasonable way can be considered as having any logical connection with or to each other.[71] Examples of laws held invalid because of multiple subject matter include an act that attempted to amend the charters of two separate and distinct municipal corporations,[72] and an act to authorize the construction of telephone lines in the state, while providing criminal penalties for divulging any private messages by any persons connected with telephone companies.[73]

On the other hand, the court has upheld an act levying excise taxes against malt beverages and wine;[74] an act removing the clerk of superior court and tax commissioner of one county from the fee system;[75] the Executive Reorganization Act of 1972, which affected numerous different agencies in the executive branch;[76] and an act amending different sections and chapters of the Official Code of Georgia Annotated.[77]

Subject Matter Noted in a Bill's Title

Required by the constitution, a "title" (formerly also called a "caption") is the formal introduction that summarizes the substantive provisions of a bill. It prefaces the main body of a bill and always precedes the phrase, "Be It Enacted by the General Assembly of Georgia." (Fig. 8 presents an example of a title of a bill.)

Georgia's Constitution of 1798 was the first state constitution to formally dictate that the body of an act cannot contain matter not mentioned in the title of that act.[78] Not only is the title a safeguard against covert and surprise legislation, but it is a practical device to notify legislators and the public of the scope and content of proposed legislation. Additionally, the title is used for the three readings of general bills in each house, unless the presiding officer or a majority of the members who will vote on the bill order that the bill be read in its entirety on the third reading.[79]

Examples of contested laws held invalid because of discrepancies between the title and body include a statute, the title of which enumerated particular land lots, while its body attempted to deal with other lots;[80] a statute, the title of which referred only to civil cases, with provisions purporting to apply to criminal cases as well;[81] and a statute whose title provided for campaign financing disclosures for certain state offices, but whose body included all county and municipal elected officials.[82]

In the majority of cases, the court appears to have been fairly liberal in its interpretations and has stated that the constitution does not require that the substance of the entire act should be set forth in the title, that every detail stated in the body be mentioned in the title, or that the title contain a synopsis of the law. Rather, a title need only indicate the general object and subject matter to be dealt with and be broad enough to protect people against covert or surprise legislation.[83]

At an early date, legislators initiated the practice of adding the words "and for other purposes" at the end of a bill's title, in hopes that this broad phrase might sufficiently cover provisions in the act which the title might not otherwise specify. And in some early cases, the court upheld portions of an act not indicated in the title, by virtue of this general clause. For example, a statute, the title of which referred only to licensing the sale of

Figure 8: *Title of Bill*

94   LC 9 7632

SENATE BILL 537

By: Senators Balfour of the 9th and Turner of the 8th

A BILL TO BE ENTITLED   **AS PASSED**

AN ACT

1	To amend Chapter 8 of Title 45 of the Official Code	31
2	of Georgia Annotated, relating to accounting for public	32
3	funds, so as to change the provisions relating to the	33
4	designation of depositories for the funds of counties and	34
5	boards of education; to repeal conflicting laws; and for	35
6	other purposes.	

7   BE IT ENACTED BY THE GENERAL ASSEMBLY OF GEORGIA: 38

8   Section 1.   Chapter 8 of Title 45 of the Official   41

9   Code of Georgia Annotated, relating to accounting for public   42

10   funds, is amended by striking Code Section 45-8-14, which   43

11   reads as follows:

12   "45-8-14. The county authorities shall designate   45

13   one or more solvent banks, insured federal savings and   46

14   loan associations, or insured state chartered building   47

15   and loan associations as depositories of all county   48

16   moneys, of moneys belonging to the school funds of the   49

17   county and the school districts therein, and of other   50

18   districts therein organized for any purpose. If the   51

19   county authorities have not provided for such a   52

20   depository, the county board of education, the trustees   53

21   of any school district, or the proper authorities having   54

22   supervision over any other public fund may designate

23   such a depository for their funds; and if there is no   55

24   applicable depository selected, the officer collecting   56

25   or holding any public funds may select a depository.",   57

26   and inserting in lieu thereof a new Code Section 45-8-14 to   59

27   read as follows: 60

S. B. 537

- 1 -

intoxicating liquors, but which possessed provisions making the sale of such liquors without a license a misdemeanor, was held invalid.[84] However, a similar statute was later sustained by the court on the sole ground that its title contained the phrase "and for other purposes."[85]

Obviously, there are limits on using the phrase in a bill's title. But the general attitude of the court has been that provisions which are germane to general subject matter embraced in the title and designed to carry into effect the purposes for which the act was passed may be constitutionally included in the body of an act, though not referred to in the title except by "and for other purposes."[86]

If a bill or resolution contains matter different from that expressed in the title, or contains provisions in conflict with the title, only that part containing such material will be declared void unless this material is so integral to the whole act that it is not severable.[87] The question has also arisen as to whether a statute is unconstitutional because its title mentioned more items than were covered in its body. The Georgia Supreme Court has held this type of statute valid.[88]

An examination of court cases involving statutes with either multiple subject matter or matter in the body not mentioned in the title suggests that most occur not because of surreptitious strategy but because of committee or floor amendments. Material may be added to or deleted from a bill during the legislative deliberations, and, through simple oversight, the title is not changed to reflect it. At this stage, it is principally the responsibility of a bill's author to consider whether proposed changes are germane to the bill's subject matter and, following all amendments, whether the bill's title accurately reflects provisions within the measure.

Amending and Repealing Statutes

Another constitutional provision for ensuring that legislators understand legislation upon which they must act is the declaration: "no law or section of the Code shall be amended or repealed by mere reference to its title or to the number of the section of the Code; but the amending or repealing Act shall distinctly describe the law or Code to be amended or repealed as well as the alteration to be made."[89] Refusing to abolish the concept of repeal by implication, the Georgia Supreme Court has repeatedly held that this provision applies only in instances where an amending or repealing statute purports to *expressly* repeal or amend a former statute.[90]

Such an approach by the court has the rather peculiar effect of rendering the requirement inapplicable in those confusing instances which it could have remedied, i.e., in cases where the amending act does not expressly refer to an earlier statute which it will modify.

Even where express repeal is attempted, however, this requirement of the constitution has apparently received a rather liberal interpretation. For example, the requirement has been held satisfied where the amending act included in its title only the title of the statute to be amended.[91] The court also has sustained an amending statute after considering its title and it as a whole, although the amended statute was not specifically mentioned. In the latter case, the court said of the constitutional requirement, "One, if not the only, object of this provision is to put everyone, legislators and the public who might be affected, on guard as to all matters connected with the subject matter."[92]

Repeals by Implication

When the legislature enacts a measure which conflicts with, but does not expressly repeal or amend, existing law, the courts generally presume that (1) it acted with full knowledge of existing law; (2) the new act must be construed in relation to other statutes of which it will become a part; and (3) statutes relating to the same subject must be harmonized wherever possible.[93] Although they express disfavor with the practice, the courts will acknowledge an implicit repeal of former law where such statutes cannot be harmonized if (1) a later statute is so irreconcilable with an earlier statute that the two cannot stand together, and (2) the later statute is manifestly intended to cover the same subject matter and to operate as a substitute for the earlier statute.[94]

In instances of conflict among statutes, the courts regard the latest expression of the General Assembly on a subject as controlling.[95] This rule applies not only to acts passed at different sessions, but those passed at the same session, in which event that act signed last by the governor will control.[96] The same principle applies if two provisions within a single act conflict. The provision last in position stands, as it is presumed to be the last expression of legislative will.[97]

The attitude of the court makes it important for a legislator to consider, when proposing a bill, whether there is an existing statute which should be expressly repealed in the new act.

Legislative Intent and Judicial Interpretation

Members of the General Assembly are constantly urged, when drafting legislation, to use precise and unambiguous language that makes their intention clearly understandable.[98] Toward this end, the attention of the legislator is directed to the many commonly used words and phrases with statutory or judicial definition, such as "may," "shall," "reasonable," "adequate," "as soon as possible," and "anything in this act to the contrary notwithstanding."[99] Even if the language should be awkward or unusual, the legislative intent manifested by a statute must be determined and enforced as law. This avoids the occurrence of absurd results not intended by the legislature. Grammatical errors may not be used as the basis for invalidating an act. A transposition of words and clauses or interposition of punctuation may be undertaken by judges when the sentence or clause is without meaning as it stands.[100]

"Judicial construction" refers to the process whereby courts analyze, construe, interpret, define, and explain a statute (either in whole or part)—both alone and in conjunction with other laws and court decisions—as well as determine the validity or invalidity of statutes. A general rule for avoiding judicial construction of legislative enactments is that the use of plain and unequivocal language obviates any *necessity* for judicial interpretation.[101] If the language used in drafting a statute is clear and not susceptible to two interpretations, the courts cannot construe the act according to the supposed intention of the legislature, but must let the act speak for itself.[102] Furthermore, if a statute is unambiguous, its wisdom of expediency is of no legitimate concern to the judiciary.[103]

However, should interpretation of the meaning or validity of any statute become necessary—due to ambiguous wording, vagueness, uncertain legislative intent, conflict with other laws, questionable constitutionality, or for other reasons—Georgia law imposes upon the courts sole responsibility for construction of statutes.[104] It should be noted that this responsibility lies with the judge or judges and is not a matter for determination by a jury.[105]

The Official Code of Georgia Annotated stipulates that when construing statutory enactments, the courts must look diligently for the intention of the General Assembly in passing them, "keeping in view, at all times, the old law, the evil, and the remedy."[106] Therefore, a basic rule of construction used by the courts is to carry legislative intent and purpose into effect if that intent is ascertainable and within constitutional limits.[107] Such intent should come from the language of the statute, hence the need for plain and unequivocal language.

On innumerable occasions, the court has ruled that legislative intent must prevail over literal meaning of words, if the two appear in conflict. Unfortunately, despite the general rule that plain and unequivocal language will preclude any need for judicial interpretation, exceptions occur where an act uses words whose meanings are generally accepted, yet literal application of them would defeat the purpose of the legislation. In these instances, the responsibility of the court is to first ascertain legislative intent in enacting a law. The court must then give the statute that construction which will effect this purpose, even if it is necessary to disregard some words within the statute.[108]

Where judicial construction is necessary to determine legislative intent, the court is not limited in the sources it may use for enlightenment.[109] For instance, it may inquire into the history of an act,[110] the surrounding facts and circumstances that influenced its passage,[111] or objective evidence gathered from polls or studies.[112] Events occurring during the progress of a statute's enactment, as disclosed by the official House and

Senate journals, may be reviewed in seeking to find the intent of the legislature.[113]

Georgia courts have held that the testimony of members of the legislature—even the bill's author—is inadmissible to show legislative intent.[114] While conceding that the opinions of members of the General Assembly might be valuable and constructive in interpreting an act passed and discovering legislative intent, the courts have nevertheless viewed such sources as both improper and impractical. Not only is there the probability that legislators would differ as to what the act meant, but also the possibility that they had varying reasons for voting for the bill in its final form.[115] Allowing such testimony, it is suggested, would be tantamount to allowing members of the legislative branch to perform a judicial function. Rather than inquire into what was in the minds of the authors of a law, the courts have said that proper judicial inquiry is into what the legislature intended when it enacted a statute.[116] Similarly, the U.S. Supreme Court ruled that the trial court's presumption—that the Georgia General Assembly, in enacting a statute, knew the facts relative to the needs and problems of the tobacco market—cannot be overthrown by the testimony of individual legislators.[117]

While testimony of a legislator is inadmissible for showing legislative intent (although occasionally it has been allowed regarding the history of a law's passage), expressions of legislative opinion through resolutions may be looked at by the courts in determining intent for passing a certain act,[118] as will subsequent acts of the General Assembly on the same subject. However, the court has viewed a resolution expressing legislative opinion as an unconstitutional attempt to perform the court's judicial function of construing the meaning or intent of a statute.[119]

Not uncommonly, an enactment of the General Assembly will contain a legislative declaration of fact, purpose, or intent, as a justification for the act, as well as a statement such as, "This Act, being for the welfare of the State and its inhabitants, shall be liberally construed to effect the purposes hereof."

In some cases, the courts have taken judicial notice of such expressions of intent, even on occasion noting, "When looking to the intent of a statute, the most significant provisions for this court are those wherein the statute itself defines its intent."[120]

In other cases, however, Georgia courts have ruled that the effect of such provisions on court interpretation of legislative intent is advisory only.[121] For instance, while the General Assembly stated that one particular statute was an exercise of the state's "police powers," the courts held the validity of this declaration, in reality, a question for the judiciary.[122] The court also disregarded the express provision within an act that an authority created by it would exercise "governmental functions," holding that the General Assembly cannot preclude the court by a legislative interpretation of its own act.[123]

The courts may turn to officials of those executive agencies which are involved in administering a particular law in question when attempting to determine legislative intent. Although the interpretation given a statute by these officials may be considered persuasive by the court, the ultimate responsibility for construction and interpretation rests with the judiciary.[124]

Constitutionality of Statutes

The constitution of Georgia provides that "legislative acts in violation of this Constitution, or the Constitution of the United States are void, and the judiciary shall so declare them."[125] The courts, however, generally entertain a strong presumption that a statute is constitutional, assuming that the General Assembly was conscious of constitutional questions at the time of enactment.[126] Also, courts presume that the legislature is aware of all applicable state and federal law when it enacts legislation.[127] Thus, legislative enactments are presumed to be constitutional by the courts, with the burden of proof placed on those who would suggest otherwise.[128] Furthermore, a long-established principle of judicial interpretation is that the authority of the courts to declare acts of the legislature void should be exercised with great caution and restraint, and should not be resorted to except in clear and urgent cases.[129]

For the courts to consider a constitutional challenge to a statute or provision, the attack must be levied by a person whose interests or rights are affected by the statute.[130] Georgia courts will not rule on the constitutionality of a law in the abstract. To attack the validity of a law, a petitioner must (1) be within the class of persons whose rights are adversely affected by the statute or (2) have suffered harm or stand to suffer harm by the mere presence of the statute upon the books. The courts require strict adherence to the rule that any attack on the constitutionality of an act, in whole or part, be stated in clear, definite, and specific terms, noting with fair precision (1) the statute or parts of a statute which are being challenged; (2) the provision of the constitution which is presumably violated; and (3) the basis of claiming the statute offends the constitution.[131] These requirements are to assure that appellate courts can determine precisely how the trial court ruled on the challenge to the act's constitutionality. Also, questions of constitutionality must be raised in the lower trial court (usually the superior court) and specifically passed on by the trial judge. Appellate courts in Georgia will not rule on constitutional attacks against a statute which are raised for the first time in an appeal from a lower court ruling.[132]

Even if a challenge is properly raised, courts will avoid passing on a statute's constitutionality when the case can be disposed of on other grounds.[133] Similarly, if two constructions of an act are possible—one which will uphold its constitutionality and one which will not—an act must be construed by the courts as constitutional.[134]

Enrolled Bill Rule

Further evidence of the judiciary's restraint in declaring legislative acts unconstitutional is its adherence to what is known as the "enrolled bill rule." A duly enrolled act, authenticated by the presiding officer of each house of the General Assembly, approved by the governor, and deposited with the secretary of state as an existing law, will be conclusively presumed by the courts to have been enacted in accordance with constitutional requirements, and no evidence to the contrary will be considered.[135] The only exception to this rule appears to involve local legislation, which can be struck down if proof of notice of proper advertising before introduction is not attached to the enrolled copy.[136]

Neither legislative journals nor other extrinsic evidence may be used in court to impeach the validity of a bill on the basis that it was not enacted according to constitutional requirements, such as being read on three separate days or having been approved by a majority of the membership. Georgia's high court has also refused to void a bill because of charges that a house failed to follow its internal rules of procedure in approving a bill.[137]

Georgia courts follow the enrolled bill rule because of (1) the respect due a coequal and independent branch of government, and (2) recognition of the great confusion that would follow if courts were permitted or called upon to conduct an independent inquiry as to whether constitutional requirements were complied with on each bill approved by the General Assembly.[138]

Severability of Unconstitutional Provisions within Acts

A statute, unconstitutional or invalid in part, is not necessarily void in its entirety. The courts will dismiss an attack that an entire statute is unconstitutional when some portions of it can be found constitutional.[139] And, although an entire act may be adjudged unconstitutional, there are certain instances where the court will partially invalidate an act, striking those provisions which offend the constitution or are otherwise invalid, while upholding the remaining provision of the act.

The courts are generally guided by the following questions in determining whether a challenged statute must be totally or partially invalidated:

1. Are the nonoffending provisions separable from the offending?
2. If so, can they be given separate legal effect, and are they sufficient to accomplish the legislative scheme and purpose?
3. Does it appear that the General Assembly intended the law to stand or fall as a whole?[140]

If the court finds that the violative sections, provisions, sentences, or phrases of a legislative act can be severed without destroying the general legislative scheme, and that the legislature did not intend for the act to stand or fall as a whole, then the court will strike only the offending provisions, leaving the remainder of the act intact. If, on the other hand, the objectionable portions are so connected with the general legislative scheme that they are indispensable, then the whole statute must fall.[141]

To illustrate, the state supreme court ruled in similar cases involving legislative membership on agencies within the executive branch, that such membership violated the constitutional separation of powers provision. In one instance, since it was possible to remove legislative membership from the board and still leave enough members to constitute a quorum and to accomplish the purpose of the legislation, the entire act was not declared unconstitutional.[142] In the other instance, however, the court ruled that the language of the statute and special voting requirements showed that the intent of the General Assembly had been to create a balance on the commission between the executive and legislative branches. Since the primary legislative intent could not be carried out without legislative representation, the court ruled that the entire act must fall.[143]

The supreme court has also ruled that where the General Assembly has passed companion acts with each part of one general legislative scheme, if one is judged unconstitutional, the companion act, though itself not violative of the constitution, must also be considered ineffective.[144]

Because of the willingness of courts to uphold portions of laws that contain unconstitutional provisions under conditions previously cited, legislative bill drafters in recent decades increasingly added "severability clauses" within bills. These clauses declared that if any section, sentence, or provision of an act should be ruled invalid or unconstitutional by the courts, it was the intent of the legislature that the remaining sections, sentences, and provisions remain in full force and effect.

Though severability clauses were not considered binding on the courts in determining whether nonoffending provisions within an act were truly separable from the offending provisions, they did place the General Assembly on record as not intending the law to stand or fall as a whole. On a number of occasions, the courts have taken judicial notice of such legislative intentions.[145]

In 1982, when the Official Code of Georgia Annotated was adopted, the need for separate severability clauses in each piece of legislation was eliminated by the inclusion in the code of a general severability section. Now, unless an act contains an express provision to the contrary, the legislature's intention is considered to be that the sections and provisions of an act are separable.[146]

SPECIAL REQUIREMENTS FOR LEGISLATION

In addition to the general requirements for legislation discussed in the preceding sections, several types of legislation must meet specific requirements for introduction in the General Assembly.

Appropriation Acts

Probably the General Assembly's single most important function each session is to authorize funding for all agencies and programs of state government. Although appropriation acts are passed in the same way as legislative statutes, there are distinct differences. For one thing, statutes continue in effect until repealed, amended, or overruled as unconstitutional. Appropriation acts, however, are valid only during the fiscal year for which enacted. A second difference is that, unlike statutes, appropriation acts are not incorporated into the Official Code of Georgia Annotated. A third distinction—one long argued by Georgia's attorney general—is that while appropriation acts authorize agencies to spend up to the maximum stated amount for purposes authorized by general law, they (1) do not mandate these expenditures, (2) cannot authorize agencies to take actions not already permitted by general law, and (3) cannot alter any agency powers derived from general law.[147]

What type of quasi-statutory language can be included within an appropriation act? Lawmakers commonly include extensive statements of intent on how a particular agency's appropriation can be spent, plus instructions to agencies and officials on what they can and cannot do.[148] The constitutionality of the practice (or the legal consequences of not following these instructions) has not been before Georgia's appellate courts. Nor have the courts ruled on the governor's use of the line-item veto to strike down instructions in appropriation acts. It is the attorney general's role to render an official opinion, at the request of an executive agency head, when legislative instructions in an appropriation act appear to conflict with that agency's discretionary power previously authorized by general law.[149]

Although also granting certain exceptions, Georgia's constitution mandates that no funds can be withdrawn from the state treasury except as appropriated by law.[150] However, this does not mean that every function or activity of a state agency must be specifically mentioned in the appropriation act. At one extreme, the legislature can appropriate a single lump sum to an agency, giving the agency broad discretion on how to spend its appropriation. At the other extreme, lawmakers can choose to control almost every aspect of agency spending through a detailed "line-item budget." Prior to 1974, Georgia's General Assembly appropriated lump sums to agencies, specifying only a few categories (such as personnel and operating expenses). However, lawmakers shifted to a line-item budget in 1974 after one agency used internal funds to implement a new program that had been turned down by the House Appropriations Committee.[151]

While state agencies carry out programs initiated by the state legislature, most are also involved in implementing federally supported programs. State agencies sometimes find they can qualify for federal grants and contracts that were not anticipated at the time the state appropriation act was considered by the legislature. To allow state agencies to take advantage of these federal funds, Georgia's constitution provides that all additional or unanticipated federal funds "are hereby continually appropriated for the purposes authorized and directed by the federal government in making the grant."[152]

As noted earlier, Georgia's constitution requires that all bills for raising revenue or appropriating money originate in the House of Representatives.[153] This provision, however, does not completely deprive the Senate of a role with respect to fiscal measures. The Georgia Supreme Court has sustained a revenue-raising measure which, though originally introduced in the House, actually came from the Senate in the form of a substitute measure. The court's rationale was that under general rules of parliamentary procedure, a substitute is merely an amendment—and thus permissible under Georgia's constitution.[154]

Among other requirements, open-ended appropriations are not allowed—each agency's allotment must be for a specific sum of money.[155] Unless specific exception is made in the constitution, no appropriation can allocate the proceeds of any tax or revenue source to a particular agency or program.[156] Although a few dedicated revenue sources (e.g., lottery net proceeds must go to education, motor fuel taxes must go to roads and bridges, federal grants must be used for the purpose authorized by the federal government, etc.) are recognized by the constitution, the overall scheme is that all other state revenues are to be deposited in the state treasury, with the governor then free to budget and the General Assembly free to appropriate based on the respective needs of state agencies and programs.

With the exception of the general appropriations bill, "all other appropriations shall be made by separate bills, each embracing but one subject."[157] When voting on an appropriation measure, the Constitution requires that a roll call vote be taken in each house.[158]

According to Georgia's constitution, "The General Assembly shall annually appropriate those state and federal funds necessary to operate all the various departments and agencies."[159] As noted earlier, no money can be drawn from the state treasury unless appropriated by law.[160] Every appropriation must expire at the end of the fiscal year for which it was enacted.[161] In the absence of an appropriation act, there seems to be no legal way for state agencies to spend money—with the exception of taxes earmarked in the constitution for specific purposes (currently only the motor fuel tax), mandatory appropriations required by the constitution, contractual obligations authorized by the constitution, federal grants, and lottery proceeds used to pay lottery prizes and operating expenses—all of which continue with or without an appropriation act.[162] For other state programs, however, it is not clear what would happen if the General Assembly failed to pass an appropriation act for the next fiscal year.*

General Appropriations Act

Each year, the General Assembly enacts a single, omnibus spending bill for state government known as the "general appropriations act." According to the state constitution, this act "shall embrace nothing except appropriations fixed by previous laws; the ordinary expenses of the executive, legislative, and judicial departments of the government; payment of the public debt and interest thereon; and for support of the public institutions and educational interests of the state."[163]

The general appropriations act (see Fig. 9) authorizes all funding for the state's fiscal year, which begins July 1 and ends the following June 30. (The fiscal year is identified in terms of the ending year—FY 97 begins July 1, 1996, and concludes June 30, 1997.) Appropriated funds not spent or contractually obligated by an agency by the end of the fiscal year lapse and return to the state's general fund as surplus.[164] Several trust funds provided for in the constitution are exempt from this requirement and can carry forth unspent funds into the next fiscal year.[165] Unspent lottery proceeds lapse to a special lottery education account in the state treasury.[166]

Georgia's constitution provides that the General Assembly cannot appropriate more money for a fiscal year than the total of (1) anticipated revenues and (2) any surplus or reserves carried over from the previous fiscal year.[167] The constitution also allows the legislature to appropriate money borrowed through issuance of general obligation and guarantee revenue debt, so long as the annual debt service (i.e., interest and repayment of principle) does not exceed 10 percent of the net revenue receipts for the previous fiscal year.[168] There is also a limit of 1 percent on guaranteed revenue debt incurred for water and sewer facilities. (Actually, in recent years interest on the state debt has been averaging 5 to 6 percent of the previous year's net treasury receipts.)

In Georgia, the budgetary process leading to a general appropriations act is a year-round process involving both executive and legislative branches. During the fall, the governor meets with state agency heads to

---

* Obviously, the governor would have to call a special session. If that failed to produce an appropriation act, most state agencies would be in jeopardy. In the short run, agency personnel might continue to work for deferred pay, or agree to receive partial pay in scrip. Because the constitution provides that the General Assembly "shall annually appropriate those state and federal funds necessary to operate all the various departments and agencies," it is likely that suit would be filed in state (and possibly even federal) court to require the legislature to perform its constitutionally mandated duty. One judicial remedy sought might be to have a judge declare the preceding fiscal year's appropriation in effect until a new one can be enacted.

Figure 9: *General Appropriations Act*

Section 14. Department of Agriculture.
A. Budget Unit: Department of

Agriculture ....$	35,951,993
Personal Services...............................$	31,024,092
Regular Operating Expenses...............$	4,153,363
Travel ....$	896,000
Motor Vehicle Purchases.....................$	446,460
Equipment..$	391,082
Computer Charges...............................$	359,078
Real Estate Rentals............................$	791,341
Telecommunications ....$	402,901
Per Diem, Fees and Contracts............$	957,050
Market Bulletin Postage ....$	860,000
Payments to Athens and Tifton	
Veterinary Laboratories ....$	2,515,782
Poultry Veterinary Diagnostic	
Laboratories in Canton, Dalton,	
Douglas, Oakwood, Statesboro,	
Carroll, Macon, Mitchell,	
and Monroe ....$	2,130,411
Veterinary Fees...................................$	412,000
Indemnities ....$	127,000
Advertising Contract ....$	175,000
Payments to Georgia Agrirama	
Development Authority	
for Operations ....$	618,360
Payments to Georgia Development	
Authority ....$	250,000
Renovation, Construction, Repairs	
and Maintenance Projects at	
Major and Minor Markets...............$	700,000
Capital Outlay ....$	0
Contract - Federation of Southern	
Cooperatives....................................$	40,000
Boll Weevil Eradication Program ....$	0
Total Funds Budgeted ....$	47,249,920
State Funds Budgeted.........................$	35,951,993

Department of Agriculture Functional Budgets

	Total Funds	State Funds
Plant Industry	$ 4,910,852	$ 4,589,852

give them a chance to explain their budget request for the coming fiscal year. Prior to the legislative session, department heads are also to explain and argue for their budget requests before the appropriations committees of the House and Senate. Inevitably, agencies request more money than will be available. Deciding which requests to fund and to what degree, within the policies and priorities of the governor, becomes an important tool for the state's chief executive.

The constitution requires the governor to present an annual budget message, a detailed report on the financial condition of the state, and the draft of a general appropriations act for the next fiscal year to the General Assembly, within five days of its convening each year.[169] The governor's proposed budget cannot exceed the state's anticipated revenue, but projecting that revenue with fair precision is an extremely complex task. Under Georgia's constitution, the governor is to make that estimate. It has long been practice for the chief executive to rely on an economist experienced in economic forecasting to project a range of expected revenue. The governor, using those figures, generally makes a conservative-to-mid-range estimate. That figure becomes the official revenue estimate, which Georgia's proposed budget cannot exceed (plus any surplus or reserve funds in the state treasury available for appropriation).

The governor's proposed state budget does not set aside funds for miscellaneous expenditures, contingencies (such as revenue shortfalls), or programs that may be proposed at that year's legislative session. Nor is money set aside for the General Assembly to allocate to programs of special interest to lawmakers. Rather, the governor's general appropriations bill allocates every dollar of the official revenue estimate for specified purposes as identified in the bill.* Funds for any new or expanded programs can only be found by taking them from funds the governor has recommended for other programs or by raising the official revenue estimate—a power that only the governor has.[170]

The General Assembly is also involved in the appropriation process. Prior to and during the legislative session, the House and Senate appropriations committees hold joint hearings, giving legislators an opportunity to hear directly from agency heads about their budget needs and to question Office of Planning and Budget (OPB) officials about the governor's recommendations. A small staff agency—the Office of Legislative Budget Analyst—works year-round to give legislators an independent

---

* Contingency and set asides may be provided if the governor sets the budget estimate below the total of anticipated revenues and, in the budget message to the General Assembly, publicly acknowledges a discrepancy between the explicit and implicit revenue estimates. Thus, funds for boosting reserves may be assured even though all of the budget estimate is allocated. Alternately, funds supporting tax cuts may be removed from expected total revenues to get the budget estimate.

source of budget information, including a "continuation budget" for lawmakers to compare with the governor's estimates of a continuation budget.* Numerous changes will be made in the governor's budget while in the General Assembly, but in the end, the final budget approved by the legislature tends to contain the great majority of the governor's recommendations.

Once the legislature enacts a new state budget, the governor has extensive authority in its implementation, with broad powers and responsibilities over how state agencies spend their funds. Many observers of state government consider the budgetary power as the governor's single most important power. To help with this responsibility, a full-time agency—the Office of Planning and Budget—exists within the governor's office. OPB conducts year-round studies of the programs and budget requests of every agency in the executive branch, but ultimately it is the governor who makes the final decisions about what will go in the general appropriations bill submitted to the legislature.

The governor has no role in reviewing or changing budget requests for the legislative and judicial branches. The chief judge of the Georgia Supreme Court and the chief judge of the Georgia Court of Appeals submit their estimate of funding needed for the next fiscal year for inclusion in the governor's budget report. Estimates for the General Assembly's budget are prepared by the legislative fiscal officer, subject to the speaker of the House and president of the Senate.[171]

Special mention should be made of one category of expenditure within the general appropriations act—the governor's "emergency fund." Each year, an appropriation is made to the governor for "emergency needs of the state agencies, which needs were not ascertainable at the time of the submission of the budget report to the General Assembly or at the time of the enactment of the general appropriations act."[172] (For FY 1995, the appropriation was $4,350,000.) An agency head requesting money from this fund must make a request in writing to the governor, who has full discretion in fulfilling the request. The only restriction on use of the emergency fund specifically mentioned by state law is that no money can be allotted to a purpose which creates a continuing obligation for the state.[173] Georgia's attorney general, however, has ruled that the money must be used for previously unbudgeted emergency needs, the recipient must be a state agency or budget unit, and the purposes for which used must be consistent with that agency's statutory authority.[174] This precludes use of the governor's emergency fund for extending a municipal water main,

---

* A continuation budget is one that factors in cost-of-living increases, anticipated changes in federal grants, and other expected changes and then attempts to show what it would cost for each agency to continue its current programs and services in the next fiscal year at the same level as in the current fiscal year.

building a radio beacon at a city airport, and paying the fees of city and county police officers to attend the police academy.[175]

State law requires the general appropriations bill to be assigned to the House Appropriations Committee. In the event that the committee makes any changes to the bill, neither the Committee of the Whole nor the full house can consider the bill until at least 24 hours after a copy of the bill as amended has been placed on the desk of each member.[176] Any funding of grant programs in an appropriations act must be identified with the word "grant" in its description, and must also be appropriated separately from any other programs (although different grants by a particular state agency shall be listed together under a heading that contains the word "grant" or "grants").[177]

Amended General Appropriations Act

The general appropriations act for any fiscal year typically is adopted late in the legislative session—usually in March or April—prior to the July 1 beginning date of that fiscal year. While economists have sophisticated forecasting models to project how the economy will perform, they must rely to some degree on guesswork. If actual revenue is more than anticipated or, more seriously, if it is less than expected, the governor and the General Assembly will have to make some adjustments. This creates the need for amending a general appropriations act.

Another important reason for making midyear corrections to the budget is that the Quality Basic Education Act requires that adjustments be made in state spending for education based on public school enrollment figures that only become known after the beginning of the fiscal year.

To deal with these situations, the General Assembly has created two reserves. On the final day of each fiscal year, the state auditor is directed to transfer an amount equal to 1 percent of the just-concluded fiscal year's net revenue collections to the midyear adjustment reserve (providing that sufficient lapsed and surplus funds are available in the treasury).[178] At the next session, this reserve can be used for any purposes when amending the general appropriations act then in effect.

A second type of budget "insurance" is the revenue shortfall reserve— the so called "rainy day" fund. On the final day of the fiscal year, after transferring funds from any surplus to the midyear reserve, the state auditor then transfers an additional 3 percent of that year's net revenue collections (providing the money is available) to a revenue shortfall reserve. This reserve is intended to make up any deficiency at the end of the fiscal year should the state fail to meet its revenue estimate.

Another way to deal with revenue shortfalls is for the governor to order OPB to cut back quarterly allotments to state agencies to bring spending into line with revenue. Or, at the extreme, the governor can call the legislature back into special session to pass an amended general appropriations act that cuts state spending to the level of a new revenue estimate.

At each legislative session, the governor submits two budgets to lawmakers. The first budget priority is to amend the current general appropriations act to cover the final months of that fiscal year. Only after that is done do lawmakers turn their attention to a budget for the next fiscal year.

Historically, the amended general appropriations act has also been called the "supplemental appropriation act," because of the common practice in good revenue years of having additional money to appropriate for the final half of the fiscal year. However, Georgia's constitution has a specific set of rules for "supplementary appropriations," and the more accurate term for the annual mid-fiscal-year budget adjustment is "amended general appropriations act."

Supplementary Appropriation Acts

Georgia's constitution provides for a second type of appropriation act— the "supplementary appropriation act."[179] This is used to provide additional funding to a particular agency to finish out the fiscal year. The constitution sets certain restrictions on supplementary appropriations. For example, all "shall be made by separate bill, each embracing but one subject." [While this would seem to require a separate act for each agency, the General Assembly on occasion has used a single supplementary appropriation act to change the appropriations of a number of state agencies.[180]] In any event, the appropriation change is only for the remainder of that fiscal year.[181]

No supplementary appropriation act can be passed until the general appropriations act has been passed by the legislature and approved by the governor, and unless (1) there is an unappropriated surplus in the state treasury, or (2) the revenue necessary to fund such appropriation has been provided for by a tax enacted for such purpose and collected into the general fund of the state treasury.[182]

Revenue, Expenditure, and Compensation Bills

Any bill changing the compensation or allowances of any elected or appointed state official or agency head must be introduced in the General Assembly during the first 10 days of a session.[183] Any bill which would significantly impact on the anticipated revenues or expenditure levels of any state agency or any cities or counties must be introduced during the first 20 days of a session.[184]

The sponsor of any bill affecting anticipated revenue or expenditure levels of state agencies must request a fiscal note from OPB and the Department of Audits and Accounts by December 1 preceding the session.[185] (This requirement can be waived by a majority of the members of the committee to which the bill is assigned.) The fiscal note must outline the fiscal effect of the proposed bill, including, if possible,

1. a reliable estimate in dollars of the anticipated change in revenue or expenditures under the bill; and
2. a statement as to the immediate and, if determinable, long-range effect of the measure.[186]

If, after investigation, it is impossible to make a dollar estimate of the impact of the proposed measure, the fiscal note must explain why such is not possible. In this event, the note must give an example based on a specific situation or reflecting the average group of persons possibly affected by the bill so as to indicate the likely cost of the bill.

No comment or opinion can be included in the fiscal note regarding the merits of the measure for which the statement is prepared, although technical or mechanical defects may be noted. Additionally, if there is a difference of opinion between the state auditor and the director of OPB, the fiscal note—which is jointly prepared—must note the areas of difference.

Fiscal notes for revenue bills must be attached to the bill and read in each house at the bill's third reading. Additionally, each General Assembly member must be furnished with a copy of the note before such bill can come up for a vote.[187]

With respect to bills changing the compensation of state officials, the state auditor is directed to prepare and furnish a fiscal note for each, unless no state funds are used, in whole or part, in an official's salary.[188] These fiscal notes must show the present compensation and allowances of an officer, any present longevity increments, and any personal expense allowances (other than mileage and travel), as well as provide a statement of the proposed increase in compensation and allowances and the total cost of such changes. Copies of these fiscal notes must be distributed to each legislator before a vote can be taken on a compensation measure.

Retirement Bills

The Public Retirement Systems Standards Law defines minimum funding standards for state and local public retirement systems, establishes legislative procedures to control the passage of bills amending or creating public retirement systems, and requires that enacted bills be concurrently funded.[189] The law was passed in 1983 to comply with the requirements of the constitution that the legislature must define pension funding standards in order to assure the actuarial soundness of such systems.[190]

Before amendments granting a benefit increase in any legislatively controlled retirement system can be made, the law requires the administrator of the system to certify to the governor and General Assembly that the system meets the minimum funding standards prescribed by the law. Any bill passed amending a system that is not certified shall not become law and shall be null and void and stand repealed in its entirety on the first day of July following its enactment.

Retirement legislation must be identified by the state auditor as being fiscal or nonfiscal. Nonfiscal retirement bills make no financial changes in a retirement system. They must be introduced within the first 20 days of any regular legislative session and bear written certification from the state auditor of their nonfiscal status. The state auditor must certify the nonfiscal/fiscal status of all amendments; a nonfiscal retirement bill cannot proceed in the legislative process if it is amended in any way causing it to have a fiscal impact.

A more rigorous procedure applies to retirement bills that have a fiscal impact. They can only be introduced during the first year of the term of office of General Assembly members and can only be passed during the second year of the legislative biennium. The time period between introduction of the bill and final consideration by the General Assembly is to permit study and perfection through joint meetings of the standing retirement committees of both houses (if necessary) and to allow enough time for a required actuarial investigation to be made through the state auditor's office. All reports and summaries must be attached to printed copies of the bill. The only allowable amendments to the bill after an actuarial investigation has been made are those certified to be nonfiscal.

A fiscal retirement bill, if enacted, can only become effective as law if it is concurrently funded. If the enacted bill is not funded, it will be null and void and stand repealed in its entirety on the first day of July following its enactment.

Special Requirements in the House

In addition to the distinctions noted earlier between general and local acts, the Georgia House of Representatives has adopted a special rule that directs that any bill relating to or affecting state revenues, general taxation, pari-mutuel wagering, alcoholic beverages, water resources, or hazardous wastes cannot be treated as local or special legislation in the House. Rather, any measure touching on such subjects must be treated as general legislation.[191] No similar rule exists in the Senate.

ENDNOTES

1. GA. CONST. art. 3, §6, ¶4(a).

2. Ibid.

3. City of Calhoun v. N. Ga. Elec. Membership Corp., 233 Ga. 759, 213 S.E. 2d 596 (1975); Employers Mut. Liability Ins. Co. v. Carson, 100 Ga. App. 409, 111 S.E. 2d 918 (1960).

4. Blackmon v. Monroe, 233 Ga. 656, 212 S.E. 2d 827 (1975); Black v. Blanchard, 227 Ga. 167, 179 S.E. 2d 228 (1971); Cragg v. State, 224 Ga. 196, 160 S.E. 2d 817 (1968). *See also* Gravely v. Bacon, 263 Ga. 203, 429 S.E. 2d 663 (1993). *But see* Franklin v. Hill, 264 Ga. 302, 444 S.E. 2d 778 (1994).

5. Gilbert v. Richardson, 211 Ga. App 795, 440 S.E. 2d 684 (1994); Kyles v. State, 254 Ga. 49, 326 S.E.2d 216 (1985); Cotton States Mut. Ins. Co. v. DeKalb County, 251 Ga. 309, 304 S.E.2d 386 (1983).

6. GA. CONST. art. 3, §5, ¶4(b).

7. OFFICIAL CODE OF GEORGIA ANNOTATED (O.C.G.A.) §28-1-15.

8. Ibid.

9. Gibson v. Hood, 185 Ga. 426, 195 S.E. 444 (1938).

10. City of Atlanta v. Gower, 216 Ga. 368, 116 S.E. 2d 738 (1960); Stewart v. Anderson, 140 Ga. 31, 78 S.E. 457 (1913); Gibson v. Hood, 185 Ga. 426, 195 S.E. 444 (1938); Tift v. Bush, 209 Ga. 769, 75 S.E. 2d 805 (1953).

11. McAllister v. State, 220 Ga. 570, 140 S.E. 2d 838 (1965).

12. Board of Commissioners of Clayton County v. Clayton County School District, 250 Ga. 244, 297 S.E. 2d 724 (1982).

13. Stewart v. Anderson, 140 Ga. 31, 78 S.E. 457 (1913).

14. Gibson v. Hood, 185 Ga. 426, 195 S.E. 444 (1938).

15. Board of Commissioners of Clayton County v. Clayton County School District, 250 Ga. 244, 297 S.E. 2d 724 (1982).

16. Tift v. Bush, 209 Ga. 769, 75 S.E. 2d 805 (1953); Walden v. Owens, 211 Ga. 884, 89 S.E. 2d 492 (1955).

17. See J. Devereux Weeks, *County Population Acts* (Athens: Institute of Government, 1976), pp. 4-9.

18. *Black's Law Dictionary* (6th ed., 1990), p. 939.

19. Lasseter v. Ga. Public Service Comm., 253 Ga. 227, 319 S.E.2d 824 (1984).

20. GA. CONST. art. 1, §1, ¶25; art. 3, §6, ¶4(c).

21. GA. CONST. art. 3, §6, ¶4(a).

22. Mathis v. Jones, 84 Ga. 804, 11 S.E. 1018 (1890). *See also* extensive citations to appellate court decisions in annotations to GA. CONST. art. 3, §6, ¶4(a) in OFFICIAL CODE OF GEORGIA ANNOTATED.

23. City of Atlanta v. Hudgins, 193 Ga. 618, 19 S.E. 2d 508 (1942); Morrison v. Cook, 146 Ga. 570, 91 S.E. 671 (1916).

24. Lorentz & Ritter v. Alexander, 87 Ga. 444, 13 S.E. 632 (1891); City of Cochran v. Lanfair, 139 Ga. 249, 77 S.E. 93 (1912).

25. Crosby v. Dixie Metal Co., 124 Ga. App. 169, 183 S.E. 2d 59 (1971); White Oak Acres, Inc. v. Campbell, 113 Ga. App. 833, 149 S.E. 2d 870 (1966); Davis v. Dougherty County, 116 Ga. 491, 42 S.E. 764 (1902).

26. Nash v. National Preferred Life Ins. Co., 222 Ga. 14, 148 S.E. 2d 402 (1966); Parrish v. Mayor and Aldermen of Savannah, 185 Ga. 828, 196 S.E. 721 (1938).

27. O.C.G.A. §1-3-11.

28. For a list of home rule powers which have been granted local governments, *see* GA. CONST. art. 9. *See also* O.C.G.A. ch. 36-35.

29. O.C.G.A. §28-1-14.

30. Smith v. McMichael, 203 Ga. 74, 45 S.E. 2d 431 (1947); Smith v. City Council of Augusta, 203 Ga. 511, 47 S.E. 2d 582 (1948).

31. Smith v. McMichael, 203 Ga. 74, 45 S.E. 2d 431 (1947).

32. Walker Electric Co. v. Walton, 203 Ga. 246, 46 S.E. 2d 184 (1948); Swiney v. City of Forest Park, 211 Ga. 154, 84 S.E. 2d 573 (1954).

33. O.C.G.A. §28-1-14.1.

34. GA. CONST. art. 3, §5, ¶8.

35. Senate Rule 98; House Rule 148.

36. Senate Rule 187; House Rule 11.

37. House Rule 53.

38. House Rule 162.

39. Senate Rules 34, 217; House Rules 33, 34.

40. GA. CONST. art. 10, §1, ¶2.

41. O.C.G.A. §§28-5-80, 28-5-105.

42. O.C.G.A. §§50-16-34(12), 50-16-39(d).

43. House and Senate Joint Rules 1, 2.

44. House and Senate Joint Rule 13.

45. *See, e.g.,* O.C.G.A. §28-10-3, §50-8-4(f).

46. Senate Rule 208.

47. *See, e.g.,* Ga. Laws 1973, p. 690; Ga. Laws 1974, p. 1457; Ga. Laws 1974, p. 1642.

48. Senate Rules 105, 115; House Rules 46, 53.

49. GA. CONST. art. 5, §2, ¶4 and art. 10, §1, ¶5.

50. GA. CONST. art. 3, §5, ¶2; Senate Rules 206, 208.

51. GA. CONST. art 1, §2, ¶9; O.C.G.A. §§50-21-1, 50-21-20 et seq.; *See* Gilbert v. Richardson, 211 Ga. App. 795, 440 S.E. 2d 684 (1994); Donaldson v. Department of Transportation, 212 Ga. App. 240, 441 S.E. 2d 473 (1994).

52. Trice v. Wilson, 113 Ga. App. 715, 149 S.E. 2d 530 (1966); Crowder v. Department of State Parks, 228 Ga. 436, 185 S.E. 2d 908 (1971).

53. Trice v. Wilson, 113 Ga. App. 715, 149 S.E. 2d 530 (1966); Sikes v. Candler County, 247 Ga. 115, 274 S.E. 2d 464 (1981).

54. O.C.G.A. §28-5-60.

55. O.C.G.A. §28-5-83.

56. O.C.G.A. §28-5-85.

57. O.C.G.A. §§28-5-100 through 28-5-105.

58. O.C.G.A. §28-5-80(a).

59. Ibid.

60. O.C.G.A. §28-5-106.

61. O.C.G.A. §25-5-80(b).

62. O.C.G.A. §28-5-82.

63. Walter McElreath, *A Treatise on the Constitution of Georgia* (Atlanta: The Harrison Co., 1912), p. 90.

64. Ibid., pp. 93, 106.

65. Ibid., p. 133.

66. GA. CONST. art. 3, §5, ¶3; Protho v. Orr, 12 Ga. 36 (1852); McCaffrey v. State, 193 Ga. 827, 189 S.E. 825 (1937); Black v. Jones, 190 Ga. 95, 8 SE. 2d 385 (1940).

67. Camp v. MARTA, 229 Ga. 35, 38, 188 S.E. 2d 56 (1972); Central of Ga. R. Co. v. State, 104 Ga. 831, 846, 31 S.E. 531 (1898); American Booksellers Association v. Webb, 254 Ga. 399, 329 S.E. 2d 495 (1985).

68. Crews v. Cook, 220 Ga. 479, 139 S.E. 2d 490 (1964); Capitol Distributing Co. v. Redwine, 206 Ga. 477, 57 S.E. 2d 578 (1950); Bembry v. State, 250 Ga. 237, 297 S.E. 2d 36 (1982).

69. Hines v. Etheridge, 173 Ga. 870, 162 S.E. 113 (1931).

70. Wall v. Board of Elections, 242 Ga. 566, 250 S.E. 2d 408 (1978); Lutz v. Foran, 262 Ga. 819, 427 S.E. 2d 248 (1993).

71. Ibid.

72. Schneider v. City of Folkston, 207 Ga. 434, 62 S.E. 2d 177 (1950).

73. W.U. Tel. Co. v. Cooledge, 86 Ga. 104, 12 S.E. 264 (1890).

74. Capitol Dist. Co. v. Redwine, 206 Ga. 477, 57 S.E. 2d 578 (1950).

75. Gainer v. Ellis, 226 Ga. 79, 172 S.E. 2d 608 (1970).

76. Carter v. Burson, 230 Ga. 511, 198 S.E. 2d 151 (1973).

77. American Booksellers Ass'n v. Webb, 254 Ga. 399, 329 S.E. 2d 495 (1985).

78. McElreath, *A Treatise on the Constitution of Georgia*, p. 93; Cady v. Jardine, 185 Ga. 9, 10, 193 S.E. 869 (1937).

79. GA. CONST. art. 3, §5, ¶7.

80. Bray v. City of East Point, 203 Ga. 315, 46 S.E. 2d 257 (1948).

81. Cade v. State, 207 Ga. 135, 60 S.E. 2d 763 (1950).

82. Fortson v. Weeks, 232 Ga. 472, 208 S.E. 2d 68 (1974).

83. Bray v. City of East Point, 203 Ga. 315, 46 S.E. 2d 257 (1948); Rich v. State, 237 Ga. 291, 227 S.E. 2d 761 (1976).

84. Sasser v. State, 99 Ga. 54, 25 S.E. 619 (1896).

85. Burns v. State, 104 Ga. 544, 30 S.E. 815 (1898).

86. Devier v. State, 247 Ga. 635, 277 S.E. 2d 729 (1981); Milhollen v. State, 221 Ga. 165, 143 S.E. 2d 730 (1965); Mikell v. Mikell, 219 Ga. 550, 134 S.E. 2d 630 (1964); Collins v. State, 206 Ga. 95, 55 S.E. 2d 599 (1949); Black v. Jones, 190 Ga. 95, 8 S.E. 2d 385 (1946); Cady v. Jardine, 185 Ga. 9, 193 S.E. 869 (1937).

87. City of Savannah v. State, 4 Ga. 26 (1848). *See also* Greer v. State, 233 Ga. 667, 212 S.E.2d 836 (1975); Sams v. Olah, 225 Ga. 497, 169 S.E. 2d 790 (1969); Fortson v. Weeks, 232 Ga. 472, 208 S.E. 2d 68 (1974).

88. Hill v. Perkins, 218 Ga. 354, 127 S.E. 2d 309 (1962). *See also* Fortson v. Weeks, 232 Ga. 472, 208 S.E. 2d 68 (1974).

89. GA. CONST. art. 3, §5, ¶4.

90. *See, e.g.,* Edalgo v. Southern Ry., 129 Ga. 258, 58 S.E. 846 (1907); Town of McIntyre v. Scott, 191 Ga. 473, 12 S.E. 2d 883 (1941); Fortson v. Fortson, 200 Ga. 116, 35 S.E. 2d 896 (1945).

91. Tison v. City of Doerun, 155 Ga. 367, 116 S.E. 615 (1923).

92. Ragans v. Ragans, 200 Ga. 890, 892, 39 S.E. 2d 162, 164 (1946).

93. Ellis v. Johnson, 263 Ga. 514, 435 S.E. 2d 923 (1993); Poteat v. Butler, 231 Ga. 187, 200 S.E. 2d 741 (1973); West v. Forehand, 128 Ga. App. 124, 195 S.E. 2d 777 (1973); Plantation Pipe Line Co. v. City of Bremen, 227 Ga. 1, 178 S.E. 2d 868 (1970); Buice v. Dixon, 223 Ga. 645, 157 S.E. 2d 481 (1967).

94. Kyles v. State, 254 Ga. 49, 326 S.E. 2d 216 (1985); Jones v. Hartford Acc. & Indem. Co., 132 Ga. App. 130, 207 S.E. 2d 613 (1974); Board of Public Education and Orphanage for Bibb County v. Zimmerman, 231 Ga. 562, 203 S.E. 2d 178 (1974); Bragg v. Bragg, 225 Ga. 494, 170 S.E. 2d 29 (1969).

95. Tomblin v. S.S. Kresge Co., 132 Ga. App. 212, 207 S.E. 2d 693 (1974); Burgamy v. State, 114 Ga. 852, 40 S.E. 993 (1902); Puckett v. Young, 112 Ga. 578, 37 S.E. 880 (1900).

96. County of Butts v. Straham, 151 Ga. 417, 419, 107 S.E. 163 (1921).

97. Stansell v. Fowler, 113 Ga. App. 377, 147 S.E. 2d 793 (1966); Tyler v. Huiet, 199 Ga. 845, 36 S.E. 2d 358 (1945). However, Georgia courts are obligated to reconcile apparent conflicts between different sections of the same statute to make them consistent with one another, if possible. *See* Undercofler v. Capitol Auto Co., 111 Ga. App. 709, 143 S.E. 2d 206 (1965).

98. Bedingfield v. Parkerson, 212 Ga. 654, 94 S.E. 2d 714 (1956); Board of Tax Assessors v. Catledge, 173 Ga. 656, 658, 160 S.E. 909 (1931); Howell v. State, 164 Ga. 204, 138 S.E. 206 (1927). For an interesting judicial observation on the language of statutes, *see* concurring opinion, Fortson v. Weeks, 232 Ga. 472, 208 S.E. 2d 68 (1974).

99. *See* O.C.G.A. §§1-3-1, 1-3-3.

100. Mansfield v. Pannell, 261 Ga. 243, 404 S.E.2d 104 (1991); Fortson v. Weeks, 232 Ga. 472, 208 S.E. 2d 68 (1974); City of Jesup v. Bennett, 226 Ga. 606, 176 S.E. 2d 81 (1970); Williams v. Linn, 108 Ga. App. 629, 133 S.E. 2d 892 (1963); Fulton Co. Federal Savings & Loan Association v. Simmons, 210 Ga. 621, 82 S.E. 2d 16 (1954).

101. Seaboard Coast Line R. Co. v. Blackmon, 129 Ga. App. 342, 199 S.E. 2d 581 (1973); City of Jesup v. Bennett, 226 Ga. 606, 176 S.E. 2d 81 (1970); Stone Mountain Memorial Association v. Herrington, 225 Ga. 746, 171 S.E. 2d 521 (1969).

102. Lunda Construction Co. v. Clayton County, 201 Ga. App. 106, 410 S.E.2d 446 (1991); Hollowell v. Jove, 247 Ga. 678, 279 S.E. 2d 430 (1981).

103. City of Calhoun v. N. Ga. Elec. Membership Corp. 233 Ga. 759, 213 S.E. 2d 596 (1975); Blackmon v. DeKalb Pipeline Co., Inc., 127 Ga. App. 395, 193 S.E. 2d 635 (1972); Froug v. Harper, 220 Ga. 582, 140 S.E. 2d 844 (1965).

104. Modern Homes Const. Co. v. Burke, 219 Ga. 710, 135 S.E. 2d 383 (1964); Northside Manor, Inc. v. Vann, 219 Ga. 298, 133 S.E. 2d 32 (1963). *See also* Douglas County v. Abercrombie, 226 Ga. 39, 172 S.E. 2d 419 (1970); Thompson v. Talmadge, 201 Ga. 867, 41 S.E. 2d 883 (1947).

105. Crosby Aeromarine, Inc. v. Hyde, 115 Ga. App. 836, 156 S.E. 2d 106 (1967).

106. O.C.G.A. §1-3-1; Franklin v. Hill, 264 Ga. 302, 444 S.E. 2d 778 (1994); Wall v. Youmans, 223 Ga. 191, 154 S.E. 2d 191 (1967); Seaboard Coast Line R. Co. v. Blackmon, 129 Ga. App. 342, 199 S.E. 2d 581 (1973). *See also* concurring opinion, Fortson v. Weeks, 232 Ga. 472, 208 S.E. 2d 68 (1974).

107. State Bar of Georgia v. Haas, 133 Ga. App. 311, 211 S.E. 2d 161 (1974); Poteat v. Butler, 231 Ga. 187, 200 S.E. 2d 741 (1973); Plantation Pipe Line Co. v. City of Bremen, 227 Ga. 1, 178 S.E. 2d 868 (1970). *See also* 1971 Ops. Att'y Gen. 71-21, 71-23.

108. Jones v. City of College Park, 223 Ga. 778, 158 S.E. 2d 384 (1967); State v. Livingston, 222 Ga. 441, 150 S.E. 2d 648 (1966); Southern Ry. Co. v. Brooks, 112 Ga. App. 324, 145 S.E. 2d 76 (1965).

109. Moore v. Robinson, 206 Ga. 27, 55 S.E. 2d 711 (1949); Ga., Fla., & Ala. Ry. Co. v. Sasser, 4 Ga. App. 285, 61 S.E. 505 (1908).

110. International Minerals & Chemical Corp. v. Bledsoe, 126 Ga. App. 243, 190 S.E. 2d 572 (1972); Wilen Mfg. Co. v. Standard Products Co., 409 F. 2d 56 (5th Cir. 1969); Sharpe v. Lowe, 214 Ga. 513, 106 S.E. 2d 28 (1958).

111. Chanin v. Bibb County and Blackmon v. Chanin, 234 Ga. 282, 216 S.E. 2d 250 (1975); Barton v. Atkinson, 228 Ga. 733, 187 S.E. 2d 835 (1972); Mayor and Aldermen of Savannah v. State, 4 Ga. 26 (1848).

112. Fleming v. Zant, 259 Ga. 687, 386 S.E. 2d 339 (1989).

113. Sharpe v. Lowe, 214 Ga. 513, 106 S.E. 2d 28 (1958); Stanley v. Sims, 185 Ga. 518, 195 S.E. 439 (1938).

114. Southern Railway Co. v. A.O. Smith, 134 Ga. App. 219, 213 S.E. 2d 903 (1975); McLarty v. Board of Regents, 231 Ga. 22, 200 S.E. 2d 117 (1973); Stewart v. Atlanta Beef Co., 93 Ga. 12, 18 S.E. 981 (1893). *See also* Friedman v. U.S., 364 F. Supp. 484 (S.D. Ga., 1973). *But see* Johnson v. Miller, WL 506780 (S.D. Ga., 1994) where Georgia legislators were allowed to testify as to intent in federal court.

115. McLarty v. Board of Regents, Transcript of Proceedings, Clarke County [Georgia] Superior Court (March 10, 1973), p. 60.

116. City of Calhoun v. N. Ga. Electric Membership Corp., 233 Ga. 759, 213 S.E. 2d 596 (1975); Ga. Railroad & Banking Co. v. Wright, 125 Ga. 589, 54 S.E. 52 (1906); Kenner v. State, 18 Ga. 194 (1855).

117. Townsend v. Yeomans, 301 U.S. 441 (1937).

118. Carter v. Oxford, 102 Ga. App. 762, 118 S.E. 2d 216; *affirmed* 216 Ga. 821, 120 S.E. 2d 298 (1961); Price v. State, 76 Ga. App. 108, 45 S.E. 2d 84 (1947); Wingfield v. Kutres,

136 Ga. 345, 71 S.E. 474 (1911). The court, however, has ruled that one legislature has no power to declare intent of a prior General Assembly in enacting a law, since that would be a legislative attempt to perform a judicial function by construing a law. Road Builders, Inc. of Tenn. v. Hawes, 228 Ga. 608, 187 S.E. 2d 287 (1972).

119. Martin v. Baldwin, 215 Ga. 293, 110 S.E. 2d 344 (1959).

120. Fender v. Fender, 249 Ga. 765, 294 S.E. 2d 472 (1982); Freeman v. W.O.W. Life Ins. Society, 200 Ga. 1, 36 S.E. 2d 81 (1945). *See also* Calhoun v. McLendon, 42 Ga. 405 (1871); Pearle Optical of Monroeville, Inc. v. Ga. State Board of Examiners in Optometry, 219 Ga. 364, 133 S.E. 2d 374 (1963); and City of Calhoun v. N. Ga. Elec. Membership Corp., 233 Ga. 759, 213 S.E. 2d 596 (1975).

121. *See, e.g.,* Thompson v. Eastern Air Lines, 200 Ga. 216, 36 S.E. 2d 675 (1946); Georgia Penitentiary Co. No. 2 v. Nelms, 65 Ga. 67 (1880).

122. Smith v. City of Atlanta, 161 Ga. 769, 132 S.E. 66 (1925). However, *see* Pye v. State Highway Dept., 226 Ga. 389, 175 S.E. 2d 510 (1970); Rives v. Atlanta Newspapers, Inc., 220 Ga. 485, 139 S.E. 2d 395 (1964); Cox v. General Elec. Co., 211 Ga. 286, 85 S.E. 2d 514 (1955).

123. Sheffield v. State School Building Authority, 208 Ga. 575, 68 S.E. 2d 590 (1952).

124. Mousetrap of Atlanta, Inc. v. Blackmon, 129 Ga. App. 805, 201 S.E. 2d 330 (1973); Mason v. Service Loan & Finance Co., 128 Ga. App. 828, 198 S.E. 2d 391 (1973); Belton v. Columbus Finance & Thrift Co., 127 Ga. App. 770, 195 S.E. 2d 195 (1972); Woodford v. Kinney Shoe Corp., 369 F. Supp. 911 (N.D. Ga. 1973).

125. Ga. Const. art. 1, §2, ¶5.

126. Luther v. State, 255 Ga. 706, 342 S.E. 2d 316 (1986); Kirton v. Biggers, 232 Ga. 223, 206 S.E. 2d 33 (1974); Buice v. Dixon, 223 Ga. 645, 157 S.E. 2d 481 (1967); Mayes v. Daniel, 186 Ga. 345, 198 S.E. 535 (1938). Furthermore, the court will not attribute to members of the General Assembly a purpose to circumvent provisions of the state constitution. McLucas v. State Bridge Bldg. Authority, 210 Ga. 1, 77 S.E. 2d 531 (1953).

127. Battallia v. Columbus, 199 Ga. App. 897, 406 S.E. 2d 290 (1991).

128. Adams v. Ray, 215 Ga. 656, 113 S.E. 2d 100 (1960).

129. City of Calhoun v. N. Ga. Elec. Membership Corp., 233 Ga. 759, 213 S.E. 2d 596 (1975); Kirton v. Biggers, 232 Ga. 223, 206 S.E. 2d 33 (1974); Black v. Blanchard, 227 Ga. 167, 179 S.E. 2d 228 (1971); Southern Ry. Co. v. Brooks, 112 Ga. App. 324, 145 S.E 2d 76 (1965). Nevertheless, when a statute is clearly in violation of the constitution, the supreme court has a duty to so determine—irrespective of the consequences. Calhoun County v. Early County, 205 Ga. 169, 52 S.E. 2d 854 (1949).

130. Smith v. State, 248 Ga. 828, 286 S.E. 2d 709 (1982); Bryant v. Prior Tire Co., 230 Ga. 137, 196 S.E. 2d 14 (1973); Northeast Factor & Discount Co., Inc. v. Jackson, 223 Ga. 709, 711, 157 S.E. 2d 731 (1967); Wilson Foundation v. Bell, 223 Ga. 588, 157 S.E. 2d 287 (1967).

131. Marchman & Marchman v. Atlanta, 250 Ga. 64, 295 S.E. 2d 311 (1982); Taylor v. Moultrie Tobacco Sales Board, Inc., 227 Ga. 384, 180 S.E. 2d 737 (1971); Ledford v. J.M. Muse Corp., 224 Ga. 617, 163 S.E. 2d 815 (1968).

132. O'Kelley v. State, 210 Ga. App. 686, 436 S.E. 2d 760 (1993); Walker v. Hall, 226 Ga. 68, 172 S.E. 2d 411 (1970); Roberts v. Roberts, 226 Ga. 203, 173 S.E. 2d 675 (1970); Shelton v. Housing Authority, 122 Ga. App. 535, 177 S.E. 2d 832 (1970).

133. Farmer v. State, 228 Ga. 225, 184 S.E. 2d 647 (1971); Cross v. State, 225 Ga. 760, 171 S.E. 2d 507 (1969).

134. Lasseter v. Ga. Public Service Commission, 253 Ga. 227, 319 S.E.2d 824 (1984).

135. Battallia v. Columbus, 199 Ga. App. 897, 406 S.E.2d 290 (1991); Wilson v. Ledbetter, 194 Ga. App. 32, 389 S.E. 2d 771 (1989); Collins v. Woodham, 257 Ga. 643, 361 S.E. 2d 800 (1987); Atlantic Coast Line Railroad v. State, 135 Ga. 545, 69 S.E. 725 (1910); Capitol Distributing Co. v. Redwine, 206 Ga. 477, 57 S.E.2d 578 (1980).

136. Richmond County v. Pierce, 234 Ga. 274, 215 S.E. 2d 665 (1975); Smith v. McMichael, 203 Ga. 74, 45 S.E. 2d 431 (1974).

137. Thompson v. Talmadge, 201 Ga. 867, 41 S.E. 2d 883 (1947).

138. Williams v. MacFeely, 186 Ga. 145, 197 S.E. 225 (1938).

139. Cunningham v. State, 260 Ga. 827, 400 S.E. 2d 916 (1991); Flynn v. State, 209 Ga. 519, 74 S.E. 2d 461 (1953); Franklin v. Harper, 205 Ga. 779, 55 S.E. 2d 221 (1949); Krasner v. Rutledge, 204 Ga. 380, 49 S.E. 2d 864 (1948).

140. Moseley v. State, 176 Ga. 889, 169 S.E. 97 (1933); U.S. v. Raines, 362 U.S. 17 (1959); City Council v. Mangley, 243 Ga. 358, 254 S.E. 2d 315 (1979).

141. Georgia Franchise Practices Commission v. Massey-Ferguson, 244 Ga. 800, 262 S.E. 2d 106 (1979); Murphy v. State, 233 Ga. 681, 212 S.E. 2d 839 (1975); Greer v. State, 233 Ga. 667, 212 S.E. 2d 836 (1975); Fortson v. Weeks, 232 Ga. 472, 208 S.E. 2d 68 (1974); Sams v. Olah, 225 Ga. 497, 169 S.E. 2d 790 (1969).

142. Greer v. State, 233 Ga. 667, 212 S.E. 2d 836 (1975).

143. Murphy v. State, 233 Ga. 681, 212 S.E. 2d 839 (1975).

144. Gay v. Laurens County, 213 Ga. 518, 100 S.E. 2d 271 (1957).

145. Rutledge v. Gaylord's, Inc., 233 Ga. 694, 213 S.E. 2d 626 (1975); Chanin v. Bibb County, 234 Ga. 282, 216 S.E. 2d 250 (1975); Stinson v. Manning, 221 Ga. 487, 145 S.E. 2d 541 (1965).

146. O.C.G.A. §1-1-3.

147. *See, e.g.,* 1967 Op. Att'y Gen. 67-189, 1973 Op. Att'y Gen. 73-80, 1977 Op. Att'y Gen. 77-87, 1979 Op. Att'y Gen. 79-46, 1980 Op. Att'y Gen. 80-118, 1984 Op. Att'y Gen. 84-19, 1991 Op. Att'y Gen. 91-26.

148. For example, in the 1994 general appropriation act, language was included stating it was the General Assembly's intent that the State Forestry Commission keep a particular nursery open and that the agency continue publishing a magazine and another publication (Sec. 59), that the Department of Public Safety buy full-size pursuit vehicles (Sec. 66), and that a technical school's satellite facility be located on the campus of a particular college (Sec. 70). In addition, numerous agencies were directed to institute new policies or to take (or not to take) certain actions. *See* Ga. Laws 1994, p. 1506.

149. *See, e.g.,* 1989 Op. Att'y Gen. 89-28.

150. GA. CONST. art. 3, §9, ¶1. Exceptions are found in GA. CONST. art. 1, §2, ¶8 (c); art. 3, §9, ¶4 (a); art. 3, §9, ¶6 (b); and art. 7, §4, ¶3 (2) (A).

151. To see how the pre- and post-1974 budgets compare, *see* Ga. Laws 1973, p. 1353 and Ga. Laws 1974, p. 1508.

152. GA. CONST. art. 3, §9, ¶2 (b).

153. GA. CONST. art. 3, §5, ¶2.

154. Mayes v. Daniel, 186 Ga. 345, 198 S.E. 535 (1938).

155. GA. CONST. art. 3, §9, ¶6 (a).

156. Ibid. See endnote 150 for exceptions allowed by the constitution.

157. GA. CONST. art. 3, §9, ¶3.

158. GA. CONST. art. 3, §5, ¶6.

159. GA. CONST. art. 3, §9, ¶2(b).

160. GA. CONST. art. 3, §9, ¶1.

161. GA. CONST. art. 3, §9, ¶4(a).

162. GA. CONST. art 1, §2, ¶8 (c); art. 3, §9, ¶4 (a); art. 3, §9, ¶6 (b); and art. 7, §4, ¶3 (2) (A).

163. GA. CONST. art. 3, §9, ¶3.

164. GA. CONST. art. 3, §9, ¶4 (c).

165. *See* GA. CONST. art. 3, §9, ¶6 (f) et seq., for a list of the trust funds.

166. O.C.G.A. §50-27-13.

167. GA. CONST. art. 3, §9, ¶4 (b).

168. *See* GA. CONST. art. 7, §4, for constitutional provisions governing state debt.

169. GA. CONST. art. 3, §9, ¶2; O.C.G.A. §45-12-74, §45-12-75.

170. 1979 Op. Att'y Gen. 79-18.

171. O.C.G.A. §45-12-78.

172. O.C.G.A. §45-12-77.

173. Ibid.

174. 1979 Op. Att'y Gen. 79-70, 1969 Op. Att'y Gen. 69-51.

175. 1969 Op. Att'y Gen. 69-51, 1967 Op. Att'y Gen. 67-322, 1965-66 Op. Att'y Gen. 66-18.

176. O.C.G.A. §28-5-4.

177. O.C.G.A. §28-5-127.

178. O.C.G.A. §45-12-93.

179. GA. CONST. art. 3, §9, ¶5.

180. *See, e.g.,* Ga. Laws 1988, p. 68.

181. GA. CONST. art. 3, §9, ¶4.

182. GA. CONST. art. 3, §9, ¶5.

183. O.C.G.A. §28-5-1.

184. O.C.G.A. §28-5-42(a).

185. Ibid.

186. O.C.G.A. §28-5-42(d).

187. O.C.G.A. §28-5-44.

188. O.C.G.A. §28-5-2.

189. O.C.G.A. ch. 47-20.

190. GA. CONST. art. 3, §10, ¶5.

191. House Rule 48.

# The Lawmaking Process

Perhaps the best method of depicting the Georgia legislature in action is to follow a bill from the time of its introduction in one of the houses through the various stages which it must pass before it can become a "law." (Fig. 10 illustrates this process.)

SOURCES OF BILLS

A member of either house of the General Assembly can introduce any measure, except revenue and appropriation bills, compensation resolutions, and resolutions to impeach; these must be introduced in the House. Only a member can introduce a bill or resolution. The governor, for example, while an important source of legislation, introduces none directly, but rather designates a legislator, usually the administration floor leader in one of the houses, to introduce administration measures.

The Georgia legislature permits multiple sponsoring of legislation by members of the same house. Georgia's constitution also allows the General Assembly to provide by statute for joint sponsorship of bills and resolutions by members of both houses, although this provision has not yet been implemented.[1]

There are no limits on the number of legislators who may sign a proposal to be introduced, although usually no more than a dozen will be listed by name on the actual bill. When many members cosponsor legislation, the major sponsors are listed by name, followed by the notation "and others." A complete list of sponsors is maintained on file with either the clerk of the House or secretary of the Senate.

DRAFTING BILLS

Although only a legislator can introduce a bill or resolution, it is not mandatory that he or she actually draft or author the measure; however,

Figure 10: *How a Bill Becomes a Law*

Need for new law or change in existing law seen by legislator, or suggested by Governor, agency, constituent, or others

1 Legislator(s) decides to sponsor a bill

2 Legislative Counsel researches law on subject and helps draft bill

During first 19 days of session, bill ready for 3d reading

During last 21 days of session, bill sent to Rules Committee, which prepares daily rules calendar

11 Bill placed on general calendar

10 In Senate only, 2d reading of bill (by title only)

12 Third reading of bill (by title or in entirety), floor debate, amendments, and motions

13 Approval of bill by majority of membership

14 Bill "engrossed" and transmitted to second house

Act becomes effective following July 1st, unless act provides different date

20 Act goes to Secretary of State for compiling, printing, and distribution

3 Legislator files bill with Clerk or Secretary

4 Bill introduced next day and read 1st time (by title only)

5 Presiding officer assigns bill to standing committee

8 Committee reports that bill "do pass" or "do pass with changes"

Committee meets to consider bill. Public hearing may be called

7 In House only, 2d reading of bill (by title only) on next day

6

Committee reports that bill "do not pass" or holds bill

15 In second house, bill undergoes same procedure

16 If second house passes bill with no changes . . .

If second house passes bill—but with changes—and neither house can agree, conference committee appointed. If its report is accepted by both houses . .

Governor may sign bill or do nothing

Governor may kill bill by veto, unless overridden by 2/3 vote of both houses

18 Bill "enrolled" and sent to Governor

17

many do. Often, private citizens, attorneys, special committees, and interest groups will draw up a proposal and seek a legislator willing to introduce it. Similarly, the governor, state agencies, and local governments will assign attorneys or legal specialists to draft a measure and seek a legislator to sponsor it.

Before introduction, however, most proposals are taken by sponsoring legislators to the Office of Legislative Counsel for drafting, redrafting, or at least review. By law, retirement bills *must* be taken to this office before being introduced.[2] This office is staffed by attorneys skilled in legislative matters and bill drafting, and offers these services to any legislator. The office has a computerized statutory retrieval system that includes the code as well as the constitution. It is used along with the bill-drafting system, so statutes can be recalled when a bill is drafted. A request by a legislator for drafting or review of a bill and any conversations between the legislator and the counsel's office are treated as privileged information and are not subject to the state's open records requirements.[3]

The Office of Legislative Counsel attempts to put proposed legislation into constitutional form, if possible. If, after drafting a particular measure, the counsel's office believes it to be of doubtful constitutionality, the author or sponsor of the bill is so informed; however, the decision as to whether to submit the proposed measure in the General Assembly is left entirely with the sponsor.

PREFILING BILLS

A bill or resolution can only officially be introduced during a legislative session. In 1994, however, the General Assembly enacted legislation allowing the prefiling of measures so that informal deliberation by legislative committee can begin before the session.

According to the legislation, any representative or senator "who will be eligible to consider the measure when introduced" can prefile legislation.[4] [Presumably this includes representatives-elect and senators-elect, though the legislation does not indicate whether newly elected members who have not yet been sworn in are included.] The proposed measure is first taken to the Office of Legislative Counsel, which prepares it in a form to indicate its prefiled status, and then to the clerk of the House or secretary of the Senate (depending on the author's house). There, the measure is given an identification number (which, at the clerk or secretary's discretion, may correspond to the number that measure will get when and if officially introduced during the session).

Copies of each prefiled bill or resolution are then sent to the presiding officer of that house, who then assigns the measure to a standing committee for consideration. [This preliminary committee assignment does not bind the presiding officer's choice of committee assignments if and when the prefiled measure is officially introduced.] The committee can then consider the prefiled bill—but it can take no official action until the bill is actually introduced and assigned to committee during the session.

INTRODUCING A BILL

To officially introduce a measure during a session, a legislator files a copy of the bill or resolution with the clerk or secretary, who assigns the bill a number and enters appropriate information about the bill in the records of that office.

A bill may also be introduced during a floor session by carrying a copy of the bill forward to the clerk or secretary at the front of either chamber. There is no formally designated "hopper" into which bills are placed for introduction, although the phrase "putting a bill in the hopper" is sometimes used to refer to the bill-introduction process.

Before being introduced, bills and resolutions must be typed or printed. They must contain the name and district of the member or members introducing the measure and a title or brief summary of the measure.

Bills drafted by the legislative counsel's office are typed into the General Assembly's computerized bill-drafting system, and the author is given copies plus an original to be submitted to the clerk of the House or the secretary of the Senate. Bills not drafted by the legislative counsel are submitted directly to the clerk or secretary, whose staff is responsible for typing the bill in correct form into the computer.

Full texts of all first drafts of bills are entered into the memory files of the computer system at the time of initial typing, and coded for insertions, deletions, and various other changes. Only the first draft of a new bill need be typed and proofread in its entirety, and if it is later amended, only the changes must be entered and proofread. The computer takes care of all necessary adjustments, including automatic respacing of lines, paragraphs, and pages.

The original copy of a bill typed in correct form is for the exclusive use of the Senate or House and the committee to which the measure will be referred.

Deadlines for Bill Introduction

A bill introduced in the Senate must have been filed in the secretary's office before 12:00 noon of the previous legislative day.[5] The House requires only that a bill be filed with the clerk no later than one hour after adjournment for introduction on the next day.[6] These rules allow time for the bill to be entered into the computerized bill-typing system and multiple copies made for distribution to members before the measure is read to the body and referred to committee.

Since logjams of bills tend to build up in legislative bodies as sessions approach adjournment, most state legislatures now impose specific deadlines for bills to be introduced during a session.[7] (Table 7 lists deadlines for specific bill introductions in Georgia.) Typically, they have provisions whereby members can introduce a measure under special circumstances beyond these deadlines, such as by securing unanimous consent or a certain vote of the whole body—usually a two-thirds majority.[8]

In the Senate, the deadline for introduction of measures which will have the effect of law is the 33d day of the session, unless written request for suspension is made to the Rules Committee, the committee reports favorably on the request, and it is approved by two-thirds of the Senate's total members.[9] The House does not have a similar deadline.

Printing of Bills

The rules of both houses require that all bills and resolutions of general application be printed and a copy distributed to each member prior to consideration.[10] This differs from the practice in some states, where bills are not reproduced until they have been referred to and approved by a standing committee.

During consideration of a measure, amendments may be proposed either in committee or on the floor. Committee amendments—including substitutes—must be printed and are incorporated into a subsequent printing of an original bill, generally on a different color of paper, with the fact noted that this version is as amended by committee.

Amendments on the floor are handled somewhat differently. All amendments in both houses must be in writing, with the author of the amendment submitting a written proposal of the change to the secretary

Table 7: *Statutory Deadlines for Bill Introductions*

Type of Bill	Deadline for Introduction
Any nonfiscal retirement bill for state, county, or municipal officials or employees[a]	20th day of session
Any retirement bill having a fiscal impact[b]	regular session, first year of biennium (odd years only)
Any bill significantly impacting on the anticipated revenue or expenditure of any state agency[c]	20th day of session
Any bill significantly impacting on the anticipated revenue or expenditure of cities or counties[d]	20th day of session
Any bill changing the compensation or allowances of any elected or appointed state officials or agency heads[e]	10th day of session
Compensation resolutions[f]	25th day of session

[a] O.C.G.A. §47-20-32. [c] O.C.G.A. §28-5-42(a). [e] O.C.G.A. §28-5-1.
[b] O.C.G.A. §47-20-34. [d] Ibid. [f] O.C.G.A. §28-5-80.

of the Senate or clerk of the House, depending on the house in which the proposal originates. In some instances, printed versions of the amendment are distributed to members on the floor, though in the House, amendments are projected on two large screens in the front corners of the chamber. However, in either house at any time, a majority of a quorum may suspend action upon any pending bill or resolution of general application until the amendments which have been offered to it have been printed and distributed.[11]

Bill Numbering and Identification

Bills and resolutions are numbered separately in the House and Senate in the order submitted to the clerk in the House and the secretary in the Senate. In both houses, bills and resolutions are numbered consecutively throughout the biennium. Thus, the first bill or resolution introduced in a house in the second year of the biennium is given the number immediately following the last bill or resolution of the preceding session.

Following the daily adjournment of each house, the clerk and secretary utilize the computerized bill-drafting system to reprint any measures that have been changed or amended in that day's session. If amendments occur in committee or on the floor, or if the committee reports a substitute measure, such changes are incorporated when reprinting the bill or resolution. Even though a bill may be so completely rewritten in committee that it bears little or no resemblance to the measure as originally submitted, the number of the bill must remain the same.

A code in the upper right corner of a bill or resolution identifies certain information on that bill for the clerk or secretary, as well as for the legislator (see Fig. 11). For instance, since most measures are drafted or revised by the Office of Legislative Counsel, a code such as "LC 14 2662" is quite common. In this case, "LC" identifies the bill as having been drafted by the legislative counsel; the "14" identifies the particular staff member who worked on this piece of legislation; and the "2662" identifies that bill for the computer, should reprinting of the bill be required.

If a measure is amended in either house, the code is changed to reflect that version of the original measure which is under consideration. For instance, the code on a bill which has been amended might now be changed to read "SB 439/FA/5." Here, "SB 439" would identify the measure as Senate Bill 439, while "FA" would show that floor amendments were incorporated into this version. The "5" in this example identifies the particular operator who typed the bill (however, this designation is only used on Senate bills).

Among the other abbreviations commonly used, "FS" identifies a measure as a floor substitute; "CA," a measure that has been amended in committee; and "CS," a measure as a committee substitute. These abbreviations may be used together where appropriate; for example, "FSFA"

Figure 11: *Identification Numbers, Authors, and Title of a Bill*

```
        93                                    SB209/FA/4

        SENATE BILL 209  ◄── Bill Number
                                                          ◄ Identification
        By:  Senators Taylor of the 12th, Bowen of the 13th and    Code
             Ragan of the 11th


 Bill Authors ───►          A BILL TO BE ENTITLED

                               AN ACT

      Title
 1   ──►    To amend Code Section 48-5-493 of the Official Code     31

 2        of Georgia Annotated, relating to the failure to attach  and   32

 3        display  certain  decals  to  mobile homes, so as to provide   33

 4        that any person who moves or transports a mobile home  which   34

 5        does  not  display  a  certain  decal  shall provide the tax   35

 6        collectors in certain counties with certain information;  to   36

 7        provide a penalty; to repeal conflicting laws; and for other   37

 8        purposes.


 9           BE IT ENACTED BY THE GENERAL ASSEMBLY OF GEORGIA:          40
     Body ──►
10   ──►     Section 1.    Code Section 48-5-493 of the Official        43

11        Code of Georgia Annotated, relating to the failure to attach   44

12        and display certain decals to mobile homes,  is  amended  by   45

13        striking  in  its  entirety  subsection  (b), which reads as   46

14        follows:

15              "(b)  (1)  It shall be unlawful for any  person  to      48

16              move or transport any mobile home which is required      49

17              to  and  which does not have attached and displayed      50

18              thereon the decal  provided  for  in  Code  Section      51

19              48-5-492.

20              (2)  Any  person who violates paragraph (1) of      53

21              this subsection shall be guilty  of  a  misdemeanor      54

22              and  shall  be  punished by a fine of not less than      55

23              $200.00 nor more than $1,000.00 or by  imprisonment      56

24              for not more than 12 months, or both.",               57

25        and inserting in lieu thereof the following:                 59

26              "(b)  (1)  Any  person  who moves or transports any      61

27              mobile home required by Code  Section  48-5-492  to      62

                            S. B. 209
                            - 1 -
```

would identify a floor substitute to a floor amendment. A Senate bill amended in the House would be identified as "HFA" (House Floor Amendment) or "HCA" (House Committee Amendment). Finally, the abbreviation "AP" (As Passed) is used to identify a bill or resolution that has been approved by both houses. As noted earlier, however, regardless of what action has taken place in committee or on the floor of either house with regard to a measure, the number of that bill or resolution remains unchanged. The code in the upper right corner merely assists in identifying the version of the bill or resolution under consideration.

Each page of a bill printed by the clerk or secretary has the lines of print numbered consecutively on the left margin, e.g., page 1, line 20, or page 3, line 2. This is for ease of reference when debating a bill in the General Assembly.

A different set of numbers appears on the right margin of a bill or resolution. These numbers are of no consequence to the legislator, as they designate identification numbers for the computer operator's use when a bill must be reprinted to add or delete words, sentences, or provisions.

DAILY LEGISLATIVE MATERIALS

There are a variety of materials, some updated on a daily basis, that are available to members of the General Assembly and to the public during the session:

1. Calendars—copies of the daily calendar of business for each chamber.
2. First Readers—measures which have been introduced and read only once (by title), with notation of committee referred to.
3. Daily Status Sheet—a single-page listing of floor and committee action taken by one house, along with those measures adopted the previous legislative day by the other house (see Fig. 12).
4. Composite Status Sheet—a multipage consolidated listing of the status of all bills and resolutions introduced that session (or carried over from the previous session in even-numbered years) through the previous legislative day. A computerized bill status reporting system is used to keep track of legislation. This sheet is updated daily and indicates all floor and committee action taken by either house on bills and resolutions, the date of such action, and the action of the governor on those measures passing both houses. (Fig. 13 presents an example of a composite status sheet.)
5. Senate Bills and Resolutions—copies of the bills and resolutions to be first considered by the Senate.
6. House Bills and Resolutions—copies of the bills and resolutions to be first considered by the House.

Figure 12: *Daily Status Sheet*

```
                          HOUSE STATUS NO. 24

                       MONDAY, FEBRUARY 21, 1994

                     TWENTY-SIXTH LEGISLATIVE DAY


                            READ FIRST TIME

   HB 1868   HIND          HB 1869   HHE          HB 1870   HSPCA2
   HB 1871   HSPCA2        HB 1872   HJUDY        HB 1873   HJUDY
   HB 1874   HJUDY         HB 1875   HJUDY        HB 1876   HSPCA2
   HB 1877   HJUDY         HB 1879   HSPCA2       HB 1892*  HJUDY
   HR 980    HRULES        HR 981    HRULES       HR 982    HHE
   HR 983    HRULES        HR 984    HRULES       HR 985    HRULES
   HR 1001*  HSIP          SB 432    HNR          SB 530    HPS
   SB 537    HED           SB 553    HLCR         SB 560    HJUDY
   SB 563    HHE           SB 602    HBB          SB 644    HSPCA
   SB 647    HED           SB 654    HSPCA2       SB 655    HSPCA2
   SB 656    HSPCA2

      * Rules Suspended in Order to Introduce


                            READ SECOND TIME

   HB 1844      HB 1845      HB 1846      HB 1847      HB 1848      HB 1849
   HB 1850      HB 1851      HB 1852      HB 1853      HB 1854      HB 1855
   HB 1856      HB 1860      HB 1861      HB 1862      HB 1863      HB 1864
   HB 1865      HB 1866      HB 1867      HB 1878      HR 963       HR 964
   HR 965       HR 966       HR 967       SB 507       SB 528       SB 541
   SB 547       SB 555       SB 607       SB 613       SB 626       SB 628


                          FAVORABLY REPORTED

          HB 1274              HB 1375   SUB           HB 1827
          HB 1829              HB 1831                 HB 1833
          HB 1834


                          PASSED/ADOPTED HOUSE

                      Yeas  Nays                           Yeas  Nays
   HB 800    FS        154    3        HB 1332   CSFA      143    10
   HB 1469             164    0        HB 1488             159     0
   HB 1499             155    0        HB 1531*            150     5
   HB 1541*  CS        119   47        HB 1547   CAFA      153     4
   HB 1557             100    0        HB 1570   CSFA      156     0
   HB 1642   FS        133   20        HB 1827             102     4
   HB 1829             102    4        HB 1831             102     4
   HB 1833             102    4        HB 1834             102     4
   HR 907    FA        140    0

      * Immediately Transmitted to the Senate


                           READ AND ADOPTED

   HR 989       HR 990       HR 991       HR 992       HR 993       HR 994
   HR 995       HR 996       HR 997       HR 998       HR 999       HR 1000


                    NOTICE OF MOTION TO RECONSIDER

   HB 1547
```

READING OF BILLS

First-time visitors to the legislative galleries frequently comment about clerks reading bills aloud on the floor of the chamber, especially since members already have printed copies of the bills on their desks. To visitors, it appears that no one is paying attention to the ritual. The requirement for reading bills traces back to British parliamentary procedure before Georgia's founding. The practice continued in Georgia following statehood because illiteracy was common and because typewriters and fast-copy printing equipment had not yet been invented.

Reading bills in the Georgia legislature—or at least their titles—continues today, not only because of long tradition, but because it helps guard against hastily called votes and—most importantly—because it is required by the state constitution.

Today, every general bill and every resolution intended to have the effect of general law or to amend the state constitution must be read three times, with each reading on a separate day, before it can be voted upon by each house.[12] The Constitution of 1983 eliminated the requirement that general bills be read in their entirety on the third reading unless the presiding officer or a majority of members voting order a full reading.

The constitution requires local bills and resolutions to be read one time (by title) before a vote, and that one full day pass between the reading and the vote. Otherwise, the General Assembly is free to set procedures by statute for considering local legislation—including a greater number of readings.[13] Any additional readings of local bills would be by title only.

First reading. The first reading of all bills and resolutions is by title and occurs the day of introduction (the legislative day following filing with the clerk or secretary). If any legislator wishes to prevent any amendments to a bill as introduced, a motion "to engross" must be made at that bill's first reading. After the measure has been read by title, the presiding officer assigns it to a standing committee. Soon afterward, the clerk and secretary prepare a list for their house entitled "First Readers," which cites the bill number, author, title, and committee assignment of each bill and resolution read for the first time that day (see Fig. 14).

Second reading. The second reading, like the first, is by title only. House rules provide that a bill or resolution "requiring three readings prior to its passage" is automatically passed to a second reading on the legislative day following the first reading.[14] This means that a bill is read a second time on the floor of the House while the bill is still in the custody of a committee (unless the committee reported the bill out the same day it received the measure).

Figure 13: *Composite Status Sheet*

NOTE: X = DENOTES CARRY-OVER BILLS WITH 1994 ACTION
SHADED AREA = 1993 ACTION

GEORGIA STATE SENATE — FINAL 1994
COMPOSITE STATUS

SENATE BILLS		Read 1st Time	Favorably Reported	Comm Amend/Sub	Read 2nd Time	Recommitted	Unfavorably Reported	Read 3rd Time	Passed/Adopted	Committee/Floor Amendments/Substitute	Lost	Notice of Motion to Reconsider	Reconsidered	Postponed	Passed/Adopted	Committee/Floor Amendments/Substitute	Lost	Amendments to Agreed to	Amendments/Substitute Disagreed to	Insists on Position	Conference Committee Appointed	Conference Committee Report Adopted	Recedes from Position	Footnotes	Sent to Governor	Date Signed by Governor	Act/Veto Number
4 Fair & Open Grants Act of 1993 - provide	(Approp) (Approp)	S 1/12 H 3/4	3/1	S 3/2 3/5				3/3	3/3	CS																	
5 Budgetary, Financial Affairs - 5-yr.strategic plans	(Approp) (Approp)	S 1/12 H 2/22	2/17	2/18 2/23				2/19	2/19																		
6 Seat Belt - driver ensure that child under 16 use	(YA&HE) (M Veh)	S 1/12 H 2/2	1/14	1/15 2/3				2/1	2/1																		
8 Property Acquisition, Lease by State - issuance of reports	(Approp) (St Inst)	S 1/12 H 2/22	2/17	A 2/18 2/23				2/19	2/19	CA																	
10 Surface, Ground-Water Use - community econ. impact analysis	(Nat R) (Nat R)	S 1/12 H 1/24	1/12 2/17	S 1/13 S 1/25				1/14 3/16	1/14 3/16	CS CS								3/16							3/23	4/5	1098
12 Firearms Dealers - cert. require-ments prior to sale, delivery	(Judy) (Pub S)	S 1/12 H 2/8	2/3 1/26	2/4 A 2/9				2/5 2/9	2/5 2/9	FA CA/FA									2/10		2/14	3/16* 2/18	3/16*	*			
20 Dietetics Practice Act - provide	(H&HS) (H&E)	S 1/12 H 2/18	2/16 1/24*	S 2/17 S 2/22	3/23			2/18 2/3	2/18	CS/FA					2/3*	2/4	CS/FA	2/8							3/22	4/8	1117
24 Recreational Bingo Games - licensing requirements	(ST&I) (Ind)	S 1/12 H 2/9	2/5 3/16	A 2/9 S 2/10	3/23			2/9	2/9	CA																	
27 DUI - driver's lic. sus-pension for 1st offense	(Judy) (Judy)	S 1/12 H 2/10	2/5 3/22	2/6 S 2/11	3/23			2/9	2/9																		
31 Cobb Judicial Cir. - additional judge of superior ct.	(S Judy) (Judy)	S 1/12 H 3/3	1/15 3/9	2/1 S 3/4				2/2 3/14	2/2 3/14	CS CS/FA								3/16			3/16	3/16	3/16		3/29	3/29	929
32 Civil Actions - period of dismis-sal for want of prosecution	(Judy) (S Judy)	S 1/12 H 2/10	2/5	A 2/9 3/11				3/9	2/9	CA																	
33 Motion for New Trial - time exten-sion for transcript of evidence	(Judy) (S Judy)	S 1/12 H 2/10	2/5 2/10	A 2/9 2/11				2/9	2/9	CA																	
34 Veh. Liability Ins. (I&L) raise minimum amt.	(Judy)	S 1/12 H			1/14*																			*			
36 Common-Law Marriage - disallow after 7/1/93	(S Judy) (Judy)	S 1/12 H 3/3	2/26	A 3/1 3/4				3/2	3/2	CA																	
37 QBE - appropriateness of sex educ.,AIDS instruction	(Ed)	S 1/12 H																									
38 Veh. Weight Requirements - allowable methods for complying	(Trans) (Trans)	S 1/12 H 2/9	2/4	2/5 2/10				2/8	2/8	FA																	
39 World Congress Ctr. - cert. hiring requirements	(C Aff)	S 1/12 H	3/2	S 3/3	1/10			3/5			3/5	3/5	3/8														
40 Public School Evaluation - cert. schools exempt	(Ed)	S 1/12 H																									
41 Torts - cert. school volun-teers immune from liability	(S Judy) (Judy)	S 1/12 H 2/26	2/12 2/15	S 2/13 S 3/1				2/16* 3/4	3/4	CS/FA					2/24* 3/14	2/25	CS/FA	3/8						*	3/22	4/13	1154
42 School Trespass - create offense	(S Judy) (Judy)	S 1/12 H 2/2	1/26	S 1/27 2/3				2/1	2/1	CS																	
43 QBE - add certain goals	(Ed) (Ed)	S 1/12 H 2/4	1/15 2/22	S 2/1 2/5	3/25			2/3	2/3	CS																	
44 In-School Suspension Classes - qualifications of persons in chg.	(Ed)	S 1/12 H																									
46 School Health Services Act - provide	(H&HS)	S 1/13 H	2/25	2/26	1/10			1/10																			
47 Mot.Veh.Insur. - prohibit requir-ing cert. glass repair companies	(I&L) (Ins)	S 1/13 H 2/19	2/16 3/8*	S 2/17 S 3/22	3/17			2/18 3/14	2/18 3/14	CS/FA CS/FA					3/16*			3/16	3/16					*			
49 County Bds. of Health - composition, powers	(H&HS) (H&E)	S 1/13 H 3/4	2/26	S 3/1 3/5				3/3	3/3	CS/FA																	
50 Theft - conversion of pmts. for real property improvements	(S Judy)	S 1/13 H	1/25	1/26	1/27			1/27																			
52 Commercial Driver's Lic. - penalty for operating without	(Pub S) (M Veh)	S 1/13 H	2/5	A 2/8				2/9	2/9	CA																	
53 Merit Sys. - sick leave accumulation, utilization	(Gov Op) (SP&CA)	S 1/13 H 2/11	2/4	2/5 2/12	2/18*			2/9* 2/10	2/10	FA														*			
54 Cert. Correctional Officers - 2 breaks during 8-hr. shift	(Gov Op)	S 1/13 H																									
55 State Officers, Employees - cond. to engage in political activities	(Gov Op)	S 1/13 H	2/9	2/10				2/11							2/11*									*			
56 Mot. Veh. Insurers - payment of benefits	(I&L)	S 1/13 H																									
57 U.S. Senators, Reps. - serve no more than 12 yrs.	(S Judy)	S 1/13 H																									
58 Dependent Children Aid - no increases for additional child	(H&HS)	S 1/13 H																									
59 Educ. Programs - availability of curriculum based assessment results	(Ed)	S 1/13 H																									
60 Fiscal Affairs - periodic program review, prog. requiring approp.	(Approp)	S 1/13 H																									

*
SB 12 2/15/94 Senate appoints Conference Committee #1; 3/16/94 Senate adopts and House rejects Conference Committee Report #1; Senate discharges Conference Committee #1 and appoints #2.
SB 20 3/22/93 Favorably reported by substitute in House; 2/3/94 Postponed in House until 2/4/94.
SB 34 1/14/93 Withdrawn from Judiciary and recommitted to Insurance and Labor Committee.
SB 41 2/18/93 Tabled; 2/24/93 Taken from table; Postponed until 2/25/93.
SB 47 3/9/93 Favorably reported in House; 3/16/93 Postponed in House until 3/17/93.
SB 53 2/8/93 Postponed until 2/9/93; 2/19/93 Withdrawn from State Planning & Community Affairs & recommitted to Governmental Affairs Committee in House.
SB 55 2/11/94 Postponed until 2/15/94.

In contrast, second reading in the Senate does not occur until the legislative day following the bill's being reported out of committee. One exception is that after the 35th day of session, second readings occur on the same day a bill is reported from committee.[15]

Third reading. General bills and resolutions have their third reading only after reported from committee, placed on the calendar, and called from the calendar by the presiding officer. Only the title of the bill or resolution need be read at this point, unless the presiding officer or a majority of the members voting direct a full reading of the bill.[16] It is only after a measure's third reading that floor debate, amendment, and voting occur.

COMMITTEE CONSIDERATION OF BILLS

Assignment of Bills

Before assigning bills to committees each day, the presiding officer reviews the title of each newly introduced bill and may even study the entire legislation. The determination of the "proper" committee to consider a bill lies with the presiding officer of each house, with the following exceptions: bills which, by statute, must be referred to particular committees,[17] (e.g., general appropriations bills, compensation resolutions, and retirement bills), local legislation, and a few other cases. The assignment is usually based on the nature of the measure or its subject matter. Occasionally, a bill may be assigned to a committee the presiding officer believes will take a desired action; for example, report the bill favorably or let it die in committee. The presiding officer is seldom, if ever, overruled

Figure 14: *First Readers*

SENATE FIRST READERS

Monday, January 10, 1994

FIRST LEGISLATIVE DAY

SB 393. By Senators Marable of the 52nd and Henson of the 55th:

A bill to amend Article 3 of Chapter 10 of Title 15 of the Official Code of Georgia Annotated, relating to civil proceedings in magistrate courts, so as to provide that deferred partial payments can be requested and ordered after judgment; to provide for applicability; to provide for related matters; to provide an effective date.

Referred to Committee on Judiciary.

SB 394. By Senators Isakson of the 21st, Clay of the 37th, Edge of the 28th and Ralston of the 51st:

A bill to amend Part 1 of Article 2 of Chapter 5 of Title 48 of the Official Code of Georgia Annotated, relating to property tax exemptions, so as to provide a homestead exemption from certain state and county ad valorem taxes in an amount equal to the amount of the assessed value of the homestead which exceeds the assessed value of that homestead for the taxable year immediately preceding the taxable year in which that exemption is first granted to a resident for certain residents of each county.

Referred to Committee on Finance and Public Utilities.

SB 395. By Senators Scott of the 36th, Robinson of the 16th and Clay of the 37th:

A bill to amend Part 2 of Article 16 of Chapter 2 of Title 20 of the Official Code of Georgia Annotated, relating to discipline in the public schools, so as to define certain terms; to provide that once a student is identified by an educator as a disciplinary problem, the parent shall be invited to a school conference and visit; to provide that after such notice has been given, any breach of discipline by the student shall result in a mandatory suspension.

Referred to Committee on Education.

SR 371. By Senators Scott of the 36th, Robinson of the 16th and Ray of the 19th:

A resolution adopting the Rules of the Senate.

Read and adopted.

on the initial choice of committee to which a measure shall be referred, although rules of both houses allow the members to override the presiding officer.[18] Much more common is a later motion to reassign a bill already in one committee to another. (Tables 8 and 9 show the workloads of committees during past legislative sessions.)

Meetings of Standing Committees

Participation in committee deliberations is an understood obligation for all legislators, although no specific Senate or House rule requires attendance. In some states, legislative rules specify that members are to be automatically dropped from committee membership if they miss a specified number of meetings (usually three) without excuse or good cause. In Georgia, however, members of each house serve on several committees, and meeting time conflicts inevitably occur, forcing members to miss some meetings. Senate rules, however, allow a senator scheduled to take part in two committee meetings occurring simultaneously to be included in the roll call portion of the minutes of the committee he or she is unable to attend.[19]

Standing committees meet on the call of the chair, generally following adjournment for the day during a session. Usually, the clerk and secretary announce the time and place for committee meetings and post schedules at their offices, although sometimes these times must be changed when legislative proceedings are unexpectedly prolonged on the floor.

At these meetings, members discuss the various bills which have been assigned to their committee. In the case of a controversial issue, a public hearing may be held to allow all interested persons an opportunity to express their views on the measure before the committee. The committee may also call on executive officials and any other persons to testify before it on the bill or to furnish it with information.

The constitution of Georgia provides that all standing committee meetings be open to the public, although it allows either house to make exception by its rules.[20] Committee meetings are open to the public in both houses, except that House and Senate rules exempt meetings of standing committees when discussing real estate acquisition, personnel matters, and charges brought against public officials or employees if a majority of a quorum of the committee or subcommittee so vote.[21] Rules of both houses provide that when two senators and two representatives on a conference committee feel that open meetings are impairing the committee's work, they may meet in executive, or closed, session if their request is approved by a majority of the membership in each house.[22]

The secretary of each standing committee is directed to keep minutes of the committee meetings, with these minutes to be matters of public record. Such minutes, however, do not generally show how each committee member votes on questions before the committee, nor do they include a statement of the committee's analysis of the bill.[23]

Table 8: *Summary of House Committees' Workload—Regular Sessions, 1989-1994*

Committee	Bills and Resolutions[a]					
	1989	1990	1991	1992	1993	1994
Agriculture and Consumer Affairs	28	27	16	30	16	16
Appropriations	44	54	36	54	52	76
Banks and Banking	19	26	16	16	9	13
Children and Youth	0	0	0	0	13	19
Defense and Veterans Affairs	1	6	10	8	11	11
Education	60	100	71	87	50	81
Ethics	0	0	0	0	0	2
Game, Fish, and Parks	22	33	12	18	20	36
Governmental Affairs	58	70	45	57	37	49
Health and Ecology	78	116	74	113	64	90
Human Relations and Aging	5	6	19	24	5	6
Industrial Relations	18	31	16	20	19	25
Industry	54	108	81	97	80	142
Insurance	62	71	48	74	44	56
Interstate Cooperation	0	0	0	0	0	0
Intragovernmental Coordination	0	0	0	0	0	0
Journals	0	0	0	0	0	0
Judiciary	184	295	219	294	202	352
Legislative and Congressional Reapportionment	0	2	0	12	3	6
Local Legislation SPCA	365	385	285	94	387	100
Motor Vehicles	72	108	75	120	66	113
Natural Resources and Environment	30	56	50	56	28	46
Public Safety	31	55	37	44	41	50
Regulated Beverages	9	13	14	28	13	12
Retirement	67	78	60	66	80	86
Rules	86	125	111	141	143	173
Special Judiciary	54	87	54	85	40	58
State Institutions and Property	56	56	48	53	56	61
State Planning and Community Affairs	71	87	85	106	57	57
Transportation	32	51	29	56	42	47
University System of Georgia	12	14	14	16	14	17
Ways and Means	109	167	91	163	145	217
TOTAL	1,627	2,227	1,616	2,332	1,737	2,017

[a]Total bills and resolutions including recommitments from other committees.

Table 9: *Summary of Senate Committees' Workload—Regular Sessions, 1989-1994*

Committee	Bills and Resolutions[a]					
	1989	1990	1991	1992	1993	1994
Agriculture	14	24	16	24	8	13
Appropriations	25	20	19	21	27	32
Banking and Financial Institutions	32	60	20	14	9	10
Consumer Affairs	8	15	9	14	13	17
Corrections	13	8	6	10	16	11
Defense and Veterans Affairs	4	9	10	8	10	12
Economic Development, Tourism, and Cultural Affairs	5	3	7	12	18	26
Education	47	72	31	56	42	69
Ethics	0	0	0	15	3	17
Finance and Public Utilities	31	41	76	123	85	91
Governmental Operations	93	126	91	98	43	22
Health and Human Services	56	70	38	63	52	68
Higher Education	9	11	18	12	9	8
Insurance and Labor	39	67	45	67	54	57
Interstate Cooperation	0	0	0	0	0	1
Judiciary	103	167	130	166	105	154
Natural Resources	49	53	46	60	43	38
Public Safety	36	53	41	32	35	50
Reapportionment	0	1	5	12	3	3
Retirement	47	71	39	44	28	42
Rules	17	22	50	67	59	68
Science, Technology, and Industry	0	0	0	0	19	33
Special Judiciary	66	86	92	114	77	85
Transportation	37	35	26	50	41	36
Urban and County Affairs	375	420	312	500	380	379
Youth, Aging, and Human Ecology	22	2	38	39	21	19
TOTAL	1,128	1,436	1,165	1,621	1,200	1,361

[a]Total bills and resolutions including recommitments from other committees.

Possible Committee Actions

A committee can dispose of a measure in a number of ways. It may

1. report the measure back to the body favorably, with or without amendments (amendments may be so extensive as to constitute, in effect, a substitute measure);
2. report the measure back unfavorably;
3. report the measure without recommendation (in the House only); or
4. not report the bill at all.

Both houses require that all committee reports be in writing, and they allow minority members of a committee to make a written report giving the reasons for their dissent.[24] The rules of the House further provide that, whenever practicable, a committee is to include with its report on a general bill or resolution a brief resume of the bill.[25] In practice, few reports are ever filed.

No committee in either house may deface or interline a measure which has been referred to it. If the committee wishes to recommend an amendment, it must do so on separate paper, noting the section, page, or line to which the amendment relates.[26] Where amendments are proposed by committee, the clerk or secretary is required to have them printed and distributed to each member. Action on any pending bill or resolution of general application may be suspended at any time by a majority of a quorum voting until the substitutes and amendments offered have been printed and distributed.[27]

When favorably reported. When a bill or resolution is (1) favorably reported by committee with no change, with amendments, or by committee substitute, or (2) reported without recommendation (in the House), it is ready for placement on the calendar and its third reading.[28] At this stage, a house could order the bill recommitted to the same committee or to another committee, could pass the measure, or could kill the bill on the final vote.

When a bill or resolution has been referred to and reported on by more than one committee, or when it has been recommitted to the same committee, the last committee report is the one which is acted upon by the house.[29]

When unfavorably reported. If the committee report recommends that the bill not pass, any member may request that the measure be placed on the house calendar for the purpose of disagreeing with this report. The individual legislator must give notice of intention to move to disagree with the adverse committee report before adjournment of the legislative day following the unfavorable committee report.[30] If that house rejects the committee's unfavorable report, the bill is passed to a third reading in the House and a second reading in the Senate, unless reassigned to committee. The house may then order the bill recommitted to the same committee or to another committee by a vote of a majority of a quorum.

If, however, the unfavorable committee report is agreed to by the house, the bill is dead for that session.

Because of the possibility of confusion, the point should be emphasized that when a vote by the whole body occurs following an unfavorable committee report on a measure, the precise question before the body is whether this unfavorable report shall be agreed to. This results, of course, in the somewhat unusual situation of a "yes" vote being in opposition to the bill in question, and a "no" vote being in its favor. A few state legislators have attempted to resolve this possible confusion by changing the form of the question before the body at this stage (e.g., "Shall the bill be read a third time?") so that a "yes" vote stands in favor of the measure in question. In actual practice, nearly all bills which receive an unfavorable committee report die at this stage.

When not reported. The rules of the House provide that, if a measure has been held by a committee for 10 legislative days without being reported, any member, after giving notice to the body, may submit a motion on the next legislative day instructing the committee to report such bill or resolution back to the House. If two-thirds of a quorum approve, the committee reports the measure, with or without a recommendation, at the next regular session. If it fails to so report, the bill or resolution is automatically returned to the House for consideration.[31]

In the Senate, there is no provision for removing a bill from committee when that committee refuses to report the bill back to the floor.

Importance of committee report. Most legislative bodies rely heavily on the work of their committees for a division of labor, which allows close scrutiny of a large number of bills. In the Georgia General Assembly, the committee report is a major determinant in the fate of most bills.

CALENDAR

Even after a committee has favorably reported a bill back to the full house, that bill cannot come before the body until it has been placed on the calendar and called up by the presiding officer. The calendar is useful not only to guide the presiding officer in calling up bills, but to alert the membership to the approximate order in which bills will be considered. It is a daily listing of the bills and resolutions that are ready to receive legislative consideration on the floor of a house, usually indicating the order in which such measures will be considered. In the House, uncontested local bills are not placed on the calendar for general bills, but are generally called up and passed on the day following their favorable report from committee. In the Senate, a separate local calendar is prepared for these bills.

General calendar. This is prepared daily throughout the entire session by the clerk of the House and the secretary of the Senate for their respective houses. In both houses, the general calendar governs the daily legislative agenda for the first 19 days of the session.[32] (See Fig. 15 for an example of a general calendar.)

Each house considers the bills introduced by its members first, then the resolutions of its members, then the bills of the other house, and lastly, the resolutions introduced in the other house. The Senate has a policy of placing the bills and resolutions left from the preceding day at the head of the next day's calendar to prevent prolonged delay in their consideration.

The House and Senate have formal rules which require a two-thirds vote to change the order of business under the general calendar, and this two-thirds vote must constitute a majority of the total membership of that house.[33] A motion to change the order of business in both houses must be voted on immediately, and no debate is allowed.[34]

Rules calendar. During the last 21 legislative days of a session, the daily legislative agenda is governed by a rules calendar prepared by the Rules Committee of each house.[35] (Fig. 16 presents an example of a rules calendar.) By this time, a greater number of bills have usually been reported from committee than can be considered on the floor during a single day, and the rules calendar specifies which of these bills and resolutions shall be called up for consideration. In preparing the rules calendar, the Rules Committee of each house draws from the general calendar, which lists all bills ready for consideration, those bills considered more important or deserving of floor consideration on the next legislative day. In the process, some bills are omitted from the list, although they are again eligible for placement on the calendar the following day. It is possible, however, for a bill favorably reported out of committee to never come up for debate or voting on the floor of that house if reported out in the last 21 days of a session and the Rules Committee chooses not to place it on the calendar.

In both houses, the Rules Committee meets sometime after that day's adjournment to set the rules calendar for the next legislative day. In the House, however, a majority of membership may vote to allow the Rules Committee to meet at any time to set a rules calendar or supplemental rules calendar.[36]

Figure 15: *General Calendar*

```
                        HOUSE GENERAL CALENDAR
                        Tuesday, February 22, 1994
                        27th Legislative Day

                              HOUSE BILLS

HB   151   Candidates; political contributions by corporations; prohibit
HB   238   Housing authorities; commissioners and resident commissioners
HB   250   Law enforcement officers; indemnification; line of duty
HB   354   Mobile barbershops; regulate
HB   537   Physicians' assistants; duties and functions
HB   596   Income tax; retirement income; exemption
HB   642   Child support; net income
HB   649   Personal care home; licensing; long-term care ombudsman
HB   652   Machine gun or firearm with silencer; penalties (Tabled)
HB   676   Telephones; certain long-distance charges; eliminate
HB   715   Local govt; cert prop in adjoining county; prohibit purchase
HB   827   Bicycles on roadways; exceptions to right side requirement
HB   832   Crimes; commission by felon using firearm (Reconsidered)
HB  1019   Superior Ct Judges Retirement; postretirement benefits; ret age
HB  1103   Service cancelable loans; certain registered nurses
HB  1136   Georgia Ports Authority; police powers
HB  1198   Drive-by shooting; define offense
HB  1204   Municipal elections; runoffs; date
HB  1222   Local sales tax; homestead exemptions; special districts
HB  1229   Pardons and paroles; certain sex offenders; notice upon release
HB  1237   Weapons; use during cert crimes; enhanced penalties (Tabled)
HB  1238   Juv Ct; 13 to 17 year olds committing cert crimes; jurisdiction
HB  1240   Motor vehicles; pedestrian's crosswalk; requirements
HB  1255   Motor vehicles; fleeing or eluding peace officer; signal
HB  1270   Lead Poisoning Prevention Act of 1994; enact
HB  1271   Criminal desecration to burial grounds; define offense
HB  1273   Budget Responsibility Oversight Committee; amend provisions
HB  1274   Fiscal notes; amend provisions
HB  1286   Boards of registrars; deputies appoint designees
HB  1290   County boards of family and children services; members
HB  1301   Child support; computation guidelines; special circumstances
HB  1304   Courts; authority to expunge certain records
HB  1306   Georgia Health Insurance Plan; enact
HB  1313   Open records law; applicability to local government records
HB  1317   Probationer arrest; powers of parole officers
HB  1327   Juvenile courts; associate judges; qualifications
HB  1328   Weapons used in commission of crime; destroy
HB  1338   Trafficking in marijuana; change provisions
HB  1358   Theft by conversion; certain rented or leased property
HB  1375   General appropriations; FY 1994-95
HB  1376   Comm driver's license; serious traffic violation; definition
HB  1390   Used cars; dealers and salvage dealers; combine state boards
HB  1394   Dispossessory proceedings; tenant at sufferance
HB  1400   Liens on aircraft; labor, materials, contracts of indemnity
HB  1403   Escape; convicted person; minimum mandatory sentence
HB  1416   Local Government Unfunded Mandate Procedures Act; enact (Tabled)
HB  1423   Forgery; cert identification cards; nonofficial
HB  1426   Emergency medical services; invalid car; applicability
HB  1432   Criminal procedure; property bond; nonresident
HB  1435   Solid waste permits; limitations on modification
HB  1436   County boards of equalization; assessments; appeals
HB  1438   Conservation use property; certain transfers
HB  1450   Candidates for nonresuscitation; amend provisions
HB  1459   Council of Municipal Court Judges; create
HB  1462   Professional Stds & Prof Practices Comm; withdrawal of applicant
HB  1465   Child custody proceedings; allegations of abuse; investigation
HB  1474   DUI; nolo plea; completion of certain program
HB  1475   Administrative procedure; proposed rules; economic impact
HB  1478   Gen Assembly; compensation and allowances; amend prov  (P.P.2/23/94)
HB  1483   Superior courts; sessions; alternative locations
HB  1504   Fulton County; board of equalization; appointment
HB  1519   Magistrate courts; constables or marshals; compensation
HB  1521   Board of Natural Resources; regulations; effective date
HB  1522   DOT; contract requirements; waiver of limitations
HB  1524   Nursing homes; imposition of remedial measures; review
HB  1525   Hospital authorities; sovereign immunity
HB  1530   Insurers; employment discrimination; prohibit
HB  1535   Motor vehicles; foglights; prohibitions
HB  1546   Handicapped parking privileges; certain Medicaid transportation
```

While the rules calendar is in effect in the Senate, it takes a three-fourths vote (providing the three-fourths constitutes a majority of the Senate) to change the order of bills on the calendar.[37] House rules are silent on changing the calendar, meaning that the vote must be by a majority of the total membership.[38]

As a final matter, the Senate rules provide that all bills are to be called up for consideration in the numerical order in which they are listed on the calendar. House rules allow the speaker to call bills from the calendar in any order.[39]

Senate consent calendars. Senate rules provide for a general consent calendar for all general bills that use population of a city, county, or metropolitan statistical area as the basis for applicability of the bills (see pp. 94-98). Population bills are placed together on a consent calendar, a copy of which is given to each senator by or before their second reading on the floor. On the day of third reading and passage, a single roll-call vote is taken on whether all bills on this consent calendar shall pass. However, before the vote, if three senators (one of whom represents a district that will be directly affected) object in writing to the inclusion of a particular population bill on the consent calendar, that bill shall be placed at the top of the calendar of bills at that time in order for third reading.[40]

All resolutions that name or rename roads, streets, highways, parks, bodies of waters, bridges, institutions, buildings, structures, and any other geographic landmark within one senatorial district are placed on a general consent calendar for commemorative resolutions. This calendar must be given to each senator by the time of third reading of the resolutions. A single roll-call vote is then taken on all resolutions on the consent calendar.[41]

FLOOR CONSIDERATION

Until this point, a bill officially has been before the entire membership of a house on each of the first two readings, but no other floor action has taken place on the bill. Once reported out of committee and placed on the calendar, it is ready for the final stage of the legislative process—floor consideration.

Floor Privileges

Before looking at this stage, it should be noted that the rules of each house limit who may enter the chamber while that house is in session. In the Senate, no one may enter the floor except

1. members (and their pages) and officers of the Senate;
2. members and officers of the House;
3. the governor;

Figure 16: *Rules Calendar*

SENATE CONVENES AT 9:30 A.M.

SENATE RULES CALENDAR

Tuesday, February 22, 1994

TWENTY-SEVENTH LEGISLATIVE DAY

HB 1214 Motor Vehicle Ad Valorem Return - false statements (F&PU-16th)
Buck-135th

SB 627 Health Planning Agency - functions (H&HS-19th)

SB 561 Appropriations - midyear adjustment reserve for education
(Substitute)(Approp-21st)

SR 485 Joint Rhodes Memorial Hall Study Committee - create (Substitute)
(Rules-39th)

SR 502 Garland T. Byrd Bridge - designate bridge across Flint River
(Trans-14th)

SR 500 Whitfield County-conveyance of certain state property (F&PU-54th)

SR 516 Martin Luther King, Jr., Boulevard - designate portion of U.S.
Highway 278 (Trans-31st)

SB 594 Lottery Proceeds - transfers to Education Account (Approp-14th)

SB 581 Appellate Court Appeals - grounds for dismissal (Judy-54th)

SR 406 Barriers to Affordable Housing Study Committee - create
(Substitute)(Rules-39th)

SR 519 State Park at Tallulah Gorge - negotiation with Georgia Power on
property (F&PU-50th)

SR 499 Department of Transportation - urge withdraw plan for airport in
Gwinnett County (Trans-9th)

SB 576 Probate Courts - may try misdemeanor marijuana violations
(Substitute)(Judy-13th)

SB 618 Housing Authority - create for certain Indian tribes (H&HS-11th)

SB 402 Driver's License Renewal - sign acknowledgment of suspension if
DUI (Amendment)(S Judy-5th)

SB 580 Orders Not to Resuscitate - legislative intent (Substitute)
(H&HS-42nd)

Respectfully submitted,

Tavid Scott

Scott of the 36th, Chairman
Senate Rules Committee

4. staff members of the offices of lieutenant governor, secretary of the Senate, clerk of the House; and of the Office of Legislative Counsel, Senate Research Office, Senate Information Office; and the Senate photographer;

5. former senators (except those registered as lobbyists or presently employed by the state);

6. such others as the Senate may allow upon written recommendation of its Rules Committee; and

7. representatives of the press, radio, and television, but only in the area at the rear of the chamber designated for them (though, in practice, photographers and film crews are accorded limited freedom of movement through the chamber).[42]

Additionally, Senate rules allow the presiding officer, at any time, to introduce any member of Georgia's congressional delegation or "any other person of national prominence." Customarily, that person will then enter the chamber and come forward to the president's podium, where he or she is introduced and allowed to say a few words to the Senate. No other person or group can be introduced or allowed to address the Senate without the approval of the Senate Decorum Committee during the first 19 days of a session, and the approval of three-fourths of the Rules Committee during the final 21 days of a session. Finally, at the time of floor consideration of any bill appropriating money, the chair of the Senate Appropriations Committee or a majority of members present may invite non-senators onto the floor to explain or answer questions on that bill.[43]

The House excludes all persons from its floor except

1. members (and their pages) and officers of the House;

2. members and officers of the Senate;

3. the governor;

4. staff members of the Office of Legislative Counsel and Office of Legislative Budget Analyst;

5. representatives of the news media and their photographers (carrying proper credentials), although no interviews are allowed while the House is in session;

6. such other persons as the House may allow upon recommendations of its Rules Committee;

7. spouses and children over 12 of House members (although they may not sit at the desk of any member); and

8. the chaplain and doctor of the day.[44]

No person who is not a member of the House is permitted to speak unless that person has been invited by resolution adopted on or before the previous day. Except for the chaplain and doctor of the day, members are prohibited from recognizing any visitor on the floor or in the gallery. This prohibition extends to the speaker, "unless he deems their presence to be of such importance as to outweigh the value of continuing the business of the House."[45]

Floor Debate and Amendment

After a bill has been called from the calendar for a third reading, members may debate its merits and offer amendments from the floor (see pp. 192-96 for a detailed description of the amending process). To speak for or against a bill, a legislator must obtain permission from the chair to address the chamber from the well of the house. Should a member already be speaking from the well, another may not speak until the first member yields the floor. However, debate is limited in both houses, and the previous question can be called by a majority of a quorum present at any time, thus precluding filibusters in either house.

A legislator in the well may be questioned by other members only should he or she yield for questions, and the choice rests with the legislator speaking from the well. Only one member at a time may ask questions after making a request through the chair. For the sake of audibility, members have microphones at their desks, which can be switched on by the clerk or secretary's staff after the legislator signals a desire to address the chair or speaker in the well.

At any time during legislative proceedings, a member may direct a "parliamentary inquiry" or "point of order" to the presiding officer. This action allows a legislator with a question regarding the specific legislative procedure occurring to seek a ruling or explanation from the chair. For instance, when a number of amendments are before the body at one time, a member may be unsure of which is being voted upon, or what the effect of one will be on another. Or, a member may have a question about the applicability of the house rules to the proceedings at hand. Rulings of the chair in these instances can be appealed to the body, but in practice are very seldom questioned. It should be noted that the parliamentary inquiry is intended to apply to procedural questions on which the chair can rule, and members are generally discouraged from using this device to make substantive arguments to influence members for or against a matter under consideration.

To conclude debate, a member may move the previous question, or the presiding officer can inquire if there is any objection to ordering the previous question. If the motion passes, further debate is cut off, except that the chairperson of the standing committee that reported the measure back to the floor is given 20 minutes, either to use entirely or to yield to other members for all or any part of this time. (Senate rules also provide that if the committee report was unfavorable, the bill's author is also allowed 20 minutes.) If there was a minority report on the measure, signers of this report are allotted 20 minutes; but those aligned with the committee majority report always speak last. In actual practice, the 20-minute time periods allowed by the rules after ordering the previous question are rarely used.[46]

The chair then asks if there is objection to the committee report on the bill being adopted; and if none, inquires if there is objection to ordering the main question. If a member objects to ordering any of these questions, an actual vote is taken.

VOTING

Voting Requirements

Georgia's constitution requires that a bill, in order to pass, must receive approval of a majority of the membership of each house. This is referred to as a "constitutional majority." The constitution also requires that the final vote for passage in each house be recorded in the journal of that body.[47]

Additionally, some actions—such as proposed constitutional amendments, overriding a veto, amending legislative rules during a session, and expelling a member—require special majorities (usually two-thirds of either the total membership or of those present).

Many of the procedural votes require only a majority of those present, provided a quorum is present. A Senate rule stipulates that amendments, motions, and procedural matters are to be decided by a majority of a quorum, unless otherwise provided by rules, and that all other resolutions not otherwise provided for require a majority of the membership for approval.[48] House rules specify that where no specific vote is provided by House rules for passage of any resolution, motion, or measure which will not become law, the vote must be by a majority of the membership, unless enacted by unanimous consent.[49]

Until voting on a bill or resolution begins, a measure may be withdrawn at any stage of the legislative process with the consent of the House or Senate. However, should a bill or resolution be rejected in the final vote in either house, it may not again be proposed during the same session, under the same or any other title, without the consent of two-thirds of the house which rejected it.[50]

Voting Procedures

Subject to constitutional and statutory provisions, as well as the rules of that house, voting in the House and Senate may be by unanimous consent, voice vote (viva voce), a show of hands (division), or a roll call (also called a vote by "yeas and nays").

Unanimous consent. This is a procedure for voting or obtaining the permission of the members of a house to allow or dispense with some action (e.g., to dispense with the morning roll call in each house). The presiding officer asks the members if there is objection to the motion or request being voted upon, and if no member voices objection, the vote, motion, or request passes. If objection is raised, the ordinary procedures for voting are then used.

Viva voce. This is a collective voice vote taken of the members present. The vote of the individual legislator is not recorded (unless a viva voce roll call has been called), and only the result of the vote—as interpreted by the presiding officer—is announced and recorded. If the presiding officer's interpretation of the result is appealed, a second vote will be taken, typically using another procedure.

Division. This is a vote by show of hands, where only the total number for and against a proposal is recorded. Historically, a division of a house was a call for the members of that house to rise and stand to one side of the chamber or the other to reflect their positions on a question. Now, when the presiding officer calls upon the members in favor of a question "to rise, stand, and be counted," the members reflect their position on the question by raising a hand.

Yeas and nays. In this vote, each member is on record with respect to how he or she voted on a question. Such roll call votes are required in both houses on all proposed constitutional amendments and on all bills appropriating money.[51] Also, when a two-thirds vote of either or both houses is required for the passage of a bill or resolution, the yeas and nays must be taken and entered in the journal. A roll call vote may be taken in either house when ordered by the presiding officer or at the desire of one-fifth of the members present or a lesser number if so provided by the house rules.[52] The Senate provides for a roll call if five members so request.[53] Senate rules also provide for a roll call on the final vote of all general bills and resolutions having the effect of law, on the adoption of all conference committee reports, and on any action that would have the effect of finalizing the Senate's action on any general bill or resolution.[54]

In the Senate, all roll call votes must be taken on the electronic voting system (if inoperative, a voice roll call is used).[55] In the House, the electronic voting system is used for yeas and nays, unless the speaker orders a viva voce roll call vote or the machine is not working.[56]

During a roll call vote, members in both houses are prohibited from attempting to explain their votes, although senators may submit a written explanation (not to exceed 250 words) and representatives a written explanation (not to exceed 200 words) for inclusion in their respective journals.[57] Additionally, during a roll call vote, no debate is permitted in either house.[58]

Voting in the House. On the desk of each representative is a switch to be used by the member assigned to that seat to register his or her vote on the electronic voting system. The votes are flashed on large tally boards placed on both sides of the House chamber, upon which the names of the members are arranged in alphabetical order. A green light signifies a "yes" vote on a particular question, while a red light signifies a "no" vote. After allowing adequate time for members to vote and to change their votes, the speaker orders the voting machine to be locked. Before locking the machine, the speaker will typically ask several times, "Have all members voted?" The vote totals are then displayed on the boards. Additionally, the vote is permanently recorded on a tape, which is pulled at the conclusion of the vote on each question by the clerk.

Voting in the Senate. The electronic voting system used in the Senate for taking roll call votes is similar in operation to that in the House, except (1) no senator's vote is shown on the tally board until all senators have voted and the machine is locked, and (2) the Senate system includes a digital countdown clock showing how much of the time allotted by Senate rules (60 seconds) for voting on each question remains before the machine is automatically locked (in contrast to the House, where the presiding officer determines when the machine is to be locked on a given vote).[59]

In both houses, utilization of the voting machine in effect dispenses with the call for verification, since each legislator's vote is clearly visible, in addition to being automatically recorded and printed. House and Senate rules provide that the vote printout may not be altered in any way nor may any votes be changed.[60]

ENGROSSMENT

When a bill is passed by the House or Senate, it is engrossed by the clerk or secretary before transmittal to the other house. Engrossment is a proofreading and verification of a bill or resolution, as passed by that house, for the purpose of making certain that the copy being certified is identical with the original bill as introduced and incorporates all amendments to the bill that have been adopted. (Fig. 17 shows the cover sheet for an engrossed bill.)

At only one other time—on the day of introduction, at the time of the first reading—is engrossment possible for a bill. At one time, both the House and Senate had engrossment procedures in their rules, but the Senate dropped these rules in 1985. If two-thirds of those voting, provided the total vote constitutes a quorum, approve a motion to engross a bill at the time of first reading, no amendments can be made to that bill while it is being considered in the House. In effect, the bill as introduced is engrossed—or certified as the final copy—and it may not thereafter be amended. No debate is permitted on this motion, except that the mem-

Figure 17: *Cover Sheet for an Engrossed Bill*

H. B. No. _____

ENGROSSING

A BILL

_____ 19 _____

The Committee of the House on Journals has exam-

ined the within and finds the same properly engrossed.

_____

Chairman

IN HOUSE

Read 1st time
Read 2nd time
Read 3rd time

And

Ayes   Nays

_____ 19 _____

_____

Clerk of the House

The Committee of the Senate on

IN SENATE

_____

Read 1st time
Read 2nd time
Read 3rd time

Recommends that this Bill

do _____

And

_____

Ayes   Nays

Chairman

_____

Secretary of the Senate

By:

ber making the motion may speak in favor of its passage for five minutes, and one other member may speak in opposition for a similar amount of time.[61]

CONSIDERATION BY THE SECOND HOUSE

Transmittal

Following passage of a bill in the house of origin, it is then engrossed (certified) and prepared for transmittal to the other house. The measure, however, cannot be transmitted on the same day that it passes in the house of origin unless two-thirds of the members voting, provided the total vote constitutes a quorum, so order. An exception to this rule is that any bill or resolution which requires action by the other house during the last three legislative days of a session shall be immediately transmitted.[62] Also, all Senate measures requiring House action on the 33d legislative day are to be immediately transferred to the House.[63] Toward the end of a legislative session, time pressure causes members of both bodies to approve immediate transmittal of measures rather frequently.

Amendments

In the second house, a bill goes through substantially the same procedures as it did in the first. If passed in the second house without change, it is returned to the first house for enrollment and can then be sent to the governor. If, however, the second house makes changes in the bill, as is often the case, several options are available.

Assuming a House bill has been transmitted to the Senate, where additional amendments are added before passage, the bill is then returned to the House, which can agree to the Senate amendments. In that case, the bill is ready for enrollment and forwarding to the governor. If, however, the House does not agree to the Senate amendments, the Senate is so notified, and it then has the option of yielding on the matter. If the Senate insists on its position, the House is notified and can itself either yield or insist on its position. At this point, the general procedure for resolving the stalemate is the appointment of a conference committee, if both houses so agree, to attempt to reconcile differences.

Conference Committees

In a bicameral legislature, lawmakers (and others) have two chances to get provisions they want into a bill—and two chances to keep provisions they don't like out. It is rare for important legislation to pass out of the first house and subsequently be accepted without change in the second house. Battles lost in the first house are fought again in the second. As a result, most major legislation is sent to what amounts to a third "house"—the conference committee.

The rules of both houses contain similar and detailed provisions regarding the appointment and functions of conference committees.[64] Since neither the president of the Senate nor the speaker of the House possesses the express power to initiate the appointment of a conference committee, it must be initiated by a member (any member) making a motion for the appointment, with this motion sustained by the body. When this happens, the presiding officer of that body must appoint three members from that house to serve on the committee. Each of the three members appointed, however, must have voted with the majority on the position assumed by his or her house on the bill, if the vote has been taken. It should be noted that the rules of some state legislatures do not require that all members of a conference committee be on the prevailing side of their house, and some even expressly state that both majority and minority views of each house must be represented on these committees.

The purpose of the conference committee is to attempt to reach an agreement or compromise on the points of dispute between the two houses on the bill. To this end, the rules provide that the committee may consider the entire subject matter of the bill and recommend revision by either house, new amendments, new bills and resolutions, or other germane changes. The Senate may instruct its conferees as to what actions they are to take. The instruction, in order to be binding, must be approved by the Senate on motion, before the members are appointed to the committee.

The conference committee cannot hold a bill indefinitely. Rules of both houses provide that if a conference committee has been in existence for five days without reporting out a bill, the full body may vote to direct the presiding officer to appoint a new committee. In the Senate, the body may instruct its conferees or take other action not contrary to the rules of that house. The motion, to be successful, must receive a majority vote of the members elected to that body. During the last five days of the legislative session, this motion may be made and passed at any time (but no more often than every three hours) whether the conference committee has been in existence for five days or not.

Before a conference committee report can be transmitted to either the Senate or the House for action, it must be approved by a majority vote of the entire membership of the committee. Once approved, the report must be printed and distributed to legislators at least one hour before action can be taken in either house. Members of the House may dispense with the written report by a majority vote of the membership, while senators can do so only on the last day of the session, by a two-thirds vote of the membership.

In the Senate, the president, acting with discretion, or on a point of order, may rule that a conference committee report is not germane to the original bill or resolution. Unless overruled by the Senate, this ruling has the same effect as a Senate vote to reject the conference committee report.[65]

The report of the conference committee must be adopted by the Senate or the House only by the vote required to pass the bill, resolution, or matter under consideration.[66] If both houses adopt the conference committee's report or settlement and enact exactly the same amended bill, it is transmitted to the governor. In case one of the houses fails to adopt the report or recommendations, the conference committee may be directed to meet and report again; or it may be dissolved and a new committee appointed. The majority of compromise reports of conference committees are accepted by the two houses.

ENROLLMENT

Enrollment is the preparation of the final copy of a bill or a resolution intended to have the effect of law, which has passed both houses in identical form (see Fig. 18). Every bill or resolution enrolled must be certified by the presiding officer of each house, the clerk of the House, and the secretary of the Senate, before it is sent to the governor for approval and signature. The enrolled copy of a bill or resolution enacted into law is permanently preserved by the Office of the Secretary of State and is the official text of the act. Thereafter, that office deposits the session acts in the archives and has them printed and distributed throughout the state.

ACTIONS OF THE GOVERNOR

Legislative actions subject to the governor's veto. Any general or local bill passed by the General Assembly must first be sent to the governor for approval or veto before it can become law. Also requiring executive approval is any resolution passed by both houses "intended to have the effect of law."[67] By statute, the legislature has added one other action requiring submission to the governor: a legislative resolution to override agency rules and regulations is subject to the governor's approval if less than two-thirds of each house vote in favor of adopting the resolution.[68]

Legislative actions exempt from the governor's veto. Georgia's governor is prohibited from vetoing any proposed constitutional amendment or new constitution approved by the General Assembly or by a constitutional convention.[69] The chief executive is not specifically restricted from signing proposed constitutional changes—although such approval would be symbolic only—and the practice in recent years has been that governors sign some amendments while leaving others unsigned.

Other legislative actions exempted from gubernatorial veto include self-convening of special sessions by the legislature, veto overrides, impeachments, election of the state auditor, and resolutions (whether simple or concurrent) not intended to have the effect of law.[70] Additionally, in a somewhat controversial procedure, the General Assembly has provided

Figure 18: *Cover Sheet for an Enrolled Bill*

ENROLLMENT

_____ 19 _____

The Committee of the House on Journals has examined the within and finds the same properly enrolled.

_____
Chairman

_____
Speaker of the House

_____
Clerk of the House

_____
President of the Senate

_____
Secretary of the Senate

Received _____
Secretary, Executive Department

This _____ day of _____ 19_____

Approved

_____
Governor

This _____ day of _____ 19_____

H. B. No. _____ Act No. _____

General Assembly

AN ACT

IN HOUSE

Read 1st time
Read 2nd time
Read 3rd time

And

Ayes   Nays

_____
Clerk of the House

IN SENATE

Read 1st time
Read 2nd time
Read 3rd time

And

Ayes   Nays

_____
Secretary of the Senate

By:

by statute that the governor's veto authority does not extend to joint resolutions vetoing agency rules and regulations should two-thirds of each house vote for the resolution (although the governor can reject the resolution if less than two-thirds of each house vote for its passage).[71]

Type of veto. With the exception of appropriations measures, a governor's veto applies to an entire bill or resolution. Unlike some states, Georgia makes no provision for the "amendatory veto" (a conditional veto which is withdrawn if the legislature makes changes in the bill cited as necessary by the governor). Similarly, once a bill has been passed by both houses, no additional legislative action can be taken before the governor acts on that measure.[72]

In appropriations bills only, Georgia's governor can veto specific funding items, while approving the remainder of the bill.[73] Termed an "item veto," this device allows the governor to delete the funding authorization for a specific budget item or program. Georgia's attorney general has held that an item veto not only eliminates funding for the particular item, but also reduces by that amount the overall appropriation to the agency in whose budget the activity was included.[74] In turn, this reduces the total state appropriation by the same figure.

Only seven states (including North Carolina, which has no provision for executive veto of any legislation) and the federal government do not allow item veto of appropriations measures.[75]

Finally, Georgia, like most other states, does not have the "pocket veto." In a pocket veto, bills sent to the governor in the closing days of a session are, in effect, vetoed unless specifically signed within a designated time period following adjournment.[76] In Georgia, the governor's failure to approve a bill within the required time period results in the bill automatically becoming a law.

Sending bills to the governor. Once both houses have passed a bill or resolution, it is enrolled and readied for transmittal to the governor's office. However, any time before adjournment *sine die*, a measure is only sent if the governor specifically requests its transmittal, or if two-thirds of the members of each house direct that a bill be forwarded prior to the governor's request. The only exception to this rule is that any local bill for which the constitution necessitates a local referendum can be immediately transmitted to the governor by order of the presiding officer of the house where it was introduced, or upon approval by two-thirds of the members of that house.[77] Following the session's final adjournment, all measures requiring the governor's approval which have not been previously transmitted are immediately enrolled and forwarded for executive consideration.

A major reason for most bills not being transmitted to the governor during the legislative session is that a decision to sign or veto would have to be made within 6 days. Because time is needed for the governor's legal staff to study the ramifications of each bill, to recommend which should and should not be approved, and to recommend the order in which bills should be signed by the governor, most general bills are sent following adjournment *sine die*, thus leaving the governor 40 days to make these decisions.[78]

Signing and vetoing bills. Once a bill or a resolution which will have the effect of law has been sent to the governor's office, the chief executive has three options: (1) to sign the measure, in which event it becomes law; (2) to veto the bill, in which event it is returned to the house where first introduced; and (3) to neither sign nor veto the measure, in which event it automatically becomes a law following a required waiting period.[79]

Georgia's governor has 6 days to take action on bills and resolutions transmitted during the first 34 days of a regular session. Any bills not signed or vetoed by the end of these 6 days become law automatically without the governor's signature.

The governor has 40 days after adjournment *sine die* to sign or veto any bills or resolutions received after the session's 34th day.[80] At the end of these 40 days, any measures neither signed nor vetoed automatically become law.

Overriding a veto. Any bill vetoed by the governor must be returned to the presiding officer of the house where it was originally introduced, along with a statement by the governor as to why the bill was rejected (see Fig. 19). If the veto occurs prior to the last 3 days of the session, the governor must return the measure within 3 days of the veto, which gives lawmakers an opportunity to immediately override the veto. If, as is almost always the case, the veto occurs during the last 3 days of the session, or during the 40 days following adjournment *sine die*, the governor has 60 days to return the vetoed measure. At the subsequent session, the legislature may consider a proposal to override the governor's veto.[81]

To override a veto, a two-thirds vote of the total membership of each house is needed. Should the General Assembly fail in its effort, the bill cannot again be brought before the legislature for the purpose of overriding the governor's action.[82]

Use of the veto. The executive veto has been used in varying degrees by different governors in Georgia (see Table 10).[83] Clearly, the veto—or threat of the veto—is a powerful legislative tool for the governor. While it may be overridden by the legislature, this is almost never done. In fact, the only instances in recent history occurred in 1974, when legislators overrode seven 1973 vetoes of local bills.[84] These vetoes were based on legal opinions as to the bills' constitutionality, but subsequent events caused the governor to withdraw his objections and signal legislators that he would not oppose an override. The small number of vetoes overridden during the past century attests to the influence of the governor, the difficulty of obtaining a two-thirds vote on controversial matters in the legislature, and the selectivity of governors in using the veto.

Figure 19: *Governor's Veto Message*

STATE OF GEORGIA
OFFICE OF THE GOVERNOR
ATLANTA 30334-0900

Zell Miller
GOVERNOR

April 21, 1994

Honorable Pierre Howard
Lieutenant Governor
State Capitol
Atlanta, Georgia 30334

Dear Lieutenant Governor Howard:

I have vetoed Senate Bill 395 which was passed by the General Assembly of Georgia at the 1994 Regular Session.

Article III, Section V, Paragraph XIII of the Constitution requires that I transmit such bills to you, together with a list of reasons for such vetoes. The bill and corresponding reasons for its veto are attached.

With kindest regards, I remain

Sincerely,

Zell Miller

ZM/cwc
Attachments
cc: Honorable Thomas B. Murphy, Speaker of the House of
       Representatives
     Honorable Robbie Rivers, Clerk, House of Representatives
     Honorable Frank Eldridge, Secretary of the Senate
     Honorable Sewell R. Brumby, Legislative Counsel
     Honorable Michael J. Bowers, Attorney General
     Honorable Max Cleland, Secretary of State

VETO NUMBER 21

Senate Bill 395 imposes the same procedural requirements for short-term school suspensions as are currently required for long-term suspensions and expulsions. It also attempts to provide for greater parental involvement when students are identified as chronic disciplinary problems. I support that portion of the bill which provides for greater parental involvement and I will request the State Board of Education to encourage school principals to provide for school visits and parent-teacher conferences for chronic disciplinary problems. What I cannot support is that portion of the bill which significantly limits a fundamental tool of the school principal--the short-term suspension--without the necessity of going through a formal hearing process.

Senate Bill 395 would require students who are chronic disciplinary problems and whose cumulative short-term suspensions within a grading period exceed 12 days be afforded a formal hearing with appeals to the local school board and potentially to the state board and the courts. This could create a logjam of disciplinary cases. It also would limit the school's ability to deal quickly and effectively with student disciplinary matters just at the time when schools must be more assertive in dealing with such problems.

Table 10: *Summary of Legislative Workload, 1987-1994*

Session Activity	Biennium Workloads							
	1987	1988	1989	1990	1991	1992	1993	1994
Bills introduced	1,574	1,038	1,542	1,316	1,556	1,497	1,559	1,239
Bills carried over from previous session	–	743	–	817	–	932	–	918
Resolutions introduced	779	811	834	984	979	936	632	930
Resolutions carried over from previous session	–	110	–	129	–	134	–	169
Total Measures Considered	2,353	2,702	2,376	3,246	2,535	3,499	2,191	3,256
Bills lost, unfavorably reported, withdrawn	23	19	11	14	16	13	9	11
Resolutions lost or unfavorable reported	8	6	7	2	3	3	0	0
Total Lost	31	25	18	16	19	16	9	11
Bills passed	808	693	714	769	608	870	632	654
Resolutions adopted	661	720	698	852	842	807	851	797
Total Passed	1,469	1,413	1,412	1,621	1,450	1,677	1,483	1,451
Bills vetoed by governor	9	9	10	18	13	27	16	4
Resolutions vetoed by governor	0	0	0	0	2	0	0	1
Total Vetoes[a]	9	9	10	18	15	27	16	5
Bills left pending at end of session	743	1,069	817	1,350	932	1,546	918	1,492
Resolutions pending at end of session	110	195	129	259	134	260	169	302
Total Measures Pending	853	1,264	946	1,609	1,066	1,806	1,087	1,794

Note: Does not include special sessions held in 1989 and 1991.
[a]Does not include line-item vetoes in appropriations acts.

Assigning act numbers to approved bills. Bills signed by the governor are given act numbers in the order in which they are approved. Surprisingly, this can become an important legislative tool for the governor. Two or more bills dealing with the same subject area may be passed at one legislative session, and they can subsequently be found to have incompatible provisions. The order in which the governor signs these bills determines which bill will take precedence, with the bill signed *last* assuming priority.[85] Working within the time limits for signing bills, the governor is thus placed in the position of determining which bill shall represent the "latest expression of legislative intent" (regardless of the order in which the legislature actually enacted the measures) and thus which bill, incompatible with another, will control.

As a final note, in the second session of a biennium (i.e., in even-numbered years), act numbers are assigned consecutively from the number of the last act in the previous session.

EFFECTIVE DATE OF LEGISLATION

In most cases, a bill is passed on different dates in each of the two houses, with approval first occurring in the house of origin. The day of approval in the second house—providing both houses have agreed on the language of the measure—is often thought of as the bill's "date of passage." This date, however, is of no particular legal significance, as the bill is then proofed, certified, and enrolled. Sometimes a month or more may lapse before a bill is ready for forwarding to the governor.

The Georgia Supreme Court has ruled that a bill becomes a law *not* when it is passed by the two houses of the legislature, but when it is approved by the governor, when it becomes law without his signature after the lapse of time specified in the constitution, or when the legislature overrides the governor's veto.[86] Thus, notations in the annual session laws following each act—such as "Approved March 25, 1994"—refer to the date that the bill became law, not the date of passage in the legislature.

The *effective date of an act* is that date on which its provisions assume the force of law, superseding any conflicting provisions of previous acts dealing with the same subject matter. The effective date of an act can differ from the date that the bill was enacted into law, depending on whether the bill provided for an effective date.

Regardless of when signed, the effective date of a general bill passed at a regular session of the General Assembly is the following July 1, unless a specific date was provided for in the legislation. Often, a general bill will specify that it shall become effective upon approval of the governor or upon its becoming law without approval. However, if there is no specific date enumerated, the bill's effective date is July 1, providing the bill was enacted into law between January 1 and June 30 of that same year. The effective date of a general bill enacted between July 1 and December 30, as in the case of bills passed at special sessions held after July 1, is the first day of January of the immediately succeeding calendar year, provided no effective date was set forth in the bill.[87]

The above provisions do not apply to local legislation or resolutions. For local legislation, a bill's effective date is immediate upon approval by the governor or upon becoming law without approval or veto, unless a specific date is provided for in the bill itself.[88] These provisions also do not apply to increases in compensation accomplished by general act, for certain county officers provided for in the constitution. The increases do not go into effect until the first day of January of the succeeding calendar year.[89]

Resolutions which do not have the effect of law become effective on the date of passage. Resolutions which have the effect of law become effective with the governor's signature or after the required lapse of time if neither signed nor vetoed.[90] Resolutions voiding agency rules and regulations become effective on the day after the governor's signing if passed by less than a two-thirds vote, or on the day following passage in the second house if approved by more than two-thirds of each house.[91] Finally, resolutions proposing changes in the constitution become effective only if ratified by the voters in a subsequent general election. Unless the resolution provides otherwise, the effective date of the constitutional change is January 1 following its ratification.[92]

ENDNOTES

1. GA. CONST. art. 3, §5, ¶14.
2. OFFICIAL CODE OF GEORGIA ANNOTATED (O.C.G.A.) §47-20-31.
3. O.C.G.A. §50-18-75.
4. O.C.G.A. §28-1-17.
5. Senate Rule 105.
6. House Rule 46.
7. For a listing of deadlines by state, see *The Book of the States, 1994-95* (Lexington, Ky.: Council of State Governments, 1994), Table 3.15, pp. 138-40.
8. Ibid., procedures for suspending bill deadlines.
9. Senate Rule 105.
10. Senate Rule 110; House Rule 49.
11. Ibid.
12. GA. CONST. art. 3, §5, ¶7.
13. GA. CONST. art. 3, §5, ¶8.
14. House Rule 46.
15. Senate Rule 114.
16. GA. CONST. art. 3, §5, ¶7.
17. O.C.G.A. §§28-5-4, 28-5-82, 47-20-34.
18. Senate Rule 115; House Rule 53.
19. Senate Rule 187.
20. GA. CONST. art. 3, §4, ¶11.
21. Senate Rule 219; House Rule 8. In Coggin v. Davey, 233 Ga. 407, 211 S.E. 2d 708 (1975), Georgia's supreme court ruled that Georgia's so-called "Sunshine Law" (O.C.G.A. §§50-14-1 through 50-14-4), which requires any meeting of a state agency to be open to the public, is not applicable to the General Assembly or its committees.
22. Senate Rule 219; House Rule 146.
23. Senate Rule 187; House Rule 7.
24. Senate Rules 117, 187; House Rules 55, 56.
25. House Rule 55.
26. Senate Rule 116; House Rule 54.
27. Senate Rule 110; House Rule 49.
28. Senate Rule 119; House Rule 56.

29. Senate Rule 120; House Rule 57.
30. Senate Rule 118; House Rule 56.
31. House Rule 58.
32. Senate Rule 30; House Rule 29.
33. Senate Rule 31; House Rule 33.
34. Senate Rule 33; House Rule 31.
35. Senate Rule 30; House Rule 29.
36. House Rule 29.
37. Senate Rule 30.
38. House Rules 29, 129.
39. Senate Rule 111; House Rule 50.
40. Senate Rule 111.
41. Ibid.
42. Senate Rule 17.
43. Ibid.
44. House Rule 12.
45. Ibid.
46. Senate Rule 161; House Rule 125.
47. GA. CONST. art. 3, §5, ¶5.
48. Senate Rule 167.
49. House Rule 129.
50. GA. CONST. art. 3, §5, ¶12.
51. GA. CONST. art. 3, §5, ¶6; art. 10, §1, ¶2.
52. GA. CONST. art. 3, §5, ¶6.
53. Senate Rule 171.
54. Ibid.
55. Senate Rule 172.
56. House Rule 139.
57. Senate Rule 177; House Rule 137.
58. Senate Rule 178; House Rule 138.
59. Senate Rule 172; House Rule 139.
60. Senate Rule 172; House Rule 140.
61. House Rule 52.
62. Senate Rule 94; House Rule 150.
63. Senate Rule 94.
64. Senate Rule 156; House Rule 146.
65. Senate Rule 156.
66. Senate Rule 156; House Rule 146.
67. GA. CONST. art. 3, §5, ¶13.
68. O.C.G.A. §50-l3-4.
69. GA. CONST. art. 10, §1, ¶5; art. 3, §5, ¶11.
70. Because resolutions can be used for many purposes, it is sometimes unclear which are not intended to have the effect of law, and thus do not need to be sent to the governor. One court ruling held that legislative adoption of a concurrent resolution suspending an executive official—as provided by statute—did not require the governor's approval, since the suspension could have been achieved by a simple resolution in each house. Gray v. McLendon, 134 Ga. 224, 67 S.E. 859 (1910).

71. O.C.G.A. §50-13-4.

72. Seventeen states allow the governor to return a bill to the legislature before taking final action on the bill, while 31 allow the legislature to recall a bill that has been sent to the governor before the governor acts. *The Book of the States, 1982-83*, pp. 212-13. (The most recent edition of *The Book of the States* does not update this information.)

73. GA. CONST. art. 3, §5, ¶13(e).

74. 1974 Ops. Att'y Gen. U74-98, 74-36; 1973 Op. Att'y Gen. U73-94.

75. *The Book of the States, 1994-95*, p. 45.

76. Ibid.

77. GA. CONST. art. 3, §5, ¶13.

78. Ibid.

79. GA. CONST. art. 5, §2, ¶4.

80. This same 40-day limit applies should the legislature take a recess in excess of 40 days during the session and should there be bills in the governor's possession for which final action has not been taken. GA. CONST. art. 3, §5, ¶13.

81. GA. CONST. art. 3, §5, ¶13.

82. Ibid.

83. See Jack B. Hood, "History of the Veto Power in Georgia," 8 *Georgia State Bar Journal* 513 (May 1972).

84. See *House Journal 1974*, vol. I, pp. 25-28; vol. II, pp. 4027-4033.

85. Keener v. MacDougall, 232 Ga. 273, 206 S.E. 2d 519 (1974); County of Butts v. Straham, 151 Ga. 417, 107 S.E. 63 (1921).

86. Floyd County v. Salmon, 151 Ga. 313, 106 S.E. 280 (1921); Ross v. Jones, 151 Ga. 425, 107 S.E. 160 (1921); Walker v. City of Rome, 16 Ga. App. 817, 86 S.E. 628 (1915).

87. O.C.G.A. §1-3-4.

88. Ibid.

89. O.C.G.A. §1-3-4.1.

90. O.C.G.A. §1-3-4.

91. O.C.G.A. §50-13-4.

92. GA. CONST. art. 10, §1, ¶6.

 **Rules of Procedure**

Effective legislators frequently are noted for their familiarity with the rules of parliamentary procedure in their house. The rule book of each house contains motions that can be used to help pass—or defeat—bills, resolutions, amendments, and other motions; and knowledge of parliamentary tactics can sometimes mean the difference between a successful and unsuccessful legislative strategy.

Georgia's constitution directs each house in the General Assembly to determine its own rules of procedure.[1] These rules serve as an addition to, and in some cases a restatement of, constitutional and statutory provisions which apply to the legislative process. Although many House and Senate rules closely follow the standard parliamentary rules used by civic and social organizations (e.g., *Robert's Rules of Order*), a large number are unique to the legislature. Moreover, while both houses have adopted many rules that are similar or even identical, significant differences exist in House and Senate rule books.

One of the first actions each house takes on the first day of each session is to adopt rules of procedure for that session. Subject to constitutional and statutory requirements, each body is free to adopt new rules, without reference to those of the previous session. In practice, however, the rules in effect at the time of adjournment at the preceding session, perhaps with minor changes, are invariably adopted.

In both houses, initial adoption of session rules of procedure requires approval by a majority of a quorum present and voting. Once adopted, any proposal to change or add to these rules must first go to that house's Rules Committee for study and recommendation.[2] In the Senate, rules may be suspended by unanimous consent when not prohibited by rules, statute, or the constitution. The House permits suspension of the rules by unanimous consent or affirmative vote of two-thirds of its members.[3] In the Senate, if the Rules Committee does not report the proposed change or addition back to the full house within two days, the proposal automatically comes before the body for consideration.[4] Proposals to amend the rules of the Senate after their initial adoption require approval of two-thirds of the members voting, providing such two-thirds constitutes a majority of members elected to that house. In the House, rules can be changed or suspended by unanimous consent or by a two-thirds vote of the total membership.[5]

Figure 20 shows two pages from the House rules book. As can be seen from this example, procedural rules govern most situations which might arise in the conduct of the legislature's business. Some state legislatures adopt a standard manual of parliamentary procedure (e.g., *Mason's Manual of Legislative Procedure*, *Robert's Rules of Order*, *Jefferson's Manual of Parliamentary Practice*) to deal with situations not provided for by state constitution, statutes, or their own rules. However, in Georgia's Senate, any questions not covered are to be controlled by "rules usually governing legislative bodies" (although no particular manual is specified).[6] House rules are silent, leaving rulings to the speaker's discretion.

This chapter looks at some of the most important rules of procedure of the two houses of the Georgia General Assembly. (The complete current rules of each house are published in the booklets supplied by the clerk or secretary.)

QUORUM

A quorum is the number of members of a body required to transact business officially in the absence of other members. The constitution of Georgia declares that a majority of the members of each house shall constitute a quorum of the General Assembly.

When there is no quorum, a small number can adjourn from day to day and take measures to compel the presence of the absent members.[7] If it is discovered that a quorum is not present, the roll is to be called and the absentees noted. A motion to this effect must first have been made and sustained by five members in the Senate or one-fifth of the members present in the House. The doors of the chamber are then supposed to be closed and the names of absentees called again. Those who do not appear at that time, and who are absent without leave, may, by order of a majority of the members present, be sent for and arrested by officers appointed by the messenger. The body may then determine upon what conditions these members are to be discharged.[8]

The rules of both houses also provide for the presiding officer to order the roll called and the vote taken by yeas and nays on any question where a division of the body discloses the fact that a quorum has not voted.[9]

Figure 20: Legislative Rules

Rule 74   DEBATE   Rule 82

chairman, to report the same back to the House, with the recommendation that the same _____ ("do pass," "do pass as amended," "do pass by substitute," or "do not pass," as the case may be).

The Speaker shall receive this report and repeat the same, and the matter shall then be before the House for action, just as though reported by any other committee.

Rule 75. Amendments offered to an amendment in the Committee of the Whole House shall not be reported to the House, but the report shall contain only the result of the committee's action on the bill, resolution, or measure under its consideration.

Rule 76. Amendments proposed by the Committee of the Whole House may be amended or rejected by the House, and matters stricken out by the committee may be restored by the House.

Rule 77. The proceedings of the Committee of the Whole House shall not be recorded on the journal of the House, except so far as reported to the House by the chairman of the committee.

DEBATE

Rule 78. When any member is about to speak in debate or deliver any matter to the House, such member shall rise from his or her seat and respectfully address himself or herself to "Mr. Speaker." No member shall be recognized by the Speaker unless the member is at his or her designated seat.

Rule 79. A member shall be confined to speaking on the matter in debate and shall not speak more than twice on any subject or more than once until every member choosing to speak shall have spoken.

Rule 80. No member of the House shall occupy the floor longer than one hour in debating any question unless otherwise ordered by the House. On the last three days of the session no member of the House shall occupy the floor longer than 20 minutes in debating any question unless otherwise ordered by the House. Any time allowed under Rule 125 shall be in addition to the time provided for in this rule. Any motion to limit or extend the time individual speeches shall be decided without debate. No such motion shall prevail unless it shall receive the affirmative votes of two-thirds of those voting, provided the total vote constitutes a quorum. Such motion may be made at any time that the movant thereof may legitimately obtain the floor.

Rule 81. If any member, in speaking or otherwise, transgresses the rules of the House, the Speaker shall call such member to order, in which case the member shall immediately sit down unless permitted to explain. If appealed to, the House shall sidecide whether to confirm the Speaker's action. If the transgressor refuses to submit to the decision of the House, the member shall be reprimanded for the first offense or fined in a sum not exceeding $100.00 for the second offense. If the member continues to refuse to abide by the decision of the House such member may be expelled from the House by a two-thirds' vote of the members. Such vote shall be taken by yeas and nays and recorded on the journal of the House.

Rule 82. If any member, excepted to shall be called to order for words spoken, the words excepted to shall be taken down in writing by the Clerk and read.

Rule 82   MOTIONS   Rule 86

The words excepted to shall then be admitted, denied, or explained by the member who spoke them. Thereupon, the question of order shall be decided and such other proceedings shall be conducted as the House may deem proper in regard thereto. If, at any time, the House is acting under the previous question, such question of order and other proceedings referred to shall not be taken up for decision until after the previous question and the main question have been disposed of, or until such future time as may then be ordered by the House. No member shall be held to answer or be subject to actions by the House for words spoken in debate if any other member has spoken or other business has intervened before the exception to the words is taken.

Rule 83. Except as otherwise stated in these rules, no member shall address the House or a member of the House or interrogate a member who is speaking, except through the Speaker. Should the member speaking decline to be interrupted, the Speaker shall cause the member desiring to interrogate to be silent.

Rule 84. No member shall refer in debate to any private conversation with another member.

Rule 85. In addressing any other member, a member may designate the other member by: "Mr.," "Mrs.," "Miss," or "Ms." plus the member's last name; or by the member's title, by his or her position on the floor, by the district he or she represents, by the county and city, or by the residence. Examples of acceptable ways to address members are: "Mr. Jones," "Mrs. Smith," "Ms. Smith," "Miss Smith," "the Representative from the First District," "Mr. Speaker Pro Tempore," "Mr. Administration Floor Leader," "Mr. Majority Leader," "the lady from DeKalb," "the Representative from Waycross," or "the gentleman from Macon."

MOTIONS

Rule 86. When any subject is before the House for consideration or under debate, no motion shall be received except the following:

(1) A motion to adjourn.

(2) A motion to lay on the table.

(3) A motion for the previous question.

(4) A motion to adjourn to a time definite.

(5) A motion to indefinitely postpone.

(6) A motion to postpone to a day certain or to a time certain if postponed to a later time on the same legislative day.

(7) A motion to commit.

(8) A motion to amend.

(9) A motion to print.

Such motions shall have precedence in the order named. After a motion is stated by the Speaker or read by the Clerk it shall be deemed to be in the possession of the House, but may by unanimous consent be withdrawn at

In many cases, no point is ever raised as to the lack of a quorum. In carrying out the opening business of a day's session and in voting on local bills and similar matters, both houses frequently ignore the lack of a quorum.

ORDER OF BUSINESS IN THE GENERAL ASSEMBLY

Each house of the General Assembly provides, in its rules, for the order in which it will conduct its business.

The daily order of business in the Senate is as follows:[10]

1. Report of the Committee on the Journal.
2. Reading of the journal.
3. Motions to reconsider.
4. Confirmations of the journal.
5. Introduction of bills and resolutions.
6. First reading and committee assignment of Senate bills and resolutions.
7. First reading and committee assignment of House bills and resolutions (also in order at any later time when no other business is pending).
8. Reports of standing committees.
9. Second reading of bills and resolutions.
10. Call of the roll.
11. Recitation of the Pledge of Allegiance.
12. Prayer of the chaplain.
13. Unanimous consents and points of personal privilege.
14. Adoption of privileged resolutions.
15. Motions to withdraw bills or resolutions from one committee and commit to another.
16. Passage of uncontested local bills and resolutions.
17. Consideration of contested local bills and resolutions.
18. General consent calendar for population bills.
19. General consent calendar for commemorative resolutions.
20. Third reading and consideration of general bills and resolutions.

Senate rules provide that the report of its Rules Committee and messages from the governor or the other house are in order at any time and may be received under any order of business.[11]

The rules of the House of Representatives set the following order of business:[12]

1. Call of the roll.

2. Scripture reading and prayer by the chaplain.
3. Pledge of Allegiance to the U.S. flag.
4. Report of the Committee on Journals.
5. Confirmation of the journal.
6. Unanimous consents.
7. Introduction of bills and resolutions.
8. First and second readings and committee assignment of House bills and resolutions.
9. Reports of standing committees.
10. Final reading and passage of uncontested local bills and resolutions.
11. First and second readings and committee assignment of Senate bills and resolutions.
12. Unfinished business of previous day's session.
13. Orders of the day.
14. Senate amendments to House bills and resolutions and reports of conference committees.
15. Motions to reconsider.
16. Points of personal privilege.
17. Third reading of bills and resolutions.

In both houses, all questions on the priority of business are decided by the presiding officers without debate.[13]

MOTIONS IN THE GENERAL ASSEMBLY

Although certain actions (e.g., reading of bills) occur automatically in each house and do not require initiation by a member, many of the most important actions require a motion from the floor.

A motion is a formal proposal made by a member to the presiding officer that some action or procedure requiring approval of the membership take place. The presiding officer then submits the motion to the full body for approval or rejection.

Various provisions in the rules of both houses of the Georgia General Assembly relate to motions in general:

1. No member can make more than one motion at a time; after offering a motion, the legislator must resume his or her seat, unless again recognized by the presiding officer.[14]
2. No member may speak on a question and then offer a motion to cut off debate without first relinquishing the floor.[15]

3. When a motion is made on the floor by any member, no second is necessary to put the motion before the body for a vote.[16]
4. In either chamber, after a motion has been stated by the presiding officer or read by the secretary or clerk, it is deemed to be in the possession of that body, but may be withdrawn by unanimous consent of that body at any time before being decided.[17]

To understand legislative procedure in the General Assembly, it is helpful to know the different types of motions that may be offered on the floor of each house. Many of these same motions can be utilized in committee meetings, but House and Senate rules only apply to their use during floor deliberation.

Precedence of motions in the two houses. Although dozens of motions can be found in the rules of each house, some of the most important apply to the stage between a bill's third reading and its final floor vote. To avoid the confusion that might result when different motions are before the body at the same time, each house has limited the number of motions that can be offered during a measure's floor consideration to nine. Moreover, the rules establish a specific order of precedence for these motions.[18] In order of priority, these motions are

1. motion to adjourn;
2. motion to lay on table;
3. motion for the previous question;
4. motion to adjourn to a time definite;
5. motion to indefinitely postpone;
6. motion to postpone to a day certain;
7. motion to commit;
8. motion to amend; and
9. motion to print.

The Motion to Adjourn

First in order of precedence is the simple *motion to adjourn*. This is one of two motions (the other being a *motion to adjourn to a time definite*) used during a session by each house to terminate legislative business for the day. (For a discussion of adjournment by concurrent resolution, see p. 54.)

Approval of the motion adjourns the House until the next legislative day and the Senate until the "next sitting day or time in course" which, unless a different time has been specified, is 10 a.m. on the next legislative day, excluding Sundays.[19] Adjournment of this type occurs independently in each house (meaning that each house concludes its daily business at different times) and does not suspend the count of legislative days for the session (as does adjournment through concurrent resolution).

The simple motion to adjourn is not debatable and cannot be amended.[20] Moreover, it can be made at any time by any member who can legitimately obtain the floor to offer the motion.[21]

There are, however, certain times when adjournment cannot take place. Once the call for the main question (i.e., a final vote on a measure) has been approved, a motion to adjourn is out of order if (1) the presiding officer has ordered that the voting machines be unlocked, (2) one vote in a voice roll call vote has been taken, or (3) a vote by division has been ordered and the hand count has begun.[22] In these situations, the motion to adjourn must await announcement of the final vote.

Two other restrictions limit the use of the motion to adjourn. In the House, once the call for the previous question has been approved, a motion to adjourn can only be made once.[23] In both houses, the motion cannot be made a second time "until further progress has been made in the business before the House (Senate)."[24]

Since the rules of each house are silent on the specific vote required for a motion to adjourn, the general requirements of each house control: a majority of a quorum voting in the Senate, and a majority of the membership in the House.[25]

The Motion to Lay on the Table

Ranking second in order of precedence in both houses is the *motion to lay on the table*. The rules of both houses state that, when this motion prevails, it removes the measure from the consideration of the House or Senate, together with all the motions attached to it at the time.[26]

The motion to lay on the table is usually made by a member who is opposed to the measure being considered. Sometimes, however, a member favoring a measure will deem it expedient to make a motion to table, lest the measure be defeated.

In neither house of the General Assembly is the motion to lay on the table, or the motion to take from the table, debatable or amendable.[27] This means that once the motion is made, an immediate vote on it ensues. Should it fail to carry, the motion can be renewed when new business has intervened between the votes.[28]

The rules of both houses prohibit the tabling of an amendment,[29] and Senate rules state that nothing can be legitimately laid upon the table that cannot be taken up again.[30] As an example, if a matter can be decided at a particular time but will be past deciding subsequently, it probably could not be legitimately tabled.

The motion to table is apparently in order at any time in both houses, except when the body has voted affirmatively that "the main question shall now be put."[31] In the House of Representatives, after the call for the previous question, a motion to lay on the table or a motion to adjourn may be made only once.[32]

To table a measure, a majority of a quorum voting is necessary.[33] However, the motion to table is not a final action. In both houses, a majority of a quorum can order that the measure be taken from the table if the body is not engaged on any other measure.[34] When removed from the table, the proposition is placed at the bottom of the calendar of bills then in order for a third reading in the Senate.[35] In the House, the measure remains in numerical order on the general calendar. During the last 21 days of the session, if a measure is tabled and then taken from the table on the same day, it remains on that day's rules calendar.[36] The rules of the two houses provide that this measure then stands before the body in the exact form, with all the motions pertaining to it, as it did when it was tabled.[37]

The Motion for the Previous Question

The *motion for the previous question* is designed to cut short the debate on a measure and to bring that measure, the "main question," to a vote. It has precedence over all other motions except those to adjourn and to lay on the table.[38]

The motion for the previous question may be stated by a member so that it applies only to a single motion or amendment; or it may be made to embrace all authorized motions, amendments, and the entire bill.[39]

Once the motion for the previous question is made, it is decided without debate.[40] The presiding officer states the motion to the body as two questions. The first is "Shall the motion for the previous question be sustained?" The rules of both houses provide that the question is to be decided by a majority of a quorum voting.[41] The presiding officer will then ask, "Shall the main question be now put?" If this question receives the required affirmative vote, then the bill under consideration is voted on by the body.[42]

The rules of both Senate and House provide that once the body has decided that the main question is to be put, no other motion is in order except one to reconsider the body's action. Even a motion to reconsider, however, is not in order when one vote has been given on a yea and nay vote, or when a division of the body has been held on a vote, or when the presiding officer has unlocked the electrical voting machine for a roll call vote.[43]

A motion to reconsider the ordering of the main question can be made only once, and its passage, in effect, repeals the ordering of both the previous and the main questions, leaving the bill under consideration open again to debate and amendment.[44]

If incidental questions of order arise after a motion for the previous question is made, they are decided without debate.[45]

The Motion to Adjourn to a Time Definite

The *motion to adjourn to a time definite* allows either house to terminate its business for a specified period of time, after which proceedings reconvene. The period of adjournment can be for less than an hour or up to three days. The constitution, however, prohibits either house from adjourning for more than three days without the consent of the other house.[46] This means that an adjournment for longer than three days can only be authorized through concurrent resolution.

The motion to adjourn to a time definite is a qualified version of the simple motion to adjourn and ranks fourth in the priority of motions. It differs from the simple motion in that it may be debated if made when the Senate and House are not actually engaged in other business. In both houses, it may be amended by substituting a day or time other than the one originally proposed.[47]

Because House and Senate rules are silent on the vote required for this motion, the general voting requirements of each apply—a majority of a quorum voting in the Senate and a majority of the membership in the House.[48]

The most frequent use of the motion to adjourn to a time definite is for daily adjournment of each house. Customarily, the majority leader in each house will offer the motion specifying the time for reconvening the next day. Usually, the motion will be to adjourn until 10 a.m. the next day, although adoption of a simple motion to adjourn would accomplish the identical result. Toward the end of a session, an earlier time for reconvening may be specified as the amount of business facing the house increases.

As a final note, neither House nor Senate rules provide for a motion to recess, nor is the presiding officer of either house given an express rule to declare a recess. Presumably, the proper procedure for taking a recess (e.g., for lunch) would be a motion to adjourn to a time definite. In practice, however, the presiding officer simply announces to the body that a recess will be taken and indicates the time for reconvening.

The Motion to Indefinitely Postpone

Next in order of precedence in both houses is the *motion to indefinitely postpone*. This seems to be the least used of all floor motions, with only four recorded instances of its use in the past 15 sessions.[49]

This motion offers an effective method of killing a bill being considered on the floor without allowing a vote on the bill's merits, since approval of the motion removes the measure from the floor for the remainder of the session.[50]

The motion to indefinitely postpone "lays open the whole question for debate," but itself is not amendable.[51] This means that not only can the motion itself be debated, but also anything related to the measure which it intends to indefinitely postpone. Approval of a majority of a quorum present and voting is necessary for the motion.[52] If the motion fails, however, it cannot be made again with regard to the same measure.[53]

Rules in both houses specify that the motion to indefinitely postpone takes precedence over, but cannot be applied to, the following motions:

(1) a motion to postpone to a day certain, (2) a motion to commit, and (3) a motion to amend. Further, the motion cannot be applied to incidental matters, such as points of order, reading reports or papers, withdrawal of a motion, or suspension of a rule.[54]

The Motion to Postpone to a Day Certain

The motion to postpone a measure to a day certain, when carried, removes the measure from the body's consideration until the time designated in the motion.

Unlike the motion to indefinitely postpone, the *motion to postpone to a day certain* does not lay open to debate the merits of the bill, resolution, or other measure being referred to. Debate is allowed on the motion itself, but both houses require that the debate be confined strictly to the proposition of postponement and to showing why one day is preferred over another.[55] Accordingly, the motion may be amended by substituting one day or time for another.[56]

The rules of the House require an affirmative vote by a majority of a quorum voting in order to carry the motion to postpone to a day certain.[57] As the Senate rules do not specify its vote requirement for the passage of this particular motion, its general voting requirement of a majority of a quorum voting applies.[58]

Should a senator make a motion to postpone to a day certain, but name a time beyond the session, the presiding officer is required to treat the motion as one to indefinitely postpone, and the rules on that type of motion would then apply. House rules declare a motion under such circumstances out of order.[59]

As is the case with the motion to indefinitely postpone, the motion to postpone to a day certain cannot be applied to subordinate or incidental questions, but only to the whole measure before the body.[60] House rules further declare that when this motion prevails, it also carries forward all amendments to the measure.[61]

If the motion to postpone a measure to a future day fails to carry when put to a vote, it cannot be renewed or made a second time on the same day.[62]

The motion to postpone consideration of a particular measure to a future day or time is used for a variety of reasons. Supporters of a bill about to be voted upon may feel that sufficient support is not present for the bill's passage. Rather than risk its defeat, they will seek postponement to gain time to build support. Opponents may seek the delay to give themselves time to build support for their side. The motion is also used to extend legislative courtesy among members. Should a measure come up before the body when its sponsor or a member known to be particularly interested in it is out of the chamber, a member may move that consideration of the measure be postponed until a time when the absent legislator can be present.

In the Senate, a bill or resolution postponed to a day certain takes its place at the bottom of the calendar under which the Senate is operating on the day to which postponed. After the 19th day of the session, if a measure is postponed for a second time, it is placed on the general (but not rules) calendar for the day to which it was postponed, which leaves the rules committee free to decide whether it will come before the full body.[63] House rules are silent on replacement of a postponed bill on the calendar of that body.

The Motion to Commit (or to Recommit)

The *motion to commit* (sometimes referred to as a *motion to recommit* if its purpose is to reassign a bill which has already been in one committee to the same or a different committee) is used to refer a bill or resolution to a particular standing (or special) committee, or to the Committee of the Whole of that house.[64]

On the day of introduction, all bills (and many resolutions) are assigned to the "proper" committee by the presiding officer. The assignment is discretionary with the president or speaker, and is not debatable, but may be challenged by the full body.[65] The author may disagree with the presiding officer's choice and wish to name the committee that would have jurisdiction of the bill. In such instance, a motion to commit—naming the desired committee—would be the proper procedure to overrule the initial assignment. It should be emphasized, however, that seldom do members challenge the presiding officer's initial committee assignment on the day of a bill's introduction. Almost always, a motion to commit or recommit is offered only after the first committee has had an opportunity to study the bill.

In both houses, a bill which has been referred to one committee may be recommitted to the same or to another committee upon approval of a majority of a quorum voting.[66] The House allows no debate on a motion to commit the bill, but Senate rules allow one senator three minutes to support the motion and one senator the same time to oppose it.[67] The Senate, however, allows instructions to be added to the motion to guide the committee which will receive the bill, and these instructions can be debated.[68]

A motion to commit or recommit may be amended in two ways. First, instructions may be added (in the Senate); second, another committee may be substituted for the one originally named in the motion.[69] However, in both houses a motion to commit to a Committee of the Whole takes precedence over a motion to commit to a standing committee.[70] Moreover, when either body is meeting as a Committee of the Whole, it is not in order to commit a matter to any other committee.[71]

Perhaps it would be well to illustrate how a measure might be recommitted. Assume that a bill that was referred to a standing committee on its first reading has been favorably reported back to the body and is now up for the third reading. Assume further, that in its debate and discussion of this bill, the body offers a large number of amendments to it. In this case, it might seem desirable to send the bill, with its amendments, back to the same or to another committee for reconsideration. A motion to commit, carried by a majority of those voting (provided the total vote constitutes a quorum), could be used to do this. The motion could, of course, include definite instructions to guide the committee in its consideration of the bill.

Because the motion to recommit, in effect, postpones the vote on a measure, it is sometimes used to prevent a measure's passage. For example, a member unfriendly to a particular bill may offer this motion to send the bill back to a committee, realizing that it will not be possible for the bill to get through the committee, back before the body, and passed before the end of the legislative session.

The Motion to Amend

An important part of the legislative process occurs during both committee and floor consideration, as bills and resolutions are "perfected" through use of the *motion to amend.* Few general bills emerge from the General Assembly without having been amended in one or both houses.

The rules of both the Senate and House specify three ways in which a measure may be amended. First, words may be inserted or added; second, words may be stricken; and third, words may be both stricken from and inserted in the measure.[72] An amendment itself may also be amended in these three ways, but the rules forbid amending an amendment to an amendment (except by unanimous consent in the House only).[73]

Germaneness of Amendments

Amendments are expected to relate directly to the matter under consideration, and both houses prohibit use of the motion to amend to introduce subject matter different from that under consideration.[74] The House specifically directs the speaker to rule out of order any amendment not germane to the measure before the House, while Senate rules direct the president to rule out of order any amendment obviously offered for the purpose of delay.[75] A similar fate awaits "irrelevant amendments" in either body.[76]

Legislators should be cautioned that adoption of nongermane amendments to a bill can later serve as grounds for the bill being declared unconstitutional because of multiple subject matter within a single act (see pp. 111-15).

Floor Substitutes

In some cases, a member may wish to offer an entire bill in the place of the one originally introduced and reported by committee. The new bill is known as a *floor substitute*, and does not have to be introduced, read, or referred to committee, but may be offered from the floor. The rules of both houses expressly classify a substitute as an amendment (so amendments to a substitute can be further amended).[77] In the Senate, no substitute can be offered to another substitute.[78]

An illustration explains the priority of voting on amendments and substitutes here. Suppose that one member of the legislature has proposed an amendment to a bill, and that another member has proposed a substitute for that same bill. Suppose that an amendment is then proposed to the substitute. The rules of both houses provide that, in this situation, the body first votes on the amendment to the original bill; second, on the amendment to the substitute; and finally, on the substitute, as amended, if the amendment was adopted. If the substitute fails to carry, a vote on the original bill follows. In the House only, if both a committee and floor substitute are offered on the same bill, a vote is taken first on the committee substitute.[79]

Legislative authorities often criticize the floor substitute because it provides a procedure for bypassing the committee system, and because it bypasses the various safeguards that ensure that legislators—and the public—know the language and effect of measures before the legislature. In some cases, "skeleton" bills with innocuous provisions have been introduced and referred to committee, and only after a bill is before the body for final voting are the substantive provisions added by substitute. Interestingly, with a substitute, the original bill number and author are retained, but the act may be changed so that there is little resemblance to the original bill. Sometimes, when this has happened, the bill's original author will take the floor to ask for the defeat of the bill (now changed through substitute).

Consideration of Floor Amendments

All motions to amend any matter before either house must be in writing and must plainly and distinctly state the language of the amendment and the part of the bill or resolution where the amendment is to be inserted or added.[80] The House has a procedure for handling amendments not used in the smaller Senate. Large screens are suspended in the front corners of the chamber for projecting amendments proposed during the floor debate on a measure. Handwritten or typed amendments can be projected onto the screens, enabling all members to read the proposed amendment and permitting the House to proceed immediately with floor debate and voting.

House and Senate rules provide that a member cannot offer an amendment to a measure after his or her house has agreed to the committee report on that measure, unless the body's agreement is reconsidered.[81] When a measure under consideration contains blanks, these blanks must be filled in before a motion can be made to amend the measure.[82] The reason for this rule, of course, is that once the blanks are filled in, the need for the amendment may not exist. Should several amendments be offered to the same measure, the last ones offered are voted on first in the House, while the process is reversed in the Senate. Actually, the rule as to priority of voting is quite broad. House rules provide that on all questions, whether in the House or in committee, "the last amendment, the most distant day, and the largest sum" shall be put first. Senate rules state that on all questions, whether in committee or in the Senate, "the first amendment, the most distant day, and the largest sum" are voted on first.[83]

A bill or resolution being amended is considered in two parts: first, the body of the bill, and second, its title. Senate rules provide that the title cannot be considered or amended until the body of a bill or resolution has been perfected.[84]

When a bill or resolution is in its final reading and a motion for division of a question has been made, the body may agree to consider it by sections or paragraphs. If this is done, the secretary or clerk, in reading the bill, is required to pause at the end of each section or paragraph, and the amendments to that section or paragraph must be offered at that time. Once a section or paragraph has been considered by the body, it is not in order to go back and amend it unless a motion to reconsider is adopted.[85] Further, the amendments to the bill or resolution which were offered by the committee to which it was referred are read by the secretary or clerk as a matter of course and without any motion being made.

A Senate rule provides that whenever a motion is made to amend a measure by striking out and adding certain provisions, the secretary must (1) read the paragraph as it is; (2) then read the words stricken out; and (3) read the whole paragraph as it would be if amended.[86] In the event that a motion is made to amend a measure by striking out a portion of it, and another motion is made to amend that portion of the bill proposed to be stricken for the purpose of perfecting it, the perfecting amendment is voted on first.[87]

House and Senate rules do not make reference to the voting requirement for approval of amendments in the house where a measure is introduced. Thus, the general voting requirements for each house apply—a majority of a quorum voting in the Senate, and a majority of the membership in the House.[88]

Amendments Made by the Other House

An important aspect of the amendment process concerns measures that are returned by the other house with amendments. A house may, of course, amend a measure sent to it by the other house. The amended measure is then returned to the house where it originated. The originating house may amend the other house's amendments and return the measure to that body.

But the originating house's amendments to the amendments of the other house cannot further be amended. The other house must simply accept or reject the amendments made to its amendments by the originating house.[89] If agreement cannot be obtained, a conference committee may be appointed to attempt to work out a compromise measure acceptable to both houses.

Assume that a bill originates in the House of Representatives and is passed by that body. It will then go to the Senate. There the Senate passes the bill with amendments. The bill will then be returned to the House of Representatives, which will then consider the amendments to the measure that have been made by the Senate. The House may, of course, accept these amendments, and the amended measure will then be transmitted to the governor. On the other hand, the House may amend the amendments made by the Senate, in which case, the bill is returned to the Senate. The House, however, may not amend its amendments to the Senate amendments.

Rules of both the Senate and House list the following motions as those which can be used regarding amendments made by the other house to its bills or resolutions. In order of precedence, they are

1. motion to amend an amendment of the other house;
2. motion to agree to the amendments of the other house;
3. motion to disagree to the amendments of the other house;
4. motion to recede from its disagreement or amendment; and
5. motion to insist on its disagreement or amendment.[90]

The Senate has one additional motion—to adhere to its disagreement or amendment—which ranks sixth in priority.[91]

The rules of the House of Representatives further provide that, when any question of disagreement with the Senate arises, the motions which are in order are (1) a motion to insist upon the House position, and (2) a motion to recede from the House position. A member can make either of these motions at any time he or she can legally obtain the floor. The motions are put to the House by the presiding officer in the order in which they are listed above, "subject to disposition by the House of any amendments affecting the matter in disagreement."[92]

The rules of each house authorize its presiding officer, when in his or her opinion an amendment made by the other body to a bill which originated in the presider's house is not germane, to rule out that amendment.[93] The presider may do this without a motion from the floor upon a point of order being made by a member. This point of order takes precedence over a motion to agree. If the presiding officer does rule out the other house's amendment on these grounds and is not overruled by an appeal from the floor, the action is considered the same as a vote by the house to disagree to the amendment.[94]

The rules of the Senate and the House of Representatives provide that the vote for the adoption of a House amendment to a Senate measure, or a Senate amendment to a House measure, must be by a majority of the membership.[95] This is, likewise, the vote requirement for adoption of a conference committee report.[96]

It might be noted that the author or proponents of a measure often announce to the body their acceptance of particular amendments. Such an announcement often forestalls or ends debate on the amendment.

The Motion to Print

Last in the order of precedence of motions applicable during floor consideration of bills and resolutions is the *motion to print*. This action allows a majority of a quorum in a house to suspend action during the time amendments are being offered on the floor so that amendments and substitutes to a pending measure can be printed and distributed to each member.[97] Although amendments must be submitted in written form to the clerk or secretary to be read before voting takes place, a member may feel that because of the length or number of amendments it is important to see the text of the amendment or substitute. This can be especially important in the Senate, which unlike the House, does not have the large screens within the chamber that allow the language of each amendment to be seen.

Other Motions

Although the rules of each house provide that when any subject is before the body for consideration or under debate no motion can be received except for the nine motions discussed above, other motions are in fact also used.[98] They are discussed in this section.

The Motion to Reconsider

Potentially, one of the most important motions to affect the legislative process is the *motion to reconsider*. This motion allows a legislative body to rescind its "final" action on a measure and, in effect, take a new vote. This has meant in some cases that a bill is passed on the floor of a house one day, only to be defeated the next day (usually following late-hour politicking) after a motion to reconsider.

According to traditional parliamentary practice, the motion to reconsider was used as a device to perfect a bill that had passed, as when a defect was discovered after a bill's approval. Reconsideration was not intended to give bills which were defeated on the floor a second chance.

While many states still maintain this restriction on the use of reconsideration, in Georgia, both approved and defeated bills can be reconsidered. Moreover, any member can move to reconsider action on a measure, regardless of having initially voted for or against it.[99]

The reconsideration process is sometimes confusing because it involves three steps: (1) giving notice that a motion for reconsideration will be made at a later time; (2) raising the motion for reconsideration, at which time a vote is taken on the motion; and (3) if the motion passes, placing the measure back on the calendar and taking a new vote.

Both houses have strict rules that any member desiring reconsideration must first give the body notice of intention to move for reconsideration. Such notice must be given during the legislative day that a vote is taken on a measure for which reconsideration is desired.[100] In actual practice, this notice is usually given immediately following a vote. For example, following the defeat of a bill, a member will say, "Mr. President, I give notice that at the proper time, I will move to reconsider the action of the Senate in defeating Senate Bill 412." The body then passes on to other business, but with the knowledge that a motion for reconsideration will later be made. Once this notice has been given, it can be withdrawn only on the same day it is given in the House. It cannot be withdrawn in the Senate.[101]

Although many members may desire reconsideration of a bill or resolution, it is only necessary that one legislator give notice to seek it. However, when it is time for the motion to be raised, any member—and not just the person who gave notice—may raise the motion.

When notice has been given, the time for making the motion to reconsider occurs during the morning order of business on the following legislative day (with certain exceptions noted below). Senate rules provide that the motion be made immediately following the reading of the journal of the preceding day's happenings, but prior to confirmation of the journal. At this time, a motion can be made to reconsider any matter which the journal contains, except those which have been previously reconsidered or transmitted to the House.[102] In the House, motions to reconsider are to be made immediately preceding the time for members to rise on point of personal privilege.[103]

In both houses, the motion to reconsider requires approval of a majority of a quorum voting. If the motion is adopted, the bill is placed back on the calendar for a new vote. In the House, the bill takes its place in numerical order on the general calendar, along with any substitute and all amendments that were a part of such bill when the motion to reconsider was passed.[104] In the Senate, during the first 19 days of the session, all bills and resolutions reconsidered take their place at the foot of the general calendar. During the last 21 days, however, bills for reconsideration that had previously passed on the Senate floor are placed at the foot of the *rules calendar*, while bills that had previously been defeated are placed at the foot of the *general calendar*.[105]

There are exceptions to these general rules. In the House, if the action to be reconsidered occurs on the 33d day of the session (the last day for transmitting general bills and resolutions for introduction in the Senate must occur before the transaction of other business) or on any of the last 3 days of a session, reconsideration may occur on the same day.[106] When the action to be reconsidered occurs on the last legislative day of the week, the motion to reconsider should be made on the following Monday or, if the House will not be in session, on the next legislative day. In the Senate, during the last 3 days of the session, and on the 33d day, notice of intention to move to reconsider must be given immediately following a vote. The presiding officer must then set a time during that day when the motion will be voted upon. Such time can be at the presiding officer's discretion, but must allow at least 10 minutes following notice.[107]

In either house, reconsideration of the vote on an amendment to a measure may take place at any time before final action is taken upon the section, bill, or resolution to which the amendment relates. Additionally, in the House, reconsideration of House actions on Senate amendments must take place immediately.[108]

The presiding officer's ordering of the main question in preparation for a final vote can also be reconsidered. However, the motion must be made prior to the unlocking of the voting machines, to the first vote cast in a voice roll call vote, or to a hand count begun of a vote by division.[109] Adoption of the motion to reconsider effectively repeals the ordering of both the main and previous questions, thus reopening the floor for debate and amendment on the pending measure. The motion can only be made once, and if defeated, the presiding officer can again order the main question.[110]

So that motions to reconsider do not indefinitely postpone the legislative process, both houses limit reconsideration to one for each "matter" in the Senate and "bill, resolution, or amendment" in the House.[111]

The Motion for Division of a Question

When an involved question, and one which contains parts which may readily be separated, is before either house for consideration, legislators sometimes want to discuss and consider the question by part rather than as a whole. To make this possible, the rules of both houses provide that any member may make a *motion for division of a question* on a subject which, in the opinion of the presiding officer, is one which may be divided.[112]

The member calling for this division must state into how many and exactly what parts the question should be divided. Each part of the divided proposition must be so distinct that, if it were taken away, the remainder of the question could stand by itself and be consistent and entire.[113] The rules of the House of Representatives include some examples which illustrate failures to meet this requirement. They indicate that a qualifying

paragraph, an exception, and a proviso are not distinct or entire parts which could be divided from the remainder of a measure. House rules also state that, when amending a measure on the floor, no member may call for a division of the question on a motion "to strike out and insert."[114]

The burden of determining whether the requirements for the division of a particular question are met is cast upon the presiding officer, who is allowed wide discretion in the determination.

COMMITTEE OF THE WHOLE

The entire House of Representatives or Senate can make up what is known as the Committee of the Whole House or the Committee of the Whole Senate. These committees are devices used by the two bodies to relax some of the formal rules, thus allowing more informal discussion and prompt action on important bills.

In actuality, the Committee of the Whole is the entire membership of either the House or Senate sitting under a different name. The rules of both houses contain separate provisions which apply to the actions of each body when meeting as a Committee of the Whole.

When used. The House rules provide that all appropriation bills shall be considered in the Committee of the Whole House,[115] but the rules of the Senate do not explicitly state conditions under which the Senate must meet as a Committee of the Whole Senate.

The speaker may resolve the House into a Committee of the Whole, without the necessity for a motion from the floor to that effect.[116] The rules of the Senate do not grant this same power to the president of the Senate.

The House or Senate may resolve itself into a Committee of the Whole if a motion is made to that effect and passed by a vote of a majority of a quorum, and when one day's notice of the intention to make the motion has been given. If the member making the motion has not given one day's notice of his or her intention to do so, an affirmative vote of two-thirds of those voting is required to pass the motion. The two-thirds must equal a majority of the total membership of the House or Senate.[117] For considering the general appropriations bill in the House, however, no previous notice is necessary; the House may resolve itself into a Committee of the Whole by the vote of a majority of a quorum, on a motion to that effect.[118]

Both houses limit individual speeches on the motion for the Committee of the Whole to three minutes.[119]

In the event that the House or Senate should refer a measure to the Committee of the Whole and then a motion to resolve the body into the committee should fail, the motion cannot be renewed. If the motion fails, the speaker or the president is required, on the following day, to have the measure reintroduced and to refer it to the appropriate committee, unless otherwise ordered by the House or Senate.[120]

Procedures when in operation. When a Committee of the Whole is formed, the speaker or president leaves the chair and appoints another legislator to preside.[121] In the House, the speaker is then free to take part in the proceedings and the speaker, as well as all other members, must vote on all questions which come before the committee, unless excused from doing so.[122] The president of the Senate (lieutenant governor) does not take part in the proceedings of the Committee of the Whole or vote on matters arising in such session.

The Committee of the Whole is prohibited from punishing disorderly conduct of its members but must report the behavior for action by the House or the Senate in regular session.[123] The chairperson of the committee, however, does have the power to clear the galleries or lobbies in case of disorderly conduct there.[124] It can be inferred from this rule that meetings of the Committee of the Whole in the two houses are generally open to the public.

As to procedure in the Committee of the Whole, the rules of the House of Representatives or of the Senate are followed with the following specified exceptions:

1. The Committee of the Whole cannot refer a matter to any other committee;
2. it cannot adjourn;
3. the previous question cannot be enforced;
4. a motion to lay on the table or indefinitely postpone is not in order;
5. a member may speak as often as he or she may obtain the floor;
6. no call of the House or of the Senate is in order; and
7. no vote can be taken by yeas and nays.[125]

Senate rules provide that in the Committee of the Whole, the secretary must first read the bill under consideration in its entirety, after which it is then read or debated by clauses or sections, with the title the last portion to be considered. This procedure may be otherwise ordered by the body.[126]

When, during a meeting of the committee, a vote on a question discloses that a quorum of the House or the Senate is not present, the committee cannot proceed with its business.[127] Further, upon the suggestion that a quorum is lacking, the chairperson must make an actual count. If he or she finds that a quorum is lacking, he or she must order that the committee immediately rise and report absence of a quorum to the House or the Senate in regular session.[128]

If, at some stage in the committee's proceedings in the Senate or House, it is desired to close the debate on a question or to limit the members' speaking time, the committee may rise and report this desire to the

Senate or House in regular session (the chairperson making the report to the president or speaker). The Senate acts on a motion or resolution to close or limit the debate, after which it may resolve itself again into a Committee of the Whole. If the motion or resolution is passed, it limits the debate only on the subject matter then before the committee.[129] The House rules only provide for it to take action as it sees fit.[130]

The rules expressly provide that the motion to reconsider may be used by members in the Committee of the Whole just as in the House or the Senate itself.[131]

When the body is meeting as a Committee of the Whole, a member may call for any papers which are in possession of his or her house and have them read for the information of the committee, unless, for some reason, the committee orders otherwise.[132]

A motion to adjourn cannot be made in the Committee of the Whole. In the event that the Committee of the Whole does not have enough time at one sitting to finish its business, a motion may be made "that the committee rise, report progress (to the House or Senate in formal session), and ask leave to sit again." As is true of a motion to adjourn in a formal session of the House or the Senate, this motion may be made at any time the member so moving can legitimately obtain the floor. It takes precedence over all other motions and is decided without debate.[133]

Should a predetermined hour of adjournment of the House or Senate arrive while its members are sitting as a Committee of the Whole, the committee then, without motion, automatically rises and the speaker or the president assumes the chair.[134]

The proceedings of the Committee of the Whole are not recorded in the *House Journal* or the *Senate Journal* except as reported to the House or the Senate by the chairperson.[135] The report contains only the result of the committee's action on the measure under consideration.[136] This limited recording of transactions in the Committee of the Whole is designed to promote greater freedom of discussion than occurs when the House or the Senate is officially in session.

After business is completed. When the committee completes the business before it, it rises and the chairperson is instructed to report the committee's action to the House or to the Senate in formal session, with the speaker or the president in the chair. The chairperson states to the speaker or president that the committee has had a certain measure under consideration and reports it back with the recommendation that it (1) pass; (2) pass as amended; (3) pass by substitute (House only); or (4) not pass.[137] The report of the Committee of the Whole has precedence over all other committee reports in both the House of Representatives and the Senate.[138] The speaker or the president repeats this report, and the matter is then before the House or the Senate for action "just as though reported by any other committee."[139]

It should be emphasized that a measure cannot be passed in the Committee of the Whole. Like any other committee, it can only report recommendations to the House or the Senate. Obviously, the action taken on a measure by all members sitting as a Committee of the Whole is likely to be the action taken by these same members sitting in formal session. But only in formal session can a measure be passed by the House of Representatives or by the Senate.

As is true in the case of a measure reported by other committees, amendments to a measure which are offered by the Committee of the Whole may be further amended or rejected by the House or Senate. Likewise, the House or the Senate may restore to a measure matters which were stricken by the committee.[140]

JOINT SESSIONS

Joint sessions are utilized for (1) the governor's annual "State of the State" address and budget message; (2) guest speakers who have been invited to address the General Assembly; and (3) electing any state officers the legislature is required by law to elect.[141] Additionally, the two houses may meet in joint session from time to time for other purposes as deemed necessary.

Procedures. To meet in joint session, both houses pass a concurrent resolution designating the day and hour of the session, at which time members of the Senate leave their chamber and go to the House.[142] There, the House doorkeeper announces their arrival to the speaker, who orders that they be allowed to enter. The president of the Senate then proceeds to the speaker's rostrum, assumes the task of presiding officer and announces that the General Assembly is in joint session. All questions regarding the order of business are decided by the president, unless overruled by the whole General Assembly. If the president of the Senate is absent, the presiding officer of the joint session would be the speaker of the House; if absent, the president pro tempore; if absent, the speaker pro tempore.[143]

A majority of the total membership of each house is necessary to constitute a quorum for the joint session.[144] Apparently, this rule is not strictly followed when no vitally important business is to be transacted.

The first thing that the presiding officer does is to have the joint resolution convening the two houses read.[145]

If there is an election to be carried out in joint session, it is not necessary to second a nomination. The presiding officer takes the vote by roll call, and a majority vote of the entire membership of the General Assembly is necessary.[146] Members cannot change their vote unless they rise and state that they voted by mistake or that their vote was recorded by mistake.[147] During the course of the business in connection with elections, no debate is allowed except on questions of order.[148]

Two motions may be made to end a meeting in joint session: "that the joint session of the General Assembly be now dissolved" or "that the joint session of the General Assembly be now dissolved to be reconvened at (a time named)." Of the two, the latter motion has precedence.[149] Either of these terminating motions is always in order, unless a roll call vote has begun. Then, it is not in order until the presiding officer has declared the result of the vote.[150]

When either of these terminating motions has been carried, the presiding officer declares the joint session dissolved, and the Senate members retire from the House. If the motion fails to carry, it cannot be made again until other business has intervened.[151]

The rules governing the procedure of the General Assembly meeting in joint session may be amended by concurrent resolution of the two houses, and when either house notifies the other of the withdrawal of its consent to any rule, that rule ceases to be in force.[152]

ENDNOTES

1. GA. CONST. art. 3, §4, ¶4.
2. Senate Rule 217; House Rule 34.
3. Senate Rule 217; House Rule 33.
4. Senate Rule 217.
5. Senate Rule 34; House Rule 33.
6. Senate Rule 216.
7. GA. CONST. art. 3, §4, ¶3.
8. Senate Rule 48; House Rule 44.
9. Senate Rule 22; House Rule 20.
10. Senate Rule 28.
11. Senate Rule 37.
12. House Rule 27.
13. Senate Rule 19; House Rule 17.
14. Senate Rule 65; House Rule 87.
15. Senate Rule 66; House Rule 88.
16. Senate Rule 64; House Rule 86. In the Senate, however, there is a specific rule that all motions in *standing committees* must have a second (Senate Rule 187).
17. Senate Rule 63; House Rule 86.
18. Senate Rule 62; House Rule 86.
19. Senate Rules 72, 42; House Rules 156, 39.
20. Senate Rule 70; House Rule 154.
21. Senate Rule 68; House Rule 152.
22. Senate Rule 69; House Rule 153.
23. House Rule 124.
24. Senate Rule 70; House Rule 154.
25. Senate Rule 167; House Rule 129.
26. Senate Rule 81; House Rule 96.

27. Senate Rule 79; House Rule 94.

28. Senate Rule 80; House Rule 95.

29. Senate Rule 78; House Rule 93.

30. Senate Rule 77.

31. Senate Rule 76; House Rule 92.

32. House Rule 124.

33. Senate Rule 167; House Rule 97.

34. Senate Rule 82; House Rule 97.

35. Senate Rule 81.

36. House Rule 96.

37. Senate Rule 81; House Rule 96.

38. Senate Rule 160; House Rule 124.

39. Senate Rule 157; House Rule 122.

40. Senate Rule 160; House Rule 124.

41. Ibid.

42. Senate Rule 164; House Rule 127.

43. Senate Rule 160; House Rule 124.

44. Senate Rule 165; House Rule 128.

45. Senate Rule 163; House Rule 126.

46. GA. CONST. art. 3, §4, ¶1(b).

47. Senate Rule 71; House Rule 155.

48. Senate Rule 167; House Rule 129.

49. Final Composite Status Sheets for 1980 through 1994 prepared by the clerk of the House and secretary of the Senate.

50. Senate Rule 86; House Rule 98.

51. Senate Rule 84; House Rule 100.

52. Senate Rule 86; House Rule 98.

53. Senate Rule 85; House Rule 98.

54. Senate Rule 83; House Rule 99.

55. Senate Rule 88; House Rule 102.

56. Senate Rule 87; House Rule 103.

57. House Rule 106.

58. Senate Rule 167.

59. Senate Rule 87; House Rule 104.

60. Senate Rule 87; House Rule 101.

61. House Rule 101.

62. Senate Rule 88; House Rule 105.

63. Senate Rule 88.

64. Senate Rule 89; House Rule 89. Rules of both houses note that a bill or resolution can be recommitted to a standing or special committee, or the Committee of the Whole. In practice, neither house assigns bills to special committees as such. Only standing committees and the Committee of the Whole consider and report on measures during a session.

65. Senate Rule 115; House Rule 53.

66. Senate Rule 93; House Rule 91.

67. Senate Rule 91; House Rule 89.

68. Senate Rule 91.

69. Senate Rule 92; House Rule 89.
70. Senate Rule 90; House Rule 90.
71. Senate Rule 125; House Rule 64.
72. Senate Rule 138; House Rule 107.
73. Ibid.
74. Senate Rule 145; House Rule 110.
75. Senate Rule 141; House Rule 110.
76. Ibid.
77. Senate Rule 139; House Rule 108.
78. Senate Rule 148.
79. Senate Rule 143; House Rule 112.
80. Senate Rule 140; House Rule 109.
81. Senate Rule 149; House Rule 116.
82. Senate Rule 142; House Rule 111.
83. Senate Rule 146; House Rule 114.
84. Senate Rule 147.
85. Senate Rule 151; House Rule 117.
86. Senate Rule 150.
87. Senate Rule 144; House Rule 113.
88. Senate Rule 167; House Rule 129.
89. Senate Rule 154; House Rule 120.
90. Senate Rules 152, 153; House Rules 118, 119.
91. Senate Rule 152.
92. House Rule 118.
93. Senate Rule 152; House Rule 118.
94. Ibid.
95. Senate Rule 155; House Rule 121.
96. Senate Rule 156; House Rule 146.
97. Senate Rule 110; House Rule 49.
98. Senate Rule 62; House Rule 86.
99. Senate Rule 94; House Rule 143.
100. Ibid.
101. Ibid.
102. Senate Rules 28, 94.
103. House Rules 27, 143.
104. House Rule 145.
105. Senate Rule 97.
106. House Rule 143.
107. Senate Rule 94.
108. Senate Rule 95; House Rule 143.
109. Senate Rule 160; House Rule 124.
110. Senate Rule 165; House Rule 128.
111. Senate Rule 96; House Rule 144.
112. Senate Rule 158; House Rule 123.
113. Senate Rule 159; House Rule 123.
114. House Rule 123.

115. House Rule 59.
116. House Rule 60.
117. Senate Rule 121; House Rule 61.
118. House Rule 61.
119. Senate Rule 121; House Rule 61.
120. Ibid.
121. Senate Rule 122; House Rule 62.
122. House Rule 66.
123. Senate Rule 130; House Rule 69.
124. Senate Rule 129; House Rule 68.
125. Senate Rule 125; House Rule 64.
126. Senate Rule 124.
127. Senate Rule 123; House Rule 63.
128. Ibid.
129. Senate Rule 131.
130. House Rule 70.
131. Senate Rule 126; House Rule 65.
132. Senate Rule 128; House Rule 67.
133. Senate Rules 132, 133; House Rules 71, 72.
134. Senate Rule 133; House Rule 73.
135. Senate Rule 137; House Rule 77.
136. Senate Rule 135; House Rule 75.
137. Senate Rule 134; House Rule 74.
138. Senate Rule 120; House Rule 57.
139. Senate Rule 134; House Rule 74.
140. Senate Rule 136; House Rule 76.
141. Joint Session Rule 1.
142. Joint Session Rule 2.
143. Joint Session Rule 3.
144. Joint Session Rule 4.
145. Joint Session Rule 3.
146. Joint Session Rules 5, 7.
147. Joint Session Rule 8.
148. Joint Session Rule 6.
149. Joint Session Rule 9.
150. Joint Session Rule 10.
151. Joint Session Rules 11, 12.
152. Joint Session Rule 13.

9 Legislative Staff and Resources

This section describes briefly the major kinds of resources and staff services available to the Georgia General Assembly, in addition to those noted in chapters 2 and 4.

LEGISLATIVE RESOURCES

Legislative Services Committee

The Legislative Services Committee is a special joint statutory committee that oversees the administration and management of the General Assembly. Since it is not a standing committee of the legislature, no bills are referred to it.

The committee may study and adopt methods and procedures for more efficient and uniform operation of both houses of the General Assembly, as well as provide for necessary services to the legislative branch. Additionally, it has complete authority over the assignment of rooms, chambers, offices, and other areas on the third and fourth floors of the state capitol, and on the mezzanine between these floors.[1]

The Legislative Services Committee is composed of 14 members: the speaker of the House (chair); president of the Senate; chairs of the House and Senate appropriations committees; chairs of the House and Senate judiciary committees; chair of the Senate Banking and Financial Institutions Committee; chair of the House Ways and Means Committee; president pro tempore of the Senate; speaker pro tempore of the House; the majority leaders of the House and Senate; clerk of the House; and secretary of the Senate (secretary for the committee). Members receive no compensation for service on the committee during legislative sessions; but, for interim meetings, they are entitled to the standard allowances authorized for other interim legislative committees.[2]

Office of Legislative Counsel

Under direction of the Legislative Services Committee, the Office of Legislative Counsel provides a variety of reference, counseling, and legislative drafting services to members of the General Assembly.

Upon request, this office will advise legislators on proposed legislation, prepare a draft bill, or review legislation prepared by the legislator. Communications between this office and legislators is privileged and confidential and not subject to the state's open records requirements.[3] Both during and between sessions, the counsel's professional staff (which includes attorneys and nonlegal specialists) advises committees and officers of the General Assembly, assisting in the preparation of their reports and recommendations. The staff researches a variety of legislative matters, upcoming policy issues, and related subjects for members, officers, and committees of the legislature. At the conclusion of each legislative session, the counsel's office publishes a summary of the general statutes enacted that year. More importantly, the office is responsible for compiling, indexing, editing, and publishing the text of the acts and general resolutions passed at that session.

The legislative counsel's office serves as staff for the Code Revision Commission, which has broad authority over revising, updating, correcting errors in, and publication of the Official Code of Georgia Annotated.[4] Additionally, the office renders opinions and provides other legal services for the legislative branch and, with approval of the Legislative Services Committee or the speaker of the House, represents the legislative branch and its interests in court litigation, with power to engage the services of others, including private counsel, to assist in these duties.[5]

Georgia law directs the attorney general to act as advisor to this office, and, on occasion, attorneys from both offices will work together.[6] While the attorney general can issue official opinions on matters of law only to the governor, lieutenant governor, and heads of departments in the executive branch, unofficial opinions will be issued to legislators on request.

Finally, the counsel's office serves as a major contact point with the Council of State Governments, National Conference of State Legislatures, and other states for the exchange of information, data, and other materials relating to Georgia law and the General Assembly.

The legislative counsel is elected by a majority vote of the total membership of the Legislative Services Committee. He or she must be an attorney experienced in legislative matters and bill drafting.[7]

Legislative Fiscal Officer

The Office of Legislative Fiscal Officer was established to oversee and centralize expenditures and fiscal accounting within the legislative branch.

Acting as bookkeeper and comptroller for the General Assembly, the fiscal officer maintains accounts of legislative expenditures and commitments. This office oversees the payment of legislative salaries, allowances, and travel expenses, and approves all purchases of supplies and other materials for the General Assembly. (Payments for expenditures over $5,000 need prior approval by the Legislative Services Committee.) The fiscal officer must prepare and sign all vouchers and warrants for expenditures of funds and make all payments from funds appropriated to the legislature. Additionally, he or she maintains an inventory of the equipment, furnishings, and nonexpendable items belonging to the legislative branch. The fiscal officer and staff are employed by the Legislative Services Committee and may be entrusted with other duties by that committee.[8]

Legislative Budget Analyst

The Office of Legislative Budget Analyst was created to give the legislature fiscal expertise of its own so that it would not have to rely exclusively on the executive branch for revenue estimates, spending projections, and departmental budgetary needs.

The budget analyst, employed by the Legislative Services Committee, assists the General Assembly and its committees—particularly the House and Senate appropriations committees—with appropriations and budgetary matters. During the initial stages of budget preparation, this office works with the Office of Planning and Budget and with legislative leaders, analyzing agency budget requests both before and after review by the governor's office. All state agencies are required to furnish any information and material that the analyst needs. The budget analyst is also present during all legislative deliberations over state appropriations.[9]

In addition, the budget analyst's office provides members of the General Assembly with independent analyses of tax measures under consideration. Following each session, the office attempts to see that departments and agencies spend the money as budgeted.

Except for the university system, any state agency must notify the legislative budget analyst of intention to apply for any new program of federal assistance. The budget analyst is then required to prepare an analysis of the program's short- and long-range impact on state budgetary and fiscal matters.[10]

Budgetary Responsibility Oversight Committee

In an effort to strengthen its capacity to oversee the budgetary process, the General Assembly enacted the Budget Accountability and Planning Act of 1993. One of the most significant changes in the law was creation of a special legislative committee known as the Budgetary Responsibility Oversight Committee. The committee consists of five members from each house appointed by the respective presiding officers for 2-year terms.

Members are appointed within 10 days of the convening of the session in each even-numbered year. To assist in its responsibilities, the committee has a full-time director and staff.

The committee is required to consult with the governor and the Office of Planning and Budget (OPB) with respect to the state's strategic planning process, which involves a long-range state plan (updated at least annually) and individual agency plans that contribute to the state plan (see p. 215). Once OPB approves state and agency plans, state law requires the plans to be sent to the Budgetary Responsibility Oversight Committee for review and evaluation.[11]

In 1993, the General Assembly established a process for an ongoing review and evaluation of all state programs and functions, with the intent that every state program be evaluated at least once every 10 years. Within 15 days of the end of a legislative session, the presiding officers of both houses send to the governor a list of state programs they would like to see evaluated. OPB and the state auditor's staff then work together to complete as many audits as resources permit. By August 31 of each year, they must report their findings to the Budgetary Responsibility Oversight Committee for review and evaluation.[12] Additionally, the committee can request a performance audit of any agency as it deems necessary.[13]

When any state agency plans to initiate any new program that will require a state appropriation, that agency must report to the committee by September 1 prior to the session at which funds will be requested. The report must contain a description, rationale, and plan for operating the program, plus an explanation of how the program conforms to the state and agency's strategic plan, and the extent to which the program's facilities and staff will be decentralized.[14] Committee members must also be furnished with the projected cost to fully implement the proposed program. The committee then uses this information to decide whether to recommend funding of the proposed program.

One of the budgetary changes enacted in 1993 requires OPB to produce a "continuation budget report" covering at least 20 percent of state agencies. By May 1 of each year, OPB must consult with the chair of the Budgetary Responsibility Oversight Committee to determine which agencies will undergo OPB's detailed analysis of their purposes, programs, and accomplishments in relation to the funding approved for the fiscal year in which the examination takes place. The committee is responsible for taking OPB's continuation budget report and the audit report for the fiscal year just ended and determining what, if any, recommendations should be made to the full membership of the General Assembly. This report must be submitted within the first week of the next legislative session.[15]

Georgia's constitution prohibits expenditure of state funds unless authorized by an appropriation act.[16] However, state agencies are involved in numerous programs funded by federal grants or contracts, and it is not uncommon for new sources of funding to become available after an appropriation act has been enacted. State law therefore directs that all federal funds received by the state are "continually appropriated in the exact amounts and for the purposes authorized and directed by the federal government in making the grant."[17] Each year, however, OPB must report to the Budgetary Responsibility Oversight Committee on any funds received and spent by state agencies that were not contemplated when the appropriation act was approved.[18]

In performing its duties, the committee can request information or reports from OPB or any agency receiving a state appropriation, and such agencies are directed by law to cooperate.[19] Each year, the committee is directed to issue a report to the General Assembly and governor on its activities and findings. The committee's chair is also directed to provide a written executive summary of the annual report to each legislator prior to the adoption of the general appropriations act.[20]

Fiscal Affairs Subcommittee

Although a fiscal affairs subcommittee is provided for each house, the primary functions of each are performed through joint meetings as the Fiscal Affairs Subcommittee. The subcommittee meets at least once each quarter, or more often at the governor's call, to review and approve budget object transfers recommended by the governor. Such transfers require the approval of at least 11 of the 20 members on the subcommittee. The two subcommittees may also meet as one at the call of the Senate president, speaker of the House, or of their own subcommittee chairs.[21]

In each house, the fiscal affairs subcommittee consists of four reelected members of the Appropriations Committee appointed by the presiding officer, the presiding officer, and five reelected members of that house selected by the governor. These subcommittees are authorized to review budget requests of the various departments and agencies at any time, with the Office of Planning and Budget, state auditor, and each department or agency directed to promptly furnish them with any requested information. The joint subcommittee must report annually to the legislature on matters coming to its attention and make recommendations for improving the efficiency of the operation and management of various state agencies.[22]

Senate Administrative Affairs Committee

This committee is responsible for (1) employing, supervising, and setting the compensation for all Senate aides, secretaries, and other personnel, including those of the Senate Research and Senate Public Information offices; and (2) supervising the purchase and allotment of Senate supplies. The committee is composed of the president of the Senate, president pro tempore, chair of the Rules Committee, secretary of the Senate, and four members appointed jointly by the president of the Senate, the president pro tempore, and the Rules Committee chair.[23]

Senate Research Office

The Senate Research Office, located in Room 204 of the Legislative Office Building, serves as an information research and resource center for all senators. The office has a full-time director, seven full-time policy analysts, and one research assistant who provide assistance to standing and interim study committees as well as to senators on an individual basis. The office maintains resource files and a library of current periodicals and publications on legislative issues.

House Research Office

The House Research Office, located in Room 205A of the Legislative Office Building, has a full-time director and a staff of six who work during the session and the interim, providing information to members of the House. The research office works with committees as well as individual representatives. The office maintains a library of research material and resources available to House members.

Legislative Interns

Under the Legislative Intern Program, graduate and upper-division students selected on a competitive basis from colleges and universities in Georgia live in Atlanta and work as staff to the General Assembly during the session. Selection and academic requirements for the interns are handled by participating schools. Work assignment and direction of interns during the session are managed by the House and Senate. For their work as interns, the students receive academic credit and are paid a stipend.

Approximately 30 interns take part in the program each session and are assigned to both the Senate and the House. Most interns are assigned to work with committees, although some may be assigned to various legislative support staff.

OTHER SOURCES OF ASSISTANCE

Office of Planning and Budget

The General Assembly receives assistance on budgetary and fiscal matters from a number of other sources within state government. A major source of expertise and assistance is located within the Office of the Governor—the Office of Planning and Budget. This office, and in particular its budget division, is responsible for

1. helping the governor draft a general appropriations bill each year;

2. conducting evaluations of state agencies and programs requested by the presiding officers of both houses;

3. developing plans for improving the economy and efficiency of state agencies;

4. carrying out the fiscal plans and policies as approved by the General Assembly;

5. preparing fiscal notes that give the expected financial consequences of certain types of legislation; and

6. in general, providing the legislature, House and Senate appropriations committees, the legislative budget analyst, and the Budgetary Responsibility Oversight Committee with assistance.[24]

The Office of Planning and Budget is required to develop and maintain (updating at least once each year) a strategic plan for the state as a whole. By law, the plan must cover a period of at least five years. This plan must have as its primary goal (1) improved fiscal responsibility and responsiveness of state government, and (2) effective and efficient delivery of services throughout the state, with an emphasis on decentralizing state government.[25]

Department of Audits and Accounts

At least once a year, the Department of Audits and Accounts (headed by the state auditor) reviews the books and accounts of every state officer, department, agency, authority, board, commission and institution, and every local school system and official receiving state aid to ensure that funds are expended and administered according to law.[26] A detailed and comprehensive report of the salaries paid to, and expenses incurred by, every person on the payroll of the state is available to legislators on request.[27]

The auditor is directed to prepare annual and, whenever required, special reports to the governor and General Assembly, showing the general financial operation and management of each state agency and whether it is being handled in an efficient and economical manner, calling special attention to any excessive cost of operation or maintenance, any excessive expense, and any excessive price paid for goods, supplies, or labor by any agency.[28] Either the House or Senate Appropriations Committee (or the governor) may direct the auditor to make a special examination and audit of all the books, records, accounts, vouchers, warrants, bills, and other papers and records, and the financial transactions and management of any agency at any time.[29] Additionally, the auditor is directed to cooperate with both appropriations committees and to furnish any information they request.[30]

The department works with the Office of Planning and Budget to prepare fiscal notes for various types of bills before their introduction in the General Assembly.[31]

Commission on Compensation

The State Commission on Compensation assists the General Assembly in setting the compensation of not only members of the General Assembly, but also "constitutional officers" and full-time heads of state agencies, authorities, boards, commissions, committees, and departments. Of the commission's 12 members, 4 are appointed by the governor, 4 by the justices of the state supreme court, 2 by the lieutenant governor, and 2 by the speaker of the House.[32] The compensation commission is responsible for reviewing salaries currently being paid state officials in Georgia and comparing these with salaries received in comparable positions within the federal government, other states, and in business, industry, and the professions. The commission is further instructed to file a written report of its findings and recommendations to the General Assembly in odd-numbered years, at least 30 days prior to the beginning of the session.

Universities

The Georgia General Assembly sometimes turns to educational and research institutions of the state for counsel and research assistance. The law schools, both public and private, are called upon from time to time for research and drafting assistance. Law professors, political scientists, public administration teachers and researchers, and other specialists also provide counsel and research assistance to committees on occasion.

The Legislative Intern Program, discussed earlier, is another example of the assistance provided the General Assembly by educational institutions. The program provides a service to legislators and an educational and work experience for the student interns.

One special resource is the Carl Vinson Institute of Government at the University of Georgia. In addition to producing this handbook, the institute has conducted a number of policy studies for committees of the General Assembly, as well as for the body as a whole. Since 1958, it has cooperated with legislative leaders in conducting the presession "Biennial Institute for Georgia Legislators" to acquaint new members with the organization and procedures of the General Assembly and provide information on issues and problems facing the state.

The Reapportionment Office, operated by the University of Georgia's Data Services Office and located in Room 407 of the Legislative Office Building, provides services to members of the General Assembly relative to redistricting required following each decennial census. The services include assisting local governments to develop city and county districts upon request by a legislator representing the affected jurisdiction. Congressional, legislative, and local district maps are also provided by this office.

National Organizations

National Conference of State Legislatures (NCSL)

This is the major organization for state legislators in the nation, with membership made up of all legislators and staff. NCSL maintains offices in Denver, Colorado, as well as in Washington, D.C. It provides research, information, and technical assistance to state legislatures and lobbies on behalf of state interests before the federal government.

NCSL responds to long-term requests for research on matters of importance to state legislatures as well as short-term requests for information. NCSL's Legislative Information System (LIS) serves as a computerized clearinghouse for sharing policy research conducted by all 50 state legislatures, NCSL, and other organizations. With this system, abstracts of articles, reports, and publications are stored and available for immediate retrieval. Additionally, the LIS database contains 50 state profiles on a variety of subjects (e.g., salaries, laws, and tax rates). Access to LIS is provided without charge and only requires a telephone hookup linking a legislative computer with the central NCSL computer in Denver.

Seminars, conferences, and other programs—in such areas as reapportionment, fiscal affairs, legislative oversight, legislative information needs, legislative management, and science and technology—are conducted each year by NCSL around the nation. The NCSL annual meeting brings together several thousand legislators and staff for a broad variety of workshops and panels.

NCSL publishes a monthly magazine, *State Legislatures*; a newsletter, *Federal Update*; and specialized reports, books, and other materials on topics of particular concern to legislators.

Council of State Governments

Another valuable source of information is the Council of State Governments, with headquarters in Lexington, Kentucky (the southern regional office is in Atlanta). On request, the council's States Information Center supplies the legislature and its committees with information on subjects of concern. Often, the library can furnish information on a subject being considered by the legislature, having gathered this information from studies and legislation of other states which have dealt previously with the matter. The council supports the Committee on Suggested State Legislation, which publishes model legislation in a variety of areas, and the Innovations Transfer Program, which identifies programs of value that have been implemented by state governments and have the potential to be utilized by other governments.

A number of council publications are worth mentioning. *State Government News*, published monthly, highlights information relevant to state legislatures, new laws, issues facing the states, and state government in general. Issued biennially, *The Book of the States* provides comparative information on constitutions, legislatures, governors, courts, and other areas of state government. The council publishes many studies on specialized areas, such as federal mandates, business tax incentives, medical care cost containment, and hazardous waste management.

PUBLICATIONS

Annually, each member of the General Assembly receives copies of the session laws enacted that year, the journal of that member's house, the state budget, the report of the state auditor, some agency regulations and annual reports, and several other publications. Some of these are distributed automatically, while others are available upon request.

Georgia Laws, Volumes I and II

These are the annual session laws compiled and published by the Office of Legislative Counsel and distributed by the secretary of state. Included in these session laws are all acts and resolutions passed by the General Assembly (general acts and resolutions are in one volume and local acts and resolutions in a second), a listing of vetoed measures, names and addresses of members of the General Assembly for the session covered, and other information.

Rules and Regulations of the State of Georgia

This compilation officially details all rules and regulations adopted by executive agencies, pursuant to law, which are covered under the Administrative Procedures Act. By law, these are to be made available upon request, free of charge, to any member of the General Assembly.[33]

Annual Reports of State Agencies

Although not every executive agency is required by law to file an annual report with the General Assembly, many are. Where an agency is required to report, state law provides that the agency simply send each legislator a notice that its annual report has been published and is available upon request.[34]

House and Senate Journals

The journal of each house is the official compendium of daily records reflecting the order of business and action taken on all legislative measures and procedural questions during the session (see Fig. 21). Listed within the journal are the authors of every measure considered by a house, the date of first and second readings of the measure, the name and date of committee assignment, and the committee recommendation on each bill or resolution reported out of committee. The journal does not record the

Figure 21: *Legislative Journal*

TUESDAY, MARCH 8, 1994   2015

HB 1619.   By Representatives Patten of the 176th, Barfoot of the 155th, Floyd of the 172nd and Dobbs of the 92nd:

A bill to amend Chapter 13 of Title 12 of the Official Code of Georgia Annotated, the "Georgia Underground Storage Tank Act," so as to define and redefine certain terms; to provide for inspections of sites by contractors or agents of the Department of Natural Resources; to permit the director immediately to issue emergency orders for corrective action without awaiting the concurrence of the governor.

The following Senate amendment was read:

Amend HB 1619 by striking on lines 24 and 25 of page 16 the following:

"~~the~~ all property of owners and operators until funds are paid and on",

and by inserting in lieu thereof the following:

"~~the property of owners and operators until funds are paid~~".

Representative Dobbs of the 92nd moved that the House agree to the Senate amendment to HB 1619.

On the motion, the roll call was ordered and the vote was as follows:

Y Ashe	Colwell	Howard	Mobley, B	Y Smith, C
Y Atkins	Y Connell	Y Hudson	Y Mobley, J	Y Smith, L
Y Bailey	Y Cox	Hughes	Y Moore	Y Smith, P
Baker	Y Crawford	Hugley	Y Mosley	Smith, T
Y Bannister	Crews	Y Irvin	Y Mueller	Y Smith, V
Y Barfoot	Y Culbreth	Y James	E Oliver	Y Smith, W
Y Bargeron	Y Cummings	Y Jamieson	Y O'Neal	Smyre
Y Barnes	Davis, G	Y Jenkins	Y Orrock	Y Snow
Y Bates	Y Davis, M	Y Johnson, D.H	Y Padgett	Y Stancil, F
Benefield	Y Dickinson	Y Johnson, E	E Parham	Y Stancil, S
Birdsong	Dix	Johnson, G	Y Parrish	Stanley, L
Bordeaux	Dixon, H	Y Johnson, J	Patten	Stanley, P
Y Bostick	Y Dixon, S	Y Johnston	Y Pelote	Y Stephenson
Y Breedlove	Y Dobbs	Jones	Y Perry	Y Streat
Y Brooks, D	Y Ehrhart	Y Joyce	Y Pinholster	Taylor
Brooks, T	Epps	Y Kaye	Y Poag	Teague
Brown	Y Evans	Y Kinnamon	Y Polak	Y Teper
Buck	Y Felton	Y Klein	Y Porter	Y Thomas
Y Buckner	Y Floyd, J.M	Y Ladd	Y Poston	E Tillman
Y Bunn	Y Floyd, J.W	Y Lakly	Y Powell	Y Titus
Y Burkhalter	Y Godbee	Y Lane, D	Y Purcell, A	Y Towery
Y Byrd	Y Golden	Y Lane, R	Y Purcell, B	Y Trense
Y Campbell	Y Goodwin	Y Lawrence	Randall	Turnquest
Canty	Y Greene	Y Lawson	Randolph	Twiggs
Carlisle	Groover	Lee	Y Ray	Y Vaughan
Y Carrell	Y Hammond	Y Lewis	Y Reaves	Walker
Y Carter	Hanner	Y Lord	Y Reichert	Y Wall
Y Cauthorn	Y Harris, B	Lucas	Y Roberts	Y Watson
Chambless	Y Harris, M	Y Maddox	Y Royal	Y Watts
Y Chandler	Hart	Y Mann	Scoggins	Y Westmoreland
Y Channell	Y Heard	Y Martin	Y Shanahan	Y White
Y Childers	Y Hegstrom	Y McBee	Y Sherrill	Y Williams, B
Y Clark	Y Hembree	McClinton	Y Shipp	Y Williams, R
Y Coker	Henson	McKinney	Y Simpson	Y Yates
Y Coleman, B	Y Holland	Y Milam	Sinkfield	E Yeargin
Y Coleman, T	Y Holmes	Y Mills	Y Skipper	Murphy, Spkr

On the motion, the ayes were 131, nays 0.

The motion prevailed.

text of bills and resolutions (except for committee or floor amendments and substitutes to a measure) but does reflect all actions taken on them by the full house.

The votes on all motions and questions coming before a house and on the final passage of bills or resolutions are reported. When a roll call vote is utilized, the names of all members and how they voted (or if they did not vote) is recorded. If the vote is by division (show of hands), the total numbers for and against the question or bill are noted. If the vote was by voice vote or unanimous consent, the journal only records whether the question or measure passed or failed.

Other journal entries are rules changes adopted by a house, results of elections for officers of that house, "housekeeping resolutions" for the biennium, copies of privileged resolutions adopted by a house, final reports of special interim study committees, messages received from the other house, copies of the governor's annual "State of the State" and budget messages, a list of the bills vetoed by the governor and the reasons for vetoing them, and the names of all lobbyists formally registered with the secretary of state.

Unlike the *Congressional Record*—which is not an official journal of Congress—individual floor remarks and debate are not recorded or published by either house, nor are "extension of remarks" permitted. However, any senator may enter a written protest against an action taken by the Senate concerning any matter. The protest must clearly set forth his or her grounds and may not impugn the motive of that house or of any member.[35] With consent of his or her house, a member may also include certain other statements in the journal, such as an explanation as to why he or she was not present to vote on a certain measure.[36]

Rules of the Senate provide that any member presenting a petition, memorial, or remonstrance shall, as concisely as practicable, indicate the name and object of the petitioner, memorial writer, or remonstrant for notation in the journal; and the paper may then be referred without reading.[37]

Responsibility for preparation of each day's journal report rests with the clerk of the House and the secretary of the Senate. Both houses provide for examination of this daily report before it is read and adopted on the following day by the whole body. The Journals Committee is responsible for this examination in the House, and the Rules Committee's Enrolling and Journals Subcommittee in the Senate.[38]

The confirmation of the journal each morning by a house officially marks the end of the previous legislative day. The rules of the Senate require the reading of the journal except if waived by either a majority vote or by unanimous consent.[39] In actual practice, this waiver is routinely granted each morning following announcement by a representative of the Senate Enrolling and Journals Subcommittee that the previous day's record has been examined and found correct.

Following a session, these daily reports are chronologically compiled and published by the clerk and secretary for their respective houses in a comprehensive two-volume set, which thereafter serves as the official record of legislative action for that session. Despite the absence of individual floor remarks, debate, statements of intent by a measure's author, and detailed standing committee reports, Georgia courts, in seeking to find the intent of the legislature, may review events occurring during the progress of a statute's enactment, as disclosed by the Senate and House journals.[40] However, the journals may not be used to impeach the validity of a bill by showing that the measure was not enacted in accordance with constitutional requirements or the rules of that house. A duly enrolled act, authenticated by the presiding officers of both houses, approved by the governor, and deposited with the secretary of state, will be conclusively presumed to have been enacted in accordance with necessary requirements, and no evidence to the contrary, even if reflected in the journal, will be considered by the courts.[41]

PUBLIC INFORMATION SERVICES

Several steps have been taken by the Georgia legislature to better convey to the public general information on the operation of the General Assembly and specific information on the status of legislation during a session.

Public Information Office

Both House and Senate have full-time staffs to provide information services to members of the General Assembly, news media, and the general public throughout the year.

During sessions of the General Assembly, each office attempts to compile day-by-day information relating to the status of bills originated in that house, committee schedules, committee recommendations on bills, and other pertinent information. Press releases are prepared on all general bills introduced in each house and on all interim committee reports. Also, each office prepares a weekly legislative wrap-up during the session and, after final adjournment, a review of legislation enacted at the session. Between sessions, the offices issue press releases and, in general, provide other information to the public and news media as requested.

Both House and Senate public information offices maintain year-round toll-free numbers for use by citizens anywhere in Georgia. These numbers may be used to leave a message for a legislator to return the call, find the status of legislation, or obtain other information (such as the schedule of committee meetings or biographical information about a legislator). To contact the House Public Information Office from outside the Atlanta exchange, call 1-800-282-5800; for the Senate, call 1-800-282-5803. Numbers within the Atlanta telephone exchange are 656-5082 for the

House and 656-0028 for the Senate. To hear a recorded message of daily events during the session, call 1-800-282-5801 for the House and 1-800-282-5802 for the Senate.

Computer Networks and Bulletin Boards

During the session, Georgia lawmakers can track the status (and view the full text) of bills and resolutions by computer from their office or home district. A local area network in the state capitol and Legislative Office Building links personal computers to GeorgiaNet—the state-owned computer network that provides online access to numerous state documents and information. Each day following adjournment, staff in the offices of the clerk of the House and secretary of the Senate record the status of every bill and resolution in the General Assembly and then upload this information to GeorgiaNet. This allows legislators and staff—as well as anyone in the state who subscribes to the network—to track legislation.

The GeorgiaNet Authority was created by the General Assembly to serve as the central source of information provided by state agencies for electronic distribution via computer network. In addition to legislative documents, GeorgiaNet plans to carry the Georgia Code (unannotated), meeting notices of legislative committees and state agencies, agency rules and regulations, proposed rule changes, attorney general opinions, executive orders, voter registration lists, and much more.

Members of the House can also call up information on bills and resolutions from their office or home district by means of an electronic bulletin board maintained by the clerk of the House.

Television and Radio

Since 1971, public television has been utilized to cover sessions of the legislature. Georgia Public Television (GPTV) has provided extensive session coverage, supplemented by interviews and analyses, enabling state citizens to view taped coverage of highlights of each day's session in the evening hours. The program, "The Lawmakers," generally airs at 7:00 p.m. on public television stations during the legislative session.

The public information offices provide a radio service through which stations across the state may get taped excerpts of House or Senate action, or receive synopses of major legislative activity without charge.

ENDNOTES

1. OFFICIAL CODE OF GEORGIA ANNOTATED (O.C.G.A.) §28-4-2.
2. O.C.G.A. §28-4-1.
3. O.C.G.A. §50-18-75.
4. O.C.G.A. §§28-9-3, 28-9-4, 28-9-5.
5. O.C.G.A. §28-4-3.

6. O.C.G.A. §28-4-5.

7. O.C.G.A. §28-4-4.

8. O.C.G.A. §§28-4-6, 28-4-7.

9. Ibid.

10. O.C.G.A. §§45-12-110, 45-12-111.

11. O.C.G.A. §28-5-5 (d)(3).

12. O.C.G.A. §45-12-178.

13. O.C.G.A. §28-5-5 (h).

14. O.C.G.A. §45-12-88.

15. O.C.G.A. §45-12.75.1.

16. GA. CONST. art. 3, §9, ¶1.

17. O.C.G.A. §45-12-91.

18. O.C.G.A. §28-5-5 (d) (5).

19. O.C.G.A. §28-5-5 (e).

20. O.C.G.A. §28-5-5 (f).

21. O.C.G.A. §§28-5-20 through 28-5-27.

22. Ibid.

23. Senate Rules 185, 187.

24. O.C.G.A. §§45-12-71 et seq., 28-4-6(b), 28-5-5(e), 28-5-42.

25. O.C.G.A. §45-12-175.

26. O.C.G.A. §50-6-24.

27. O.C.G.A. §50-6-27.

28. O.C.G.A. §50-6-24.

29. O.C.G.A. §50-6-4.

30. O.C.G.A. §50-6-23.

31. O.C.G.A. §§28-5-2, 28-5-42, 28-5-52, 47-20-32 et seq.

32. O.C.G.A. §45-7-90 et seq.

33. O.C.G.A. §50-13-7.

34. O.C.G.A. §45-6-4.

35. Senate Rule 61.

36. Senate Rule 177; House Rule 137.

37. Senate Rule 44.

38. Senate Rule 29; House Rule 28.

39. Senate Rule 36.

40. Stanley v. Sims, 185 Ga. 518, 195 S.E. 439 (1938); Sharpe v. Lowe, 214 Ga. 513, 106 S.E. 2d 28 (1958).

41. Collins v. Woodham, 257 Ga. 643, 361 S.E.2d 800 (1987); Atlantic Coast Line Railroad v. State, 135 Ga. 545, 69 S.E. 725 (1910); Capitol Distributing Co. v. Redwine, 206 Ga. 477, 57 S.E.2d 578 (1980). The only exception to the "enrolled bill rule" appears to be the matter of notice of advertisement for local bills (which, incidentally, is not recorded in the journal of either legislative body). Richmond County v. Pierce, 234 Ga. 274, 215 S.E.2d 665 (1975); Smith v. Michael, 203 Ga. 74, 45 S.E.2d 431 (1974).

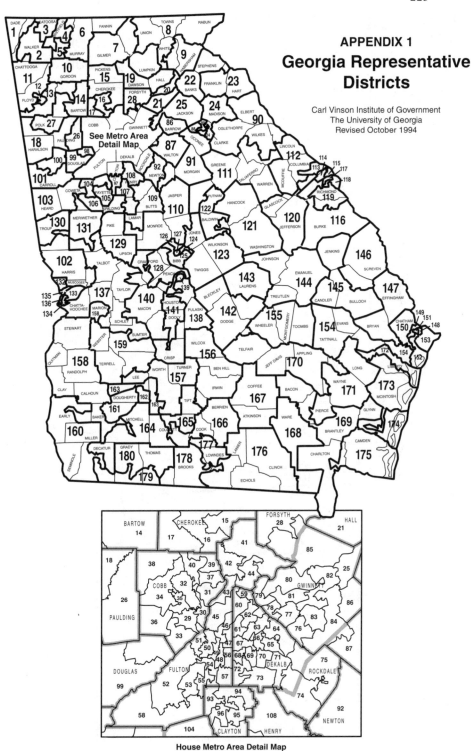

APPENDIX 1
Georgia Representative Districts

Carl Vinson Institute of Government
The University of Georgia
Revised October 1994

House Metro Area Detail Map

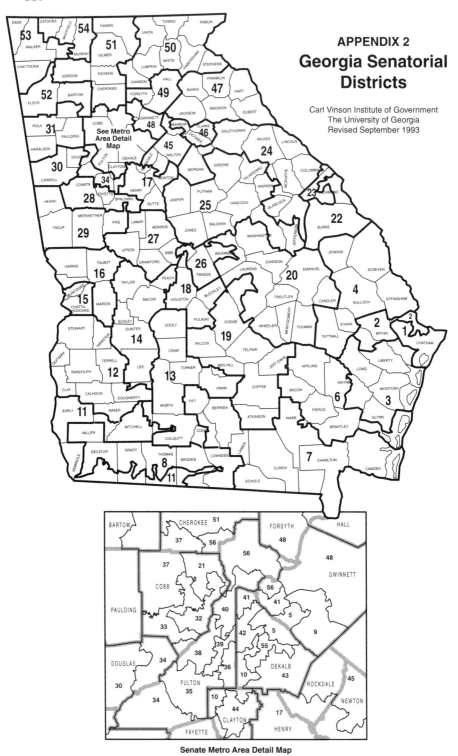

APPENDIX 2
Georgia Senatorial Districts

Carl Vinson Institute of Government
The University of Georgia
Revised September 1993

Senate Metro Area Detail Map

Index